Book mini... ...

God with Us

A Walk Through the Gospels

by

Margaret Montreuil

In God's extravagant love,

Margaret

xulon PRESS

Credits

The bullet points at the beginning of each chapter that give a chronological outline of the life of Christ, including geographical notes and Scripture references, are taken from *THE NIV HARMONY OF THE GOSPELS: With Explanations and Essays*, Robert L. Thomas, Editor; and Stanley N. Gundry, Associate Editor (Harper and Row Publishers, San Francisco, Copyright ©1988 by Robert L. Thomas and Stanley N. Gundry). Used by permission of the copyright holders, all rights reserved.

All other quotations are used with permission as follows:

1. All Scripture quotations are taken from the HOLY BIBLE, NEW INTERNATIONAL VERSION®. NIV®. Copyright ©1973, 1978, 1984 by International Bible Society. Used by permission of Zondervan. All rights reserved.
2. Chapter 13: Excerpt from the book, *The God Who Comes* by Carlo Carretto, Orbis Books, ©1974. Used by permission of Orbis Books.
3. Chapter 34: *The Finale,* the third book in the series *The Singer Trilogy* by Calvin A. Miller, InterVarsity Press, ©1975, 1977, 1979, 1990. Used by permission of InterVarsity Press.
4. Chapter 36: Poem/lyrics from *God and Man At Table Are Sat Down* by Dr. Robert J. Stamps, ©1972. Used by permission.
5. Chapter 39: The partial lyrics from *"Why"* by Michael Card, *Immanuel: Reflections on the Life of Christ*, Thomas Nelson Publishers, ©1990.
6. Chapter 42: Excerpts taken from *Reliving the Passion* by Walter Wangerin, Jr., Copyright © 1992 by Walter Wangerin, Jr. Used by permission of Zondervan Publishing House.

This devotional is one of a two-book set.
The novel, *God in Sandals: When Jesus Walked Among Us*
is a creatively passionate story of the life of the Son of God
during that unique and holy time when he lived
with us as one of us.

You are welcome to contact the author at:

www.margaretmontreuil.com

A free *Group Leader's Guide* is available for *God with Us*
on the author's web site.

This book is dedicated to Lord Jesus and his Bride.

Preface

Today, greater demand has arisen for more meaning and purpose in our lives—for spirituality. At the same time, the uncertainty of our days has drawn many to seek hope and answers through Christian literature with more depth. The re-publishing of books considered spiritual classics has begun to help meet that need—writings of devout Christians from past centuries who were in love with God and who knew how to adore him and meditate on the mysteries and wonders of God's absolute, bounteous love. Books such as these answer the needs of our times—and of our hearts.

An "experiencing God" book such as *God with Us: A Walk through the Gospels* is about Jesus himself—and the love he lived and gave.

As a devotional companion to the Gospels, as well as a companion to the novel, *God in Sandals,* this devotional book was written to delight those who wish to meditatively follow in the footsteps of Jesus' earthly life. *God with Us* is designed to practice the ancient method of praying with Scripture: to imaginatively meditate, to reflectively ponder and personalize, and to listen to God with a journal. *God with Us* facilitates devotional, contemplative prayer. This prayer is often called the Prayer of Love, or the Gaze of Love. This particular form of prayer is not a matter of seeking blessings or help from God but is, rather, seeking God himself.

Through contemplative prayer
which is most truly expressed as
desire for God,
we are invited to come,
to look upon the One
Who draws us with everlasting love.

Just as Jesus responded to his first two followers when they pursued him that day by the Jordan River, this book also invites those seeking him to "come and see"—to see and know Jesus himself. It is *his* invitation. It is because our pursuit of God is more truly his pursuit of us that this book is a meeting place. Each chapter has the following sections:

1. <u>Chapter title and a short, set-apart Scripture text</u> introduce the chapter's theme.
2. The bulleted list at the beginning of the chapter references the Scriptures and locations for the events of Jesus' life covered in each chapter. This list provides a quick reference tool to distinguish "fact" from "fiction" for the reader of the novel's corresponding chapters. The Scripture references for all four Gospels are listed in chronological order in the book's 45 chapters. This Scripture list is an excellent reference or guide for those who wish to read the Gospels, in a harmony of all four Gospel accounts, in chronological order.
3. ***A Contemplative View*** contains poems, imaginative narratives, and reflective prose to deepen understanding surrounding the mysteries and realities about Jesus and his love.
4. ***Wonder Just a Little*** invites you to reflect through questions and thought-provoking ideas meant to awaken wonder.
5. ***What Do You See?*** gently guides you to imaginatively enter into a Gospel event to see and hear Jesus and "encounter" him through meditative, contemplative prayer.
6. ***Journal*** exercises are provided to help you better understand and record insights, and to experience listening to God with a journal.

Introduction

Many have undertaken to draw up an account of the things that have been fulfilled among us, just as they were handed down to us by those who from the first were eyewitnesses and servants of the Word. Therefore, since I myself have carefully investigated everything from the beginning, it seemed good also to me to write an orderly account for you, most excellent Theophilus, so that you may know the certainty of the things you have been taught.

Luke 1:1-4, in his letter to Theophilus

Since Luke penned these words about two thousand years ago, there have been countless books and writings on the life of Jesus. But it seemed good to me also to write an orderly and thoughtful account of what the eyewitnesses, those early servants of the Word, saw and heard. May the writings in this book become for you a contemplative journey of reading and prayer as you and Lord Jesus retrace his footsteps across the pages of the Gospels.

Margaret Montreuil, a Word servant
January 26, 2003

Content

1 - Mary's Son

For to us a child is born,
to us a son is given;
and the government will be on his shoulders.
And he will be called Wonderful Counselor,
Mighty God, Everlasting Father, Prince of Peace.
Of the increase of his government and peace
there will be no end.
He will reign on David's throne and over his kingdom,
establishing and upholding it with justice
and righteousness from that time on and forever.
The zeal of the Lord will accomplish this.
Isaiah 9:6-7

- Who is Jesus? *John 1:1-18; Matthew 1:1-17; Luke 3:23b-38; Isaiah 9:6-7*
- Jesus' birth is foretold to Mary (Nazareth): *Luke 1:26-38*
- Mary visits Elizabeth (Judean hills): *Luke 1:39-56*
- Birth of Jesus (Bethlehem): *Luke 2:1-7*
- John's birth, Zechariah's prophetic song, and John's growth and early life (Judean Hills): *Luke 1:57-80* [See Chapter 5]
- Angels praise and shepherds witness (Bethlehem): *Luke 2:8-20*
- Circumstances of Jesus' birth explained to Joseph (Nazareth): *Matthew 1:18-25*
- Circumcision and presentation of Jesus at the temple (Jerusalem): *Luke 2:21-38*

A CONTEMPLATIVE VIEW

In Love's Disguise

Through waters of pain and blood
God's blessings flood!
The Messiah's birth, He's come at last
But without a single trumpet blast

In answer to our deepest longing
He slips into our world disarming
All that keeps us far from Him
He's come to annihilate our sin

Can He smell the beasts and dung?
Or know His angels have just sung?
Did He hear Eve's groans of pain?
And feel the shock of air like icy rain?

God with skin, so velvet soft—
Is scratched by straw and bound by cloth
The curse of Eden forgotten by joy;
in this wonderful, tiny, baby boy

In awe the angels' Maker now—
fills tiny lungs—and, so, they bow
They tremble at His needy cry—
for this is none but El Shaddai

Eternity and Time meet as one—
The Ancient of Days is Mary's son
To our breast we bring Him near—
and hold Him close, so very dear

Creator of Life is in our care;
for our pain He too will share
For since the days of the Fall,
None has seen God's face at all

Now in the manger crude He lies
Wrapped in Love's disguise

**

Expectant after Gabriel's visit, Mary awaits *The Promise*. For nine months, her hopes grow with the holy Seed within. Can she understand this mystery? She's never *known* a man. Her child, the angel said, was God's only begotten Son—the one of whom the prophet wrote: *"For to us a child is born, to us a son is given."*

WONDER JUST A LITTLE

Let this sink in. Almighty God became an embryo, grew into a baby boy, grew into a youth, grew into a man. He was like each and every one of us. We take this for granted because we really can't grasp this wonder. Let's ask ourselves a few questions. Why did God choose to come to earth as a baby? Why did he become a vulnerable, needy, baby boy? He could have visited the earth as a man as he had done before. What motivated him to do this? What purpose did it serve that he became one of us—including the need to cut teeth, learn to crawl, walk, and talk? He grew in wisdom—which means he learned.

Can you imagine the Word of God eventually picking up words of Aramaic from his parents in order to speak? He is wisdom itself! By his Word, all things exist.

Can you see his parents' delight in their toddler's first steps? Imagine, the engineer of the universe toddled. It's simply too overwhelming to comprehend.

This mystery of God's incarnation is far too comfortable a notion in our minds. We are way too numb. Once in a while our hearts are awakened with wonder. A shock of truth makes its way through the layers of indifference. When Jesus walked on water, he shocked a few people. He did this after years of being an ordinary person, hidden in the ordinary lives around him. But Jesus was no ordinary human being. He was fully God as well as fully man. That is why he came the way he did. He wanted to be fully human.

We must ask another question. Why did he live that hidden, ordinary life for so long? Thirty years? What do these things tell us about God's *inner* life—his *heart*—about his *motives*?

Is it possible God simply wanted to love and be loved? He wanted to be known, and he knew we couldn't know him because he was too far above and removed from us. Did he want to be handled and held? Intimately known? There is something very tender about God's desire to be loved in this way. Why did God desire to experience all that we experience?

Imagine what this meant to a simple carpenter named Joseph. The Lord of heaven and earth, as a baby, began a face-to-face, long-term, intimate relationship with him as "his son." Vulnerable for the first time, God completely entrusted himself to the very creatures he made. Mary and Joseph were chosen for the most privileged roles of the Ages. How could an ordinary man, called to be an ordinary dad, be the "dad" to Divinity? How could a young woman bear the Creator in her womb?

Did Joseph and Mary know they held their own Maker when they held little Jesus? Did Joseph realize that when he taught Jesus how to work with his hands, that his son's hands had made him? Did Mary and Joseph ever tremble at the scope of responsibility placed upon their shoulders? Perhaps Jesus' full identity remained a mystery to them during his life. If they could have fully comprehended the truth, they couldn't have raised Jesus as a normal child.

Yet this great mystery—the earthly life and mission of Jesus—was the drastic means God took, the tremendous lengths he went to, to bring "Eden" life to us. Eden means delight.

How God longs for intimacy with us. He couldn't give any more of himself than he did in the *way* he came to us, and he couldn't have better proved his love to us than in the *way* he showed it to us. Now we know God's unrelenting, surpassing, surprising, everlasting love.

WHAT DO YOU SEE?

Read Luke 2:1-19. Enter into the story of Jesus' birth. Close your eyes and imagine being there. Smell the cave, feel the cool dampness. Listen to the sounds of the night. Do you hear a baby's cry? What conversation passes between Mary and Joseph? What happens when the shepherds come? What is it like to be there?

This prayer exercise was given to a group of four people. After spending a little time together in quiet, the group then shared what their experiences had been:

- I didn't see anything, but I heard Baby Jesus crying. It really affected me to think of God crying—as a vulnerable baby.

- While I pictured Mary holding Baby Jesus, I saw Jesus' little hand grasping hold of Mary's finger, like babies do sometimes. Then another image came to me: Michaelangelo's painting on the ceiling of the Sistine Chapel. Both God and Man are reaching for each other, their fingers stretching for the other's. What a contrast this seemed to that image and that of the small infant and mother. Then I stayed with the image of the Child sweetly clinging to Mary's finger. I am so glad God came to us this way!

- I saw the bloodied straw from childbirth. I've never thought about the reality of the situation so much. We always see the sweet nativity scene of the birth of Christ. I think sometimes the stories in the Bible are so familiar that they lose the shock value of the way it really was. By seeing the bloody straw, I felt very touched to think about how God chose to enter into our human experience so fully.

- I focused on Joseph. I felt a connection with him; how he must have felt to be a part of the birth of Jesus, yet not to be able to be on the same intimate level of the experience with Jesus as was Mary.

JOURNAL

Record in your journal your thoughts, prayers, and experience from your time of meditation. What stands out from the experience? What about the story of Jesus' birth moved or stirred within your heart? What is God saying to you today about these things? What do you wish to say to him? Using your journal, commune with him.

He knows how we feel

2 - Starlit Hope

Where is the one who has been born king of the Jews?
We saw his star in the east and have come to worship him.
Matthew 2:2

• Visit of the Magi and Herod's jealousy (From the east to
Jerusalem): *Matthew 2:1-8*

A CONTEMPLATIVE VIEW

History has named the mysterious visitors who came to worship
the Child Jesus the "Magi." Also known as the "Wise Men," they
came from Persia or perhaps from as far east as Arabia. Their story
became part of Holy Scripture, a colorful, dramatic event in the
Gospel. Christian folklore and songs about them are a familiar part
of our lives. As far as theologians have determined, the Magi were
not kings, as some have thought, but were, more likely, astrologers.
As explorers of the universe, they were considered "seers" in their
own land. What we do know for sure is that they saw Heaven's
"birth announcement," interpreting the bright, new star as a sign of
the birth of a divine Jewish king. They understood the phenomenon
as their invitation from the Universe to "come and see."

And, they responded. They came, full of hope, to the land of
Israel.

Their past, color of skin, place of birth, culture, religious
upbringing—none of that mattered to God—only that they were on
a journey of desire. What was the star that they followed? Could it

21

have been a comet? Was it low in the heavens? Did it actually guide them? Or, did they strike out to Jerusalem because of ancient Jewish writings that guided them in understanding, coupled with the appearance and location in the heavens of the new star? Did they see planets in some special conjunction, and come to a conclusion about the message they conveyed based on their astrological beliefs? We can only guess. All we know for sure is that their worshipful visit to young Jesus was a dramatic, profoundly mystical event.

Because it was a part of God's story of redemption, we want to understand its import.

We know that the Magi came to adore the Son of God, bearing symbolic gifts appropriate for him: gold—for his royalty; myrrh—for his humanity; and frankincense—for his divinity. And we know for certain that God drew the wise, mystic seekers from the East to himself.

These men who traveled from afar were seekers of the King of the Universe. They were men not content to stay put in their own comfortable world, but they traveled a great distance to find the Person they believed the newborn king to be. They did not care to experience the gods of their own making, or to send others to find what they themselves needed to find. Theirs was a journey of desire and hope—placed inside their hearts from above. Just as the star lit the sky above their heads, so the Creator lit the fire of desire within their souls—to journey on a path of faith and hope to him.

WONDER JUST A LITTLE

Hope and desire. What are these powers so strongly intertwined within the human heart? They are no less than God's own hope and desire towards us, wooing us to him.

The story of the eastern Magi is a parable for today: of our scientists, politicians, students, of all seekers of truth—for everyone, for all time. Within each living soul is a deep yearning to know truth, to learn, and to discover. We were born to wonder! Animals and plants do not care to marvel at the sunset; nor do they care a bit about what makes the world go around. Why do people? Why did

God make us this way?

What did the Magi know about the God of Israel? Had they read the ancient Jewish prophecies about the promised redeemer? Did they realize that those prophecies predicted that the Light of the World would come from Israel itself? What drew them there? Why did they travel such a long distance to find the Answer to their seeking? What does this amazing story, this moment in history, mean?

Apparently, the wise men didn't come for political reasons, personal ambition, or curiosity. We realize that their worshipful visit was part of a dramatic scene in God's living play. His Story. It was, to over-simplify its meaning, a surprise. It seems rather strange that God would bring pagan seers to witness and worship the birth of his Son—letting the strangers in on what all of Israel was blind to. But then, God the Father let a few simple shepherds in on his happiness that first night too. It does seem to be in character with the kind of outlandish things he does with the most unexpected, unlikely people.

The God of Israel wooed the strangers there, making them take part in the history of his participation with humankind. We don't know God's reasons. But everyone who has sung the songs about the mystic traveling gentlemen at Christmastime know this much— they were on a spiritual quest. The Magi's story shows us how God draws us to himself, and when we respond, he reveals himself so that we really *do* find and see him. God is the Reward for our wandering, longing hearts and eyes, and is the Answer to our heart's deepest questions.

WHAT DO YOU SEE?

In prayer, imagine you are one of the Magi traveling to find the King for whom the star shined. You've journeyed a long distance. You arrive in Jerusalem, thinking you would find the child in a palace. You meet with King Herod. You are directed to the nearby town of Bethlehem. You see the humble home of the young child, Jesus. Then you see *him*. Why have you come to see him? Why have you been drawn to desire him? To what end or for what purpose has this long journey been?

For another perspective of this event, imagine what the visitors' coming, their adoration and their gifts, meant to Mary and Joseph, in charge of raising Jesus. Perhaps it was as much for them that God brought about such an event. What a spectacular sign this was to them of Jesus' supernatural beginnings. Perhaps the presents of gold, frankincense, and myrrh—with the memory of the eastern visitors—was another sign to them of God's strange and wondrous doings, his reminder and confirmation to them that Jesus was the Promised One.

JOURNAL

This chapter hints of the reality of God's *Larger Story*—God's pursuit of us. In what ways does your faith journey relate to the eastern seekers? Ask the Lord to show you some of the signs he's used or ways he's led you close to himself. Perhaps there was one big sign, event, or condition that strongly drew you to seek to know him better.

Ideas for journaling: 1) Write a summary or a time-line graph (with major life events or experiences) showing how God has met you or how he has pursued you, throughout your life. How have you discovered him in response? 2) Write a letter to God in your journal about what it means to know him. Then ask God what it means to him to know you.

3 - Grace Child

And the child grew and became strong;
he was filled with wisdom,
and the grace of God was upon him.
Luke 2:40

- Visit of the Magi in Bethlehem: *Matthew 2:9-12*
- Escape into Egypt and murder of boys in Bethlehem (Bethlehem and Egypt): *Matthew 2:13-18*
- Return to Nazareth (Egypt and Nazareth): *Matthew 2:19-23; Luke 2:39*
- Growth and early life of Jesus (Nazareth): *Luke 2:40*

A CONTEMPLATIVE VIEW

Mary and Joseph knew Jesus was straight from Heaven but could they have grasped the reality of *God-in-their-arms . . . God crawling . . . God learning to talk . . . God being obedient to them?*

Who was this boy they watched over and raised? Could they understand his having "no beginnings?" Did they wonder how he would fulfill all that was prophetically expected of him? How did they treat him on a day-to-day basis? What was it like to raise such a child?

Every believer is one with God through faith in Jesus. We believe that the Father, Son and Holy Spirit is in us and we are in union with God. These are mysteries we believe through faith but cannot fully comprehend.

The same is true for Mary and Joseph. Jesus was God's only begotten son whom they raised. The Scriptures say nothing about Jesus' life from the age of twelve to thirty. Because of a few things recorded in Scripture, we know Jesus was the oldest of the children in a large family in Nazareth, a town in the rolling and beautiful hills of Galilee. Joseph supported the family through carpentry and Jesus helped him. Since Joseph isn't mentioned during Jesus' public ministry, we assume his foster-father died within those eighteen years. That means that Jesus probably assumed the responsibility of providing for his family. Jesus lived in Nazareth, where he was called "the Carpenter." Jesus told stories about things he was most intimate with: articles such as plows, yokes, furniture, and houses. He grew up with simple, hardworking people like farmers and shepherds. Jesus experienced ordinary life to the fullest.

But what in the world was it like to raise him? If only we could ask Joseph and Mary a few questions . . .

Joseph, what was it like to be the father of God's Son? Did you ever spend time together under a starlit sky and talk of Heaven? Did you overhear any of his prayers? What were they like?

Did he laugh easy and hard? What did he most like to do? Did he cry very much? Did he keep things inside? Did he ever complain to you about anything? Did he share his hopes and dreams with you?

When he was young, did he follow you around?

Did he ever bang his thumb with a hammer or did he get slivers in his fingers?

Did he sing around the house, or whistle at work? Did you insist he redo his projects to get them perfect? Or were they perfect each time? Was his measuring accurate or could he skip that step altogether?

Did he have any pets? Did he like to catch bugs and frogs and such? What did he do if a snake was around?

Did he ever wrestle with you, or anyone else, just for fun? Did he ever tell jokes? Or play them on others?

Had you ever known him to "turn his cheek" to playmates, or peers, especially when he was older?

Did you discuss with him the "facts of life" when he was a growing young man?

Did anyone ever complain about him?

What kind of enjoyable things did the two of you do? Did he coyly smile when he knew more than you?

Was he ever afraid? Or did he have nightmares, or call out from a dream? Did his brothers and sisters ever "tell on him" or did they never have a reason to? Was it a lot easier to raise Jesus than your own? What did he most like to study? Did he like words or numbers best? How was his memory with the Scriptures? Did he enjoy his studies or did he put them off?

Did you usually think of him as God's son and not your own?

**

Mary, what was it like to mother your Maker? Did your heart leap when he first smiled at you? What was it like when he cooed? Did he fuss to get your attention? Did you watch him learn to crawl and feel pride when he took his first steps? Did the dark nights seem darker when he cried? Or did the sun stop shining when he was sad? Did he often need your comfort?

Did he help you around the house? Did you have to tell him to do something more than once? How was he at picking up after himself? Was he open and talkative, or did he keep to himself? What did he like to talk about most?

Did he have a favorite color? Did you ever see him walk on water? Did you always have leftovers?

Did he have a special friend he grew up with? Was he shy around girls or have any girls as friends? Did he ever give you advice—or ask for yours?

What kinds of things made him laugh? Did he ever pick flowers and surprise you with them? Did he ever go to his brothers' or sisters' defense in the neighborhood?

What was the Feast of Passover like with him year after year? Did it make you feel at all anxious? How did he act during the meal? Did he talk to you about his theological opinions? When he was older, did he tell you about his disappointments, dreams, or pain? When you were alone with him, did he share from his heart?

Did you ever tell him he should get married?

James, Simon, Jude, Joses, and at least two sisters . . . What was it like having Jesus for a brother?

WONDER JUST A LITTLE

Luke uses one sentence to speak volumes about the humanity of Jesus: "And the child grew and became strong; he was filled with wisdom, and the grace of God was upon him." Here is the first human being to grow up unhindered by sin. Yet, surely, he was "hindered" by the sin he saw all around him. Can you imagine what it might have been like to be the brother or sister of Jesus? Can you imagine the differences between Jesus and his siblings in that household? Can you see the strains or grace it may have produced? If we go a little deeper, we can see how it must have been for Jesus as he grew up. He must have graced others with his patience and forgiveness early on. Surely, his motives and thinking made him quite different from everyone else around him. Yet his mission wasn't to try to change anyone by his example or teaching— although during his three years in ministry, he did so.

His main reason for coming was to die. Isn't it amazing that he spent so long just being one of us—just living his own life among us, without trying to change the world while doing so? He changed the world all right. But think about how.

He brought Grace through his own goodness and doing, not by even asking us to try to change ourselves.

WHAT DO YOU SEE?

Imagine a typical day in Jesus' life with his family in Nazareth. Let the images flow freely through your heart and mind. Perhaps you will picture them sitting around Joseph in the evening, an oil lamp or two lit, while he reads the Scriptures to his family. Or, imagine Jesus working beside his father at their trade. In this way, see how the Lord became one of us and experienced ordinary life. What new insights does this give you about him?

JOURNAL

Even Jesus learned and grew. He developed as a normal human being. What is your earliest recollection of God? Did you know God when you were a child? Describe what this was like. Do you know that God is always drawing you with everlasting arms of kindness? Do you know that the Father doted over you when you were little? Sometimes it is hard to realize that God is a parent to us and takes pride in us, even cries for joy over us. Your childhood was (or is) very precious to God. You may wish to read Psalm 139:13-18 as a reminder. Just as God loved his own son, Jesus, so God loves each of his children. Each and every day of our lives has been written in the book he keeps of our life.

Those who have experienced neglect and abuse as children or as innocent victims have a special and tender place in God's heart. How terribly he grieves over these things that happen. He is our Father in heaven and longs for us to know his love—and his healing power. The world can be such an evil place because free will, when in sin, is a powerful force against the Good of our Father. Although not as a child, Jesus did experience abuse. As we know, the Sin of humankind gave him what he did not deserve. He is our merciful and understanding Healer.

Record in your journal the insights or reflections you've experienced from this chapter. Perhaps you'd like to ask Joseph, Mary, or other members of Jesus' family a few of your own questions. What would it be like to visit with his sisters, his grandmother or grandfather, or aunt? It does bring us to ponder things about Jesus we may never have thought of before. It is good to do—after all, Jesus spent most of his life as a member of an ordinary family. Our family life is important to God.

4 - "My Father's House"

"Son, why have you treated us like this?
Your father and I have been anxiously searching for you."
"Why were you searching for me?" he asked.
"Didn't you know I had to be in my Father's house?"
Luke 2:48b-49

- Jesus' Passover at age 12 (Jerusalem): *Luke 2:41-50*
- Jesus' growth to adulthood (Nazareth): *Luke 2:51-52*

A CONTEMPLATIVE VIEW

Jesus, Son of God, son of Mary, and legal son of Joseph . . .

On my twelfth birthday, my father presented me with a seam-less prayer cloak my mother had made, with the fringe hem and knotted strands at its corners. It was just like his. Wearing the *tallit* meant that I was a "son of the law" and would wear it from then on. Walking to the synagogue that evening, I was wrapped in it like a chick in its mother's soft, warm wings. Never had I been more excited over a gift. I had not known how moved I would be by the wearing of it, although I had anticipated it for a long time.

During a special service, I took in hand the Word and, as a man, led the Hebrew liturgy of our forefathers, as well as dedicating myself to the service of the Most High. Leading up to this sacred day in my life, I had studied the ancient words of Torah and memo-rized more than the required portions. My rabbi told me that I was

31

gifted in that the Word found its way fully into my mind and heart. Since my father had overseen my progress, he and the rabbi presented me to the congregation as one of their new members, having now *come-of-age* before their eyes. I would, from then on, sit in the main assembly room with them. I would take my turn reading from the sacred writings as a full member of the congregation. In keeping with tradition, I began with the *Shema*, read portions of the law, and ended with the following prayer:

"O my God and God of my fathers, on this solemn and sacred day, which marks my passage from boyhood to manhood, I humbly raise my eyes unto you, and declare with sincerity and truth, that henceforth I will keep your commandments, and undertake and bear the responsibility of my actions towards you. In my earliest infancy I was brought within your sacred covenant with Israel: and today I again enter, as an active responsible member, into this congregation, in the midst of which I will never cease to proclaim your holy name in the face of all nations."

I meant the prayer literally, with all of my heart, mind, soul, and strength.

Torah commanded that every able-bodied man attend three feasts a year, every year, at the temple: Passover, Pentecost, and Tabernacles. I hoped to never miss any of them. I knew that the commandments were not something I must sacrifice or obey as a duty, but that it was my greatest joy and deepest desire to perform. I wanted to attend the feasts in Jerusalem and was most happy for the command. I felt this way about all of Torah—it was like honey to my tongue.

Our people love Jerusalem, and to worship the God of our fathers in his house of prayer. On the occasions when it is impossible to go, a prayer of sorrow is added to the liturgy at the Passover meal, along with everyone shouting: "Next year in Jerusalem!"

That entire year leading up to my "coming of age as a *son of the commandments*," along with the intensified studies, I longed for Jerusalem. As it turned out, that year's pilgrimage became one of the best I remember. Our songs of ascent on that last day of the week of traveling—as we neared Jerusalem—made me feel as my ancestors must have felt before the Red Sea parted: *I must quickly get from here to there, but how?* The caravan moved too slowly for me. As it turned out, when we came close to Jerusalem, we stopped for the night in a village on the outskirts, and set up our camp. I took heart in that at daybreak I would be in the temple.

I was up before everyone else in our tent, but the pre-morning darkness did not hinder me from striking out on my own. It was a short walk to the great sprawling wall.

My heart beat faster when the trumpets sounded and the gates opened. Up and up I climbed, for there were many stairs at that particular gate. At the top, I saw the pinnacle with all of its gold, glittering in the sun. After lifting my prayer shawl over my head and removing my sandals at the entrance of the men's court, I went in.

A few white-clad priests formed a choir on fifteen wide steps. They began to sing songs of praise. It captivated me. I reverently walked farther in and dropped to my knees. I was at peace, in bliss, caught up in the sense of holiness. "God of my Fathers, your name is holy," I prayed. "I belong to you. What would you have me to do? Show me the way, Holy One."

Two gentle and love-filled words answered me within my heart. "My Son."

And bowing low, I answered, "My Father." And my love, too, went up to him, just like the incense of smoke that curled its way up into the pink and lavender-streaked sky that morning.

I expected him to show me the way. And, so, I both forgot and *found* myself in my Father's house for three days.

WONDER JUST A LITTLE

Did Jesus grow to know his Father through faith as we all do?

What was it like for Jesus, whose heart was innocent, loving, and good, to grow up witnessing and experiencing sin and sorrow all around him? Did he experience, with keen awareness, God as his Father? Did he learn early that his Father God walked closely with him, as he had with Adam and Eve in Eden?

The "ministry" of Jesus took up a mere three years of his life. Over ninety percent of Jesus' life was lived as a non-eventful, ordinary one. Nearly all of his years were spent as a son, a brother, a neighbor, a friend, and a tradesman. If you lived in his town, you might have known him as the man who fixed your oxen's yoke, or sold you a sturdy table, or perhaps he was your son's playmate when your children were young; or he might have been your uncle.

What was he like before he began preaching and healing the sick? Why did so few people from his hometown believe that he was a prophet? This is truly amazing, the fact that the Messiah, the Savior, the King of Kings and Lord of Lords blended right in to ordinary, common, everyday life—for thirty years. That's what's wonderful about the "silent years" of Jesus' life. The silence of the Scriptures speaks volumes—Jesus, filled with grace, living in perfect union with the Father, and was, for so long, an ordinary man. Jesus experienced all that is common to us. In this way, he was truly one *of* us, and one *with* us.

WHAT DO YOU SEE?

Jesus had brothers and sisters, yet how often do we consider this? Imagine being one of them. Let your heart go . . . picture yourself in that household. Ask the Lord to guide your time of meditation, and let the Spirit give you "spiritual eyes and ears" to experience what life close to Jesus in an ordinary, everyday way, might have been like. See him as a person who lived in joy and pain, as well as in everyday humdrum. What might it have been like to know Jesus as a brother and to grow up with him in your home, in your life, in the everyday? Of course he is now spiritually present, but what might it have been like with him face-to-face then?

Would he ever tease? Would he come to your aid? Would he give you advice? Scold you? Listen to your problems? Help you figure things out? Would he let you make mistakes and do things your own way? Do you think you'd be jealous of him—he might have been "goodie- goodie-two-shoes," while you were growing up. He might also have been the most trusted friend you'd ever have your entire life long.

On the other hand, what do you think it was like for him, the

Lord as one of us, to be a friend, or a brother? We know he was one to at least six siblings. What might the human experience mean to him now, our glorified Lord, friend, and brother?

JOURNAL

Sometimes we think that what pleases the Lord the most is our service. Perhaps we feel we should be a missionary, or be involved in ministry, but because of our family needs or situation, we think God has us "on the shelf." But remember, Jesus spent most of his life at home, seemingly doing nothing "in ministry" for God. So, what if we stay at home and do nothing out of the ordinary but obey God in the everyday, small things of life? Is this important? Ask the Lord what value this is to *him.*

Reflecting on the above questions, be open to the flow of God's thoughts to you and write them in your journal.

God loves us and wants us to be content and quiet. When we are quiet, He can speak to us in simple and profound revealation -

We can notice His gifts. I feel the peace He intends -

5 - Heaven's Carpenter

"I baptize you with water for repentance.
But after me will come one who is
more powerful than I,
whose sandals I am not fit to carry.
He will baptize you with the Holy Spirit and with fire."
Matthew 3:11

- John's birth foretold to Zechariah (Jerusalem, in the temple): *Luke 1:5-25*
- John's birth (Judean hills near Jerusalem): *Luke 1:57-66*
- Zechariah's prophetic song (Judean hills near Jerusalem): *Luke 1:67-79*
- John's growth and early life (Judean desert): *Luke 1:80*
- "The people were waiting expectantly . . .": *Luke 3:15*
- John's ministry is launched (Judean desert): *Mark 1:1; Luke 3:1-2*
- John, Jesus' forerunner, prepares the way for him (Judean wilderness near the Jordan River): *Matthew 3:1-10; Mark 1:2-8; Luke 3:3-18*
- Jesus comes from Galilee for baptism (Judean desert at the Jordan River): *Matthew 3:13*

A CONTEMPLATIVE VIEW

Jesus Was More Than Meets The Eye

Jesus left his glory and home in Heaven
thirty years before he left house and home in Galilee.
Leaving everything behind once more,
the carpenter of Nazareth,
a master in his trade,
a creative artist at best,
with an eye for beauty
and a knack for practicality,
laid aside his hand-tools one day
to build God's kingdom on earth.

What kind of a man might Jesus have been before his public life? Did he have close friends? What was his personality? The person Jesus, outside of his mission, is not revealed to us. For some long-forgotten reason, nobody who saw or knew him thought it was important to describe what he looked like!

Isn't it amazing to ponder the Creator of all things as a carpenter? The original materials: the stone, metal, and wood he worked with, were things his God-hands had made.

Was he gentle with his customers? Did anyone ever complain about his work, or his prices? We don't know what his hands fixed or made during his time in Nazareth; we can only imagine. Perhaps it was yokes, tables, doors, and such. But he was most certainly handy.

In three years of ministry, look at what came from his creativity—love, forgiveness, new beginnings, hope, grace, freedom, joy, truth, peace, and eternal life (which is the ability to know and enjoy God). In truth, this list is endless. Jesus was far more than a carpenter. In three short years after Nazareth, he forever changed the course of the world.

WONDER JUST A LITTLE

Have you ever considered that Jesus probably hung a door?
A door of wood. As a carpenter, I mean.
Have you ever considered that Jesus hung as a Door?
On a piece of wood. As a Savior, I mean.
He could have worked on a bridge.
Why not? Who else would? They didn't have road-construction workers, did they?
About that bridge . . . He built one between heaven and earth.
What about gates for sheep? Well, by now you see what I mean.

Then there are the nails to consider.
Isn't it something that he let someone pound those crude spiked objects of his trade into his own eternally capable hands? Hands more than familiar with what to do with a nail. And, what about his love? It's true that there was no need for nails at all. We agree with Michael Card's much-loved lyric: "His love would have held him there."
It's true. But nails were used as well as a beam of wood. Hung on a tree, was the "Tree of Life."
But there are brighter thoughts about Heaven's carpenter if we consider his "early works."
The Creator enjoyed himself when he made our world. His creation shows his glory and intelligence—and his personality. It's true. Just like any artist, there is a reflection of the person in his work, especially in *creative* works.
Here's just a few of God's originals.
Stars. Millions of them. Totally out of reach. The moon and sun—they are wondrous things to look at, plus depend on. He hung them and told them their jobs. He made high, snow-capped mountains—ever wonder why? Flat ground would have been simpler. The jungles. The glaciers. Overhead he placed a vast canopy called "sky," making things beneath it ever changing. He made the wind to use, but never control.
Flowers. Oh, the many kinds. Such artistic, beautiful designs! Red poppies, little white bells on the lily-of-the-valley. Roses, lilacs, petunias, daisies, carnations, tulips . . . the colors, the shapes,

the fragrances. They are lovely. And that's what they're for—to be lovely. Even if a valley full of them is never seen. It's that extravagant way of his with beauty.

Oceans. For those magnificent bodies of water, he gave rules to follow. Underground rivers and lakes, with secret passageways and storage places that only he knows about. The teeming-with-life rainforests. The wind-swept deserts. And these are just settings for the creatures he came up with.

He put the roar in a lion, and fitted him with a handsome mane. On a gentler side, he put the mew in a kitty and told her to be independent and to take lots of naps. He laughed out loud when he made the ostrich, knowing she would need a small head with which to hide. When he got around to making the penguins, he was still in a humorous mood. Not meant to be funny or odd, he cleverly stretched the neck of the giraffe—it was actually the trees that influenced him on that. The camel's hump wasn't an accident; it was a bit of ingenuity. He spotted ladybugs, striped the zebras, made a gorgeous spread of feathers for the peacock—a flair of grandeur having taken his fancy at that moment. And the spider—her strong, yet delicate, intricate web—what surprising engineering went into that little creature! Oh, the Lord had an amazing time in his workshop in heaven.

When he made the oxen—those large beasts that would bring ease to mankind's labors—he thought ahead to the hand-made plows and yokes with which he would fit them.

He taught the ants to build cities, instructing them to live an orderly life, and to be selfless. With a chuckle, he gave the green frog bulging eyes on the top of his head. Just for fun, he made monkeys, and told them to play all day, every day.

He put the delicate artwork in the wings of the butterfly. But, amazingly, he started out with a worm and a cocoon. It does seem strange. He showed the birds how to fly. He encouraged them to come up with their own songs. Porcupines were made not to cuddle, nor were the jellyfish meant to hold. Turtles and horses—could creatures be any more different? What a wild imagination!

Then, after all this, the grandest of all moments arrived. Pensive but joyful, he took dirt.

Bent over the ground, with loving hands, he formed a person.

And he breathed into his nostrils, imparting his own life into the man.

It was thousands of years later, in a workshop in Nazareth, that the Creator busied himself with wood, nails, and such. And, although he was a skilled, conscientious, hard-working carpenter, fair in business, gracious in manner, and true to his word, it wasn't until years later that anyone realized that he was much more than met the eye. He was, in reality, Heaven's carpenter.

WHAT DO YOU SEE?

Imagine the day Jesus put away his tools for the last time in Nazareth. Imagine what he might have been feeling at that time. Can you see his hands, his face? Can you see him as he contemplates what lies ahead of him? What do you think he thought regarding his cousin, John? Do you think Jesus was excited to "receive" what his Father had to say and do through his fiery prophet, his cousin John?

The meaning of ministry is *knowing God and making God known*. Jesus set off from his home of thirty years to publicly minister full time. He would no longer live an obscure, hidden life. What might he have felt as he left?

JOURNAL

What are your thoughts as you ponder how Jesus lived as a carpenter? Of all the ideas in this chapter, what most stirred your heart? What was your time of meditation like? What did you see and experience? End your journaling time by telling the Lord what you think of him.

That His craft was slow, quiet, contemplative, not pushy or showy.

6 - Holy Immersion

And a voice from heaven said, "This is my Son,
whom I love; with him I am well pleased."
Matthew 3:17

- John's person, proclamation, and baptism (Judean desert and the country around the Jordan River): *Matthew 3:1-6; Mark 1:2-6; Luke 3:3-6*
- John's messages to the Pharisees, Sadducees, crowds, tax collectors, and soldiers (Judean desert and the country around the Jordan River): *Matthew 3:7-10; Luke 3:7-14*
- John's description of the Messiah (Judean desert and country around the Jordan River): *Matthew 3:11-12; Mark 1:7-8; Luke 3:15-18*
- The beginning of Jesus' public ministry (Judean desert at the Jordan River): *Matthew 3:13-17; Mark 1:9-11; Luke 3:21-23a*

A CONTEMPLATIVE VIEW

John the Baptist, at the Jordan River . . .

I have come to call that day "the day of days." Yet it began as a typical one during those many months I spent south of Jericho when God sent me to preach and baptize his people.

I knew that the time was ripe for the sons and daughters of Jacob to come near to the true, living God, and to make room for him in their hearts. I could no longer stomach that our people were

43

being led by imposters in Judea, who compromised our inheritance and set religious traps for their own gain. Rome oppressed us, but the wolves of Judea added more than greed to the mix of worship in the temple. It was in God's loving jealousy that I preached and baptized his flock.

I knew from childhood that I was the one to prepare the way for the Messiah. And the Spirit of the Most High encouraged me, revealing that his days were near, even at hand. I baptized the people in water, but he would baptize them with fire. All this had been shown to me. And so I proclaimed his words with the fire of my mouth, which was what the God of Jacob had given me.

On what I thought was an ordinary morning, my disciples reported that a group from Galilee had arrived the evening before just before sunset. Some had sought accommodation and food in the small nearby village, near the Jordan River, and some had come ahead here, to the river, and settled in camps.

The villagers were not slow to take advantage of the situation. Shelters of sticks, grass and mud, plus a number of guestrooms in houses, sprang up to accommodate them, not without cost. By word of mouth, a steady stream of people had been coming to us for what turned out to be more than a year. New groups of pilgrims quickly replaced the ones before.

You would have thought that on that day, the day for which my entire life had been groomed, I would have *felt* his presence. Known he was so near. Seen him coming. But I did not.

I had not noticed him until he stood in front of me, head bowed, hands clasped in prayer, ready for baptism. Next in the line of penitents, his eyes were cast down, or maybe they were shut. I supposed that the man before me was so deeply in prayer that he hadn't known it was his turn to be immersed. It wasn't until one of my disciples tapped him on the shoulder, encouraging him to draw close to me, that he then looked up. When our eyes met, my heart leapt. At once my entire being cried within me, "It's *him!*"

Many years had passed since I'd seen Jesus, my second cousin. At first, he said nothing to me. His hands were still folded together in prayer when more of my disciples moved closer, concerned that something was upsetting me. He, in turn, looked at me with an open face, awaiting my instructions, unmoved by the fact that we were cousins. I was glad that he did not smile or make light conversation about seeing me again, because the moment had taken on such a solemn import within my spirit that I could hardly breathe. He simply waited for me to say or do something. It seemed an eternity passed while I tried to find my tongue, for all I could do was look at him. It was probably only seconds that passed; but in that brief span of time I realized that he was the One we expected. The Messiah. The One with "no beginnings." Mary's son. My cousin.

Oh, my Lord of heaven and earth. Lord of heaven and earth!

I was not about to baptize him. With a racing heart and shaking knees, I glanced at my disciples as they approached me. They had sensed something happening to me. Something strange. But I managed to wave them off.

Jesus, seeing this, bowed his head again. He wanted me to proceed. But I couldn't. It was absurd.

"I need to be baptized by you, and do you come to me?" I finally managed to speak.

Looking up again into my face, he took hold of my shoulders and, leaning close to me, luminous eyes only inches from mine, said in a low voice, "Let it be so now. It is proper for us to do this to fulfill all righteousness."

I stared blankly back. But he nodded his head to say he meant it, encouraging me to do as he wished.

The water was nearly waist-high. As I recall, I nodded in agreement and raised my hands to put them on his shoulders. He did not wait for them, but knelt so that his head disappeared beneath the surface. As he went down, I gently stayed my hands on top of his head. When I removed them, he came up out of the water, head still bowed, hands clasped in prayer as before. Water trickled in streams from his hair and beard.

Suddenly the loudest thunderclap I have ever heard tore open heaven above us. Fear gripped everyone but him. The signs in the heavens seemed appropriate to me. I couldn't help but smile. I stepped reverently back from him and lifted my hands in worship.

Clouds parted and a beam of sunlight shone down on us. A dove-like manifestation of the Holy Spirit gracefully descended and lit upon him. A voice from heaven followed: "You are my Son, whom I love; with you I am well pleased."

Smiling, Jesus lifted his face to heaven, eyes closed. It was terribly bright all around us. He stayed thus for quite some time. Afterward, he looked at me, and his look was such a look of gladness, the likes of which I've never seen on any other face. His delight was so contagious that I found myself caught up in the same ecstasy as he. The light around dimmed to normal, the dove disappeared, and what remained was the two of us full of smiles. We embraced.

Jesus thanked me, kissed both cheeks, and slowly walked out of the river. He quietly stepped along the shore, bent to find his sandals and put them on, and then proceeded on his way, walking around and between kneeling people. All eyes were fastened on him. Some of the people reached out to touch his hem as he passed by. Some softly blessed him or praised God as he walked along. He disappeared from our eyes over a small hill, behind an outcrop of wild brush.

Awe had filled all of us and no one stirred after his disappearance.

The entire drama had unfolded so suddenly, without any hint or sign of its coming, that it took me a few minutes to recover enough to know that I, too, must retreat from the place. Overcome by the experience, I excused myself from my disciples and the people for the day.

My entire life had brought me to this moment. My cousin, of whom my mother had spoken so well of years before, was the Son of God. I wanted to let the awe of it fill my soul. I went to my cave and worshiped until the next morning. When I returned to the Jordan, I looked for him. But it was more than forty days before I saw him again.

**

Since Eden's paradise was lost, God's designs for redemption waited for the right time. And this was it. It came about, as is customary, that a courier be sent ahead of a king to announce his arrival. That proclamation was heard upon God's chosen land two thousand years ago. For months, the courier stood beside a gentle river that flowed through the dry, barren landscape, crying out to thirsty hearts that God's kingdom was coming to them.

Through John the Baptist, God's Spirit cried out, "Come! Come to the waters! Come, wash, and draw near to me. Turn from your lifeless, sinful lives—I want to see your faces."

Answering the call to be baptized, Jesus humbly immersed himself in the waters of repentance. Of course there was no sin in him, but he would fulfill all righteousness. In him, in his death, we would find resurrection. And so, Jesus said yes to his Father. He would take the sins of the world upon himself through death, be buried, and rise to live a resurrected life. This is what his baptism symbolized.

Jesus knew his mission fully.

And so it was that John and Jesus began to reveal the coming of God's Kingdom. Soon the *land* would spring forth with vibrant life from rivers of blessing, from the Anointed One, and his Grace would be poured out upon them—from his words and actions—from his *Life*.

WONDER JUST A LITTLE

For thirty years, sensitive to his Father's will, Jesus waited. He did not step out into ministry until the time was right. When his cousin began to preach and baptize in the wilderness, Jesus knew his time was drawing near. He understood John's mission: to prepare the hearts of the people for his own ministry.

Can you imagine the thoughts and feelings Jesus might have experienced when he first heard the news of his cousin's preaching and baptizing activities? What a wonderful moment it must have been when John and Jesus stood face-to-face in the river and the Spirit of God came upon them. In that glorious moment, the Mystery of heaven was manifested—the Father, Son, and Holy Spirit. John's heart would have leapt as he stood with Jesus. Had he not leapt within his mother's womb thirty years before when encountering the Son of God's first coming to him?

How wonderful this moment was! For the dove of the Spirit lit upon the Son of Man, and the Father's voice was heard. How could anyone fully comprehend the wonder of that event? That moment in the eternal annals of history was a shining moment for God. And so, too, for us.

It was for Jesus' sake, not only for those present, that God the Father's voice sounded audibly. "You are my Son, whom I love; with you I am well pleased."

Why did the Father say this to his Son? Did Jesus need to hear this? Didn't he already know where he'd come from? That he was God's only begotten Son, having come from heaven? Is it possible that Jesus lived his life in faith, like we all must, and that he understood his own identity through faith? Could it have been a slow unfolding during his lifetime, bringing him to this moment in his own life? His Father's words were not, "He is my beloved Son," rather, they were, "You are my beloved Son." This was a moment they gloried in one another.

Jesus surrendered to all that the waters of baptism meant. In the total emptying of himself, he lived only to love others, and all his life was the giving of himself.

WHAT DO YOU SEE?

Read the Scripture passages that surround the events of Jesus' baptism. Ask the Holy Spirit to guide you to experience being there. Imagine that you are a witness, maybe even one of those who had come to hear John the Baptist. Let God prepare your heart, for the Lord is always coming to us in new ways. Let yourself feel the marvel of this moment in history.

JOURNAL

Jesus, the Lord, was baptized and took upon himself the mission to give himself—his very life—to redeem us. Can you appreciate this sacred hour in the life of Jesus and the world? Summarize in your journal insights or thoughts that are meaningful to you about Jesus' baptism.

7 – Triumph in the Desert

"If you are the Son of God . . ."
Luke 4:3b

- Jesus' temptation in the desert (Judean desert): *Matthew 4:1-10; Mark 1:12-13a; Luke 4:1-13*
- Angels minister to Jesus (Judean desert): *Matthew 4:11; Mark 13b*

A CONTEMPLATIVE VIEW

"If you are . . ."
Satan put this question to Jesus about his identity. Was it a matter to be proved, even to himself?

The first of three tests: "If you are the Son of God, tell these stones to become bread."
There was something familiar about these words—they were like these: "Eat the fruit of the tree, Adam and Eve, then you will be like God, knowing good and evil."
They had failed their test and eaten. Here, now, was Jesus to redeem the sin.
Jesus replied that man does not live on bread alone, but on every word that comes from the mouth of God. And he did not succumb to his own will but waited in obedience to his Father.

"Did you see that? My son, my son, he is obedient unto death!" God the Father exclaimed to everyone in heaven. "He will not fail

49

in his mission. Truly, my son, he is the Bread of Life!"

Atop the pinnacle of the temple, the second test came. After taking Jesus there in a moment of time, the devil said to him, "If you are the Son of God, throw yourself down. For it is written: 'He will command his angels concerning you, and they will lift you up in their hands, so that you will not strike your foot against a stone.'"

But Jesus answered, "It is also written: 'Do not put the Lord your God to the test.'"

"Oh blessed day!" A trumpet sounded with Elohim's shout of happiness. "My son, my son! Did you see that, you angels, did you hear what he said? Although he has humbled himself and lives by faith, as do all men on the earth, yet he knows who he is! He cares not for the opinion of others, but for mine alone. He will save all the fallen! Do you see my son? He is the Lord and Holy One of Israel, the Messiah, the King of the Jews, one in my Spirit, whose glory fills my temple!"

Immediately, the third test came. The devil took Jesus to the summit of a high mountain and showed him all the kingdoms of the world and their splendor. "All this I will give you, if you will bow down and worship me."

Now this was the hardest of all three tests. How very tempting to bypass all the work, the pain, to bypass even the cross! How easily Jesus could gain what he'd come to reclaim. But there was not a moment's hesitation. Jesus knew who he was and what he had come to do, and exactly how he would have to do it.

"Away from me, Satan! For it is written: 'Worship the Lord your God, and serve him only.'"

And his heavenly Father sang in triumph a wondrous blessing upon his son, "You have all authority both of heaven and earth. You, my son, are my voice, my hands, my heart! Go and take your inheritance back from the Prince of darkness!"

After the devil left Jesus, angels came to revive him. They gave him heavenly bread to eat. They soothed his weary soul and told him that his Father was pleased, and that he had all authority of heaven and earth in his hands.

WONDER JUST A LITTLE

Is it true that spiritual trials precede spiritual greatness? Deserts have proven many saints over the ages. Wilderness experiences turn the faithful into heroes. It was true for the Patriarchs, Abraham, Moses, the whole of Israel, and has been true of Christians as well. This was true even for Jesus.

Where Israel failed in the desert—Jesus did not. His identity was proven there. He left the ordeal with the full power and authority of heaven. He was ready.

Isn't it incredible to consider that God, in Jesus, was tested like we all are? That is how very far God came to reach out to take us by the hand, to lead us safely home. He put himself in harm's way, to suffer just as we suffer, to be tried, just as we are tried. And, in him, we triumph against the evil that comes against us.

It's really a wonder that Jesus had to go through a time of testing at all. God doesn't enjoy the deserts any more than we do. He'd prefer to spend time with us in the Edens of our love with him. But in the times of the desert, our love is proven and made strong—just as it was for Jesus.

WHAT DO YOU SEE?

Read the Scriptures about Jesus' testing in the desert. Now watch over the events as though you stood beside God the Father in heaven. Or watch over Jesus as one of his angels. Does this give you new perspective? What does it mean to you that Jesus endured these temptations?

In the prayer Jesus taught us he said, "Our Father . . . give us our daily bread . . . forgive us as we forgive . . . lead us not into temptation . . . for yours is the power, and the glory, and the kingdom, forever and ever." How deeply he experienced these elements of his prayer from his time in the desert.

JOURNAL

We are ever reaching. We must discover who we are in God and our hearts ask, "Who am I? Why am I here?" These questions recur over and over in our lives. Also, we experience temptations that try to draw us away from God even in our searching.

Record in your journal what you have learned and experienced while pondering Jesus' temptation in the desert. Look back to times when you've experienced temptations, or times when you felt God let you fall through his fingers. Sometimes we live long enough to become thankful for those times. Sometimes we find ourselves in the middle of it and cannot see clearly at all. Can you find a truth in Scripture to get you through the ordeal? Can you trust in God's heart, even though you cannot see what his hand is doing—and he seems so far from you? In these times of testing and proving, we become just like Jesus.

8 - The Unveiling Begins

"Come," he replied, "and you will see."
John 1:39a

- John's testimony about himself to the priests and Levites (Bethany near the Jordan River): *John 1: 190-28*
- John's testimony to Jesus as the Son of God (Bethany near the Jordan River): *John 1:29-34*
- Jesus' first followers (Bethany on the east side of the Jordan River): *John 1:35-42*

Note: Jesus' dream in the novel, *God in Sandals*, is not in the Gospels. However, you may find its source of inspiration from Revelation 19:11-16; Psalm 24:7-10; Zech. 14:3-4; Ezek. 44:2-3; Zech. 9:9; Matt. 21:5; Acts 1:9-12.

A CONTEMPLATIVE VIEW

God's Unveiling

From the heights of glory
to the desert valley of human need
came our God.
In full stride,
in power and authority,
the Holy One from heaven came to us.

When the Lord first appeared at the banks of the Jordan, his heart was full of secrets he would, in three short years, reveal. But the most wondrous thing that he showed us—the greatest mystery of all he'd come to disclose, that most desired—was himself. The Desire of ages. The face of God humankind has always longed to see, suddenly appeared before them.

No one knew exactly who Jesus was that day that John said, "Behold . . ."

John knew about Jesus because the Holy Spirit told him beforehand, "The man on whom you see the Spirit come down and remain is he who will baptize with the Holy Spirit." But perhaps John had been just as surprised as everyone else.

After Jesus' time in the desert, he returned to the Jordan where he was baptized. Upon seeing him, the prophet John testified about him, "I have seen and I testify that this is the Son of God."

Right after this, two of John's disciples were strongly drawn to Jesus. About him their teacher had said, "He is the Lamb of God, who takes away the sins of the world!"

And, although they couldn't yet understand what John was saying, the veil between God and humankind began to fall away.

So, John and Andrew were the first to follow after and seek Jesus. When Jesus turned around and asked them what they wanted, they asked him, "Where are you staying?"

They didn't know what else to say. But they wanted to be with him, to follow him. They had seen what their hearts were made for. And Jesus knew their hearts. Jesus' first words to his first followers were: "Come and see."

Oh, Heaven! That is the invitation into the mystery, the glory, and the wonder of our God.

Our hearts beat faster now. Our eyes see clearer now. God smiles on us, just as Jesus smiled on his two first followers. For truly, God himself had come to give his eternal blessing to his own:

"The Lord bless you and keep you;
the Lord make his face shine upon you;
and be gracious to you;
the Lord turn his face toward you
and give you peace." Numbers 6:24-26, *Aaron's Blessing*

God wants to shine his face toward us—to smile—at us. He gave this blessing to Moses to give to Aaron with which to bless his people. And when Jesus came, this became the most wonderful reality. Jesus came to shine the face of God upon us! This was the unveiling—the beginning—of God's love and redemption made known.

WONDER JUST A LITTLE

"The next day John saw Jesus coming toward him and said, "Look, the Lamb of God, who takes away the sin of the world! This is the one I meant when I said, 'A man who comes after me has surpassed me because he was before me.' . . ."

Let this moment come alive in your heart. If you were there, what would you have thought? You would have looked at the man being pointed out. Of course you would. You would have sized him up in your mind and heart. What is his demeanor like? What is he doing as you look at him? Why is he at the Jordan to be baptized, you ask yourself. He's just like the rest of us, you say. What is the meaning of the Baptist's strange words, you wonder. You are a person who has grown up in the tradition of animal sacrifices. How many countless lambs have been offered up to God for the peoples' sins over the many years? And, so, you ask, how can a single person be a Lamb of God?

This name by which the Baptist called Jesus had tremendous significance—for it held the clue to the purpose for which the Son of God had come to earth. After the Passover meal with his disciples and the new covenant in his blood was established, this title would mean more to those who had heard John's first announcement about Jesus as the Lamb of God.

Jesus was God's own atonement sacrifice for sins—once and for all.

Today we have the benefit of hindsight. We have the gift of the Holy Spirit within us, giving us the revelation of John's testimony about Jesus. Those at the Jordan that first day did not because it was just the beginning of God's unveiling.

Scripture says that when Jesus returns, riding the clouds of heaven, the hem of his white robe will have been dipped in blood. On earth, during his reign in the Messianic Age, the lion and lamb will peacefully lie down together. No more blood, nor pain, nor sorrow. All this is a wonder, when we view God's *Larger Story*. How we long for the days of Eden restored. How deeply our souls long for the fullness of intimacy with God to be ours again.

John the Baptist testified about Jesus' identity and directed the people to *behold* him. Just like Jesus' first disciples, we want to follow him and be with him. Jesus invites each of us to daily "Come and see."

WHAT DO YOU SEE?

Do you see Jesus excited and delighted to be with John and Andrew? Can you imagine them sitting with Jesus all afternoon, conversing with him? What things do you think they talked about? Afterwards, Andrew went to his brother, Simon, and said, "We have found the Messiah." Andrew's response after one day with Jesus was that he believed he was the long-awaited Hope of Israel. He couldn't wait to bring his brother, Simon Peter, to him.

Try to imagine these events and enjoy the experience. Can you see the excited faces, can you see Jesus talking with his hands, using Scriptures to draw hearts in? How is it the two men so quickly knew that he was the Messiah? Jesus didn't disclose this until much later, and then he told them it was a secret.

JOURNAL

How would you describe the Lord to someone who knew nothing about him? Write this out in your journal as though you were writing a letter of introduction to someone who had never heard about Jesus. Who is Jesus to you personally?

9 - "Follow Me"

. . . Finding Philip, he said, "Follow me."
John 1:43b

- Jesus calls Philip to follow him (Bethabara in Judea): *John 1:43*
- Philip finds Nathanael and brings him to Jesus (Cana in Galilee): *John 1:44-48*
- The first disciples of Jesus go with him. They are: John, Andrew, Simon Peter, Philip, and Nathanael (Traveling from Jordan to Galilee): *John 1:49-51*

A CONTEMPLATIVE VIEW

Oh, to Follow You, Jesus!

Jesus, when you first saw Simon, you nicknamed him your "little rock."
Your beloved Peter.

Peter was the "first believer" to proclaim faith in you—
as Messiah and Son of the Living God.
The moment your faces met, you knew he'd be the first stone laid—
in your spiritual temple.

Upon him, and his first "witness" of you, the rest of us are stacked.

A fisherman of men, he'd follow in your wake.
He was a born fisherman.
And you knew all about him right from the start, before he uttered a word.
As his Maker, you knew him at first sight.

Jesus, when you met Philip, it was you who went after him.
Finding him, you said at once, "Follow me."
You'd never said these words to anyone before.
You knew what Philip wanted eons before he did.
Jesus, how did it feel?
How was it when you saw Philip's whole face brighten when it dawned on him
that you were the One, standing before him, with a glint of knowing in your eyes,
that you were the One whom he had longed for his entire life?
How did it feel, Lord, to be face-to-face with a true follower who had followed you in heart even before seeing you with eyes?

What was it like to share your joyful looks with one another?
Oh, what a sight it would be to see the two of you standing there
You with your spiritual nets cast all about him—that wonderful net of yours,
that invisible power of love, for it was cast by you all about him.
We know now about your mysterious drawing that makes us drop everything
because we want only you.

Jesus, it must have been a joy for you when you met Nathanael,
for surely you had known his longing, heard his heartfelt prayers
for God's Anointed One to come. Had his prayers drawn

you near?
No wonder he and Philip shared a holy bond.

Was this whole surprise—that is, your coming to them—
planned before Time?
Had you dreamed up that wonderful day when you three
met by the fig tree?—
the fig tree of Israel, the symbol of your nation?
Glory, Lord, for all the many details, symbols,
and meanings in which you so delight to fulfill!
What a sentimental, dramatic God you are!

Lord, when our hearts hear you say, "Follow me,"
everything in life becomes true and beautiful.
You know each person you've created even before we are
born.
You know who we will be.
You know that we will become ourselves upon our discovery of your love.
When we know who you are and that our deepest desires are
for you,
then we learn to know ourselves and why we exist.

Lead us, Lord, lead us.
Oh, to follow you, Jesus!
Carry us away with you to our heart's home.
Oh, to follow you, Jesus!

WONDER JUST A LITTLE

It is amazing to read the Scriptures of the beginnings of Jesus'
public life. His first followers didn't become disciples right away.
At first they simply followed him around for a time and then
returned to their homes and their trades. It took awhile before these
early followers joined Jesus in his ministry. Yet, they certainly were
excited about this man from Nazareth upon their first meeting.
After that one afternoon with Jesus, why did Andrew run and get

his brother and excitedly say, "We've found the Messiah!"? And, a day or so later, Philip ran to find his friend, Nathanael, and said to him, "We have found the one Moses wrote about in the Law, and about whom the prophets also wrote . . ." Yet, it wasn't until more than two years later before these same men proclaimed their belief that Jesus was the Messiah. Jesus waited until close to the end of his ministry to confirm his identity as Messiah to them.

There was something wonderful about their first encounters with Jesus . . . for their hearts knew then, way before their minds knew, just who Jesus was. What made their hearts marvel upon first meeting the Lord? Why did they need signs, wonders, and explanations over and over to have faith in him later on? These are things to ponder.

After Nathanael excitedly proclaimed Jesus as "the Son of God and the King of Israel," Jesus said, "I tell you the truth, you shall see heaven open, and the angels of God ascending and descending on the Son of Man." Jesus liked to call himself the "Son of Man" (Daniel 7:13-14), a title which both veiled and unveiled his identity. Those who heard Jesus call himself by this name may have thought he meant the promised One spoken of by Daniel. It was revealing and still concealing, depending upon a person's faith and readiness. Those whose hearts were ready to follow him and those who looked into the Scriptures knew his self-designation meant that he claimed to be that promised One.

. To call himself the "Son of Man" suggests he enjoyed the reality that he, fully divine, had become a man. A son of humanity, one of us, these days were like no other in his own eternal life! He delighted in becoming a part of the very world and people that he made.

Isn't it amazing that Jesus called himself "Jacob's ladder?" This, too, is something great to ponder. For this "ladder" is the way to heaven from earth. Certainly, his new followers marveled at his words about that.

For those with ears to hear, Jesus clearly reveals himself. He calls us to follow him, and as we do, we will know him more and more.

WHAT DO YOU SEE?

John 1:43 says, "The next day Jesus decided to leave for Galilee. Finding Philip, Jesus said to him, "Follow me." There were probably reasons Jesus searched for Philip, reasons not explained in the Scriptures. We know that Philip excitedly brought Jesus to his friend, Nathanael. Can you see the humor and delight on Jesus' face when he sees how Nathanael turns from a skeptic to a saint in a moment, because of Jesus' answer to a question, "How do you know me?" Jesus cuts through Nathanael's caution and reluctance with one simple comment! And it is because Jesus has known Nathanael before they met in person—just as Jesus had already "known" Simon Peter.

Imagine Jesus looking for you and finding you. Imagine yourself as either Nathanael or Philip—and enter into the story. Can you hear the voice of Jesus, his laugh, his humor? Can you see his intense look when he calls you by name? How does he know you? How does this make you feel towards him? This is truly how he is with each of us—for he's always known us.

JOURNAL

Record your thoughts, prayers, reflections, or experiences from the thoughts presented in this chapter and from your time of meditation. Ask Jesus what he enjoys about you.

10 – The Extravagant Bridegroom

He thus revealed his glory,
and his disciples put their faith in him.
John 2:11b

- Jesus' first miracle: water becomes wine (Cana in Galilee): *John 2:1-11*

A CONTEMPLATIVE VIEW

No one at the wedding banquet knew that the Divine Bridegroom was a guest there. Nobody realized what surprise the Father in heaven had in store that day. Neither did the two bridegrooms know beforehand what transformation was about to occur. The one just married sat beside his bride at the table, his heart sinking as the wine vessels were drained. The other unrecognized Bridegroom dreamed of his Bride as he quietly watched the wedding celebration, a patient knowing filling his heart.

This was the setting for Jesus' first delightful and wonderful miracle.

As with most miracles, this one came out of crises. It wasn't a life-threatening situation, not a matter of "life and death." It was a threat to the life of a party. The crisis and panic was in the eyes of the bridegroom and his family. It involved shame for them and disappointment for their guests. But was this just cause for Divine intervention?

"Father, do you want me to do something here?" Jesus prayed

after his mother pressed him to help. She had that look in her eye—that look!

At once, Jesus knew.

He spied the six large clay water jars, sitting in a row nearby. At the start of the meal, the guests were provided with water to spiritually purify themselves before they ate. There was plenty of water left in the jars to serve Jesus' purpose, but he instructed the servants to fill them to the brim. Then, without any dramatics, Jesus told them to serve the water-become-wine to the headmaster, and then to all the guests.

Here, now, were gallons and gallons of this "purification" water turned into wine! The servants were in awe. The headmaster was puzzled. The bridegroom and his family were relieved and amazed. And all the guests had fun!

Jesus, Mary's son, had turned lifeless water meant for a purification rite into free-flowing, heart-lifting wine.

What a surprise! Laughter and dancing faces off with religious legalism!

Who knows what is holy in God's eyes? Jesus came to bring freedom and life—rich, abundant, overflowing blessedness. Turning gallons of water into wine was an appropriate beginning to his public ministry.

Enjoy life with me! I've come to set you free. L' Chaim!

Let's open our hearts to receive God's extravagant favor and kindness! God's love and the desire of his heart was given away during his first miracle two thousand years ago. And his gifts continue still, repeatedly, in many forms and ways. The Divine Bridegroom hasn't changed a bit.

WONDER JUST A LITTLE

Even as believers, sometimes the love of God escapes our grasp for the simple reason that it just seems too good to be true. Often, we miss the real message of Jesus' first miracle. We miss the true gift in this story—God's extravagant, non-legalistic grace. As Christians, we know that we have been called out of darkness and into the light. Not sure how to respond, we become self-righteously pious, and our faith and love for God become a legalistic and ideal-istic taskmaster. God never intended this to happen.

There is nothing legalistic, boring, or even "religious" about Jesus. That's not the life Jesus came to bring us. If we truly knew God's heart, we would realize that he is an extravagant, fun-loving, lively, and passionately happy, uplifting Person.

"God prefers mercy to sacrifice," Jesus said, quoting Scripture. Just what does that mean in our modern-day language? It means that God has a forgiving and loving heart and doesn't require us to work hard to please him. It means love is the religious expression God desires us to experience. It means that God wants our hearts to become like his.

Well, what is he like? Look closely at this miracle. What did the Lord do? What was his purpose? How much wine did he make? Have you ever heard the argument that Jesus' miraculous wine was unfermented? (The people of his day would not have been impressed!) Anyone who believes this has missed the point entirely! God have mercy!

The real reason why God performed this miracle is a wonder. It was for one reason only—to bring people joy. He wants to change 'lifeless living' into a celebration of life. He wants to change our tasteless water into rich, abundant wine. The message is not that he wants us to become drunkards. His miracle holds spiritual meaning. Jesus showed us that God delights to delight us.

Just think about how the Lord gave his all to and for us. This is the God who loves us and wants us to come near. If we would just relax and come near and let him have what he wants. If we would place ourselves upon his breast, breathe deeply and listen intently, then we'd know. He's crazy in love with us. That's the truth. He's not looking for us to perform or abstain from enjoying ourselves.

The thing the Lord hates is to see us stay far from him and look for "life" through everything else but him. What he wants for us is to enjoy real life—which is to know and enjoy him. This is the message of Jesus' wonderful, miraculous wine.

In your presence is fullness of joy; in your right hand
there are pleasures forevermore.
Psalm 16:11

WHAT DO YOU SEE?

Enter into the story of the wedding banquet at Cana. Become one of the characters in the story. Watch and experience the miracle. What are Jesus' reactions—his facial expressions when he sees how surprised the servants are when they witness this miraculous transformation of water to wine? Watch Jesus as he interacts with the people who, because of him, greatly enjoy themselves. How does Jesus act during the party, especially after the miracle? Can you see him enjoying himself too? Ask the Lord to reveal his true heart to you.

JOURNAL

If you love God and want to please him, then you can, in practical ways, follow your love for him. If you have God first in your life and love him above all else, then you can follow that inner leading, because your own heart is in union with God's. Don't let others tell you what you should or shouldn't do. Don't allow yourself to be trapped in a cage when God invites you to fly the heavens with him. You don't know what he has in store for you; it may be entirely different than what he has in store for others. Grow up in Christ's love. Let him show you how to live! He is carefully leading you to become the person he's always wanted you to be. And you are unique. No one is like you. Not one. And just remember, his priority for you is to set you free and to bring you close to him, so that the two of you enjoy each other. Our faith is a journey, and how we live it will change as we change.

Write your thoughts and experiences from this chapter in your journal. What is God saying to you through the story of the wedding wine and Jesus' extravagance?

11 - God's Temple

But the temple he had spoken of was his body.
John 2:21

- Jesus' first stay in Capernaum with his relatives and early disciples (Capernaum): *John 2:12*
- First cleansing of the temple at Passover (Jerusalem): *John 2:13-22*
- Early response to Jesus' miracles (Jerusalem): *John 2:23-25*

A CONTEMPLATIVE VIEW

Rabbi Jesus, son of Joseph, entered a special court area, having humbly and respectfully removed his sandals outside the gated threshold of the arched, open-aired place—an area within the temple complex designated for prayer. It was a wide, rectangular-shaped court, used more as a sanctuary. Its four sides were flanked by marble columns with arches that stretched along its sides, dividing the open space from the outer halls. Along these halls flowed hundreds of pilgrims walking from one court to another. It was normally quiet in this inner court-sanctuary, as well as in its passageways, except during the feasts when voices were raised in prayer, chanting, and songs carried ever so beautifully to those quietly shuffling by. But it was not a place for gatherings or conversation, even in the busiest times of the feasts.

In recent years, however, the sounds in this court had changed.

Jesus' disciples followed their rabbi, one of many others there that day. His head was covered by his prayer shawl, with only a part of his face showing. The shawl's tallit—the four cornered strands of delicately knotted string—fell against his light wool tunic. Once inside, his gait quickened to a purposeful stride. The place had been turned into a marketplace. He spotted a rather heavy rope that had been used for bundling merchandise and stooped to pick it up. While maintaining his stride, he twisted it, forming it into a whip. Suddenly, without warning, Jesus gave it a hard crack upon the stone floor. His eyes flashed fury. He drove out the sellers and buyers alike, to the left and right, as he wielded his crude but effective lash above their heads, and upon them, if they happened too close to him. Out of his mouth flew shouts of indignation. Within a matter of minutes, the place looked like a great storm had passed through. Birdcages were thrown open, upturned tables rested on their sides. Merchandise, coins, broken stools and cartons, all sorts of things, were strewn about. Circling high in the open air, near the tops of the arches, were gray and white doves, their rushing wings the sound of something otherworldly, like angels hovering watchfully overhead.

When his rage was spent, with a sorrowful groan, Rabbi Jesus threw his rope down. The doves had either settled or flown away, and a heavy silence fell upon the onlookers as though the dread of God had descended. Fearful surprise filled every heart. Shaking his head, and muttering a prayer, Jesus strode out of the place, while the stunned crowd divided, making a path for his exit.

"Who is he?" more than one voice asked.

"The Prophet of Nazareth."

"He works miracles and heals the sick," a swarthy shepherd from Galilee answered.

A religious leader lifted his voice as Jesus was about to pass him. "What miraculous sign can you show us to prove your authority to do all this?"

Jesus stopped to look squarely at his challenger. With Heaven's authority and confidence, he answered in a strong, loud voice that underlined his words, "Destroy this temple. And I will raise it again in three days."

His famous dare later proved, beyond all shadow of doubt, by what authority he had come. His proof was this: He was, himself, the living temple of God.

**

Lord Jesus knew that the religious leaders did not understand his words or his heart that day in the temple marketplace. Even so, he let his actions speak for themselves. God's love cried out to be heard, dramatically and passionately. It was a long time before anyone understood the reality of what had transpired that day.

Jesus was willing to play "the fool." The religious leaders, rather than listen to him, scorned him. How sadly wise he must have felt that day in the temple courts. He knew the rulers would take his Presence and destroy it. In fact, Salvation (the meaning of his name) counted on it. How else would he become their Passover Lamb? How else would the entire temple and its rituals performed there bring to fulfillment their meaning? The temple and its traditions were in place waiting for him to come. Without him, none of it held any real sense. Everything pointed to his mission.

Within the Son of God resided the fullness of the Creator of the Universe, the God of Israel. At the time of his wholehearted strike against polluted religiosity, he prophesied about his death and resurrection. Heaven's authority was upon him. The living temple of God would be raised on the third day after his saving work on the cross.

WONDER JUST A LITTLE

The dwelling place of God's personality, God's Spirit, God's heart and mind, resided fully in Jesus. His own people didn't recognize their Lord. Today, the same is true. When God abides in his people, he's often not recognized.

Just before Jesus' first temple (his body) was destroyed, he said, "If you love me, you will obey what I command. And I will ask the Father, and he will give you another Counselor to be with you forever—the Spirit of truth. The world cannot accept him, because it neither sees him nor knows him. But you know him, for he lives with you and will be in you. I will not leave you as orphans; I will come to you. Before long, the world will not see me anymore, but you will see me. Because I live, you also will live. On that day you will realize that I am in my Father, and you are in me, and I am in you. Whoever has my commands and obeys them, he is the one who loves me. He who loves me will be loved by my Father, and I too will love him and show myself to him." (John 14:15-21)

Jesus still walks the earth in humble disguise. He walks in us. Like the Jerusalem temple, we are meant to be in communion and in union with him. We, too, are the house of God that Jesus is so passionate to defend.

The Lord hates religious trappings that have a form of worship but which lack true devotion. Being in love with God—that grace which springs forth from an overwhelming response to his love and favor—this is what God wants for us in "our temples." How he loves us.

WHAT DO YOU SEE?

Jesus had, beating in his heart, the burning zealousness of God. He acted the part of a "broken-hearted" lover that day in the temple courtyard. He used a whip of love to clear away devotion-gone-wrong. Can you see this? Imagine being there. What kind of message did Jesus act out that day in the temple? Imagine his face, his movements, the sound of his voice echoing around the temple. Do you see the whip in his hand, his prayer shawl falling from his head? Do you see people running out of his way?

Secular scholars have judged Jesus to be an young angry man who lost his temper. Just like those at the temple that day, they are missing the point. Christian teachers have pointed out that Jesus' actions were God's righteousness cleansing the holy place. This is true. Christian counselors have explained that Jesus was upset over the "spiritual abuse" by the selfish leaders, explaining that Jesus was defending those who had come to the temple, out of faith and obedience, so that they wouldn't be taken advantage of. This is also wonderfully true. But most obvious is that Jesus was greatly moved by the defilement of the holy temple of God. It was a place to meet with God: the dwelling place of his Father, the holy place in which the Spirit of God came to be with his people. Turning it into a marketplace showed no respect for God's presence. The temple was meant as a place to be in communion with God—not for commerce, or anything else. What do you see in the heart of Jesus as you imagine the scene?

JOURNAL

As a believer, each of us is a temple of God. Sometimes Jesus comes in, stirs things up, and purges us. He does this because of his deep, affectionate love. He'd rather have us hot than lukewarm. Is there anything not right within your heart or in your life that keeps you from him? He wants to be in loving communion with us, so that we may enjoy his presence.

There are many facets to the Lord's love for us. In this chapter we see the Lord's zeal for holiness. Does this zeal make you feel guarded, or does it draw you? Have you been trying to please him rather than coming to really know him? With the understanding that Jesus' heart is full towards you, what things do you perceive may hinder your closeness with him? Write about these things in your journal and ask the Lord for his insight regarding them.

trust
fears

12- Seeing God's Kingdom

Jesus declared,
"I tell you the truth,
no one can see the kingdom of God
unless he is born again."
John 3:3

• Nicodemus' interview with Jesus (Jerusalem): *John 3:1-21*

A CONTEMPLATIVE VIEW

During the Feast of Passover in Jerusalem, Jesus came boldly into the public eye. Beginning with the cleansing of the temple, he acted the part of a high-spirited prophet of God. Like John the Baptist, Jesus spoke openly about the nearness of God's Kingdom, of God coming to them. But the religious authorities shunned both John and Jesus.

It was the masses of people who flocked to Jesus.

"Many people saw the miraculous signs Jesus was doing and believed in his name. But Jesus would not entrust himself to them, for he knew all men. He did not need man's testimony about man, for he knew what was in a man" (John 2:23b-25).

Jesus did not *entrust himself* to them. What does it mean to "entrust oneself" to another? Were there no souls found worthy of his wondrous friendship?

Yes, there were some souls with whom Jesus entrusted himself, with whom he was friends. There was John, the beloved apostle;

Peter, whom Jesus endearingly nicknamed his "little rock;" James, who, early in his life, was martyred for Jesus' entrustment; Mary of Magdala won Jesus' heart entirely; Mary of Bethany certainly held his affections, for he defended her for "wasting" her time and money on him. Yes, there were some who won his trust. And they have become our most revered examples—we want to be just like them.

But the multitudes in Jerusalem that week of Passover followed Jesus everywhere for the wrong reasons. Jesus had certainly astounded them with his divine power. He gave them what they could only have dreamed of—some were healed of diseases, while others gained freedom from oppression. The blind could see, the deaf could hear, and the crippled learned how to dance.

They believed in him. Perhaps some even believed the truth about who he was, that he was the long-awaited Messiah. But superficial faith, the fleeting approval of the sightseers, meant nothing to Jesus. He knew that their hearts were self-centered, that they were not regenerated.

So when Nicodemus, a member of the ruling council, came to him in secret, Jesus told him that his heart, his life, needed regeneration. He said, "You must be born again."

Anyone can obtain Jesus' favors and blessings. No matter who a person is or what a person has done, the Lord will bless, forgive, heal, and help whoever comes to him. His love extends to all the nations, to every living soul; his mercies are new every morning. But how does one win his entrustment? How can one experience his intimate and wondrous friendship?

He told Nicodemus how.

Knowing that the Pharisee did not believe in his and John's teaching, he offered a good, close look into the heart of God. This was an open invitation to holy friendship. Jesus explained how true faith, the kind that would win God's entrustment and friendship, could be his.

Revealing the mystery of salvation, the Savior explained to his late-night visitor, the very scope of his life and mission. And what true faith in him would bring. What revelations Jesus disclosed to this man! If Nicodemus had gone to Jesus for the sake of theology, he heard the most profound. If he sought to better *know* Jesus, who he and his peers mistrusted, their meeting's conversation became an amazing bridge. Jesus laid himself across that chasm, openly disclosing everything about himself to Nicodemus.

That night Jesus had gently said to him, "You should not be surprised by my saying, 'You must be born again.' The wind blows wherever it pleases. You hear its sound, but you cannot tell where it comes from or where it is going. So it is with everyone born of the Spirit."

Was Nicodemus ever born again? Did his life show the signs of *Ruach-ha-Kodesh*, the Holy Spirit, the *wind* of God having passed through? Apparently, he did. This Pharisee ended up courageously defending Jesus when he was accused and brought to trial. He claimed Jesus' body and took care of his burial—regardless of what anyone thought. He saw God's kingdom, and knew its King. There were signs of the Holy Wind having passed through and into his life.

WONDER JUST A LITTLE

What makes God care so much about humankind that he made himself so utterly vulnerable to us? He actually cares what we feel about him, and why. His love for us is entirely selfless, because all he wants to do is give himself so fully to us. This is why Jesus came.

Freedom to choose him, to believe in him, means everything to him. He could have made us love him automatically; he could have made us with built-in obedience natures. But love isn't love unless it is freely given and freely received.

Have you ever met anyone who told you she or he was very spiritual, yet they had no relationship with Jesus as their Lord? Spirituality is popular these days. But how many people are like the multitudes that "believed" in Jesus? How many religious people have their theology all neatly in place but have never really understood the heart of their Lord? What about the millions of souls who would rather not think about God at all, who are only concerned with this life? It is a wonder that all the signs of God's kingdom go unnoticed; blindness covers eyes and hearts.

Isn't it a wonder how so few have really understood him? Spiritual birth happens as a result of impregnation—God's Spirit impregnates a person's soul. The result is: true life for that person. It is a quickening. This same powerful quickening raised Jesus' body from the dead! It comes from faith (in our Savior's work on the cross). Seeing Jesus lifted up brings us to truly see. How, then, can we *not* love him? This is what it means to be "born again."

WHAT DO YOU SEE?

Imagine the late evening Nicodemus came. We don't know where he and Jesus met. It could have been on a rooftop, while on a walk, or they could have been with others indoors. How do you imagine the scene? You may wish to slowly read the words Jesus used to explain to Nicodemus the way to eternal life. Look closely at this man who came to speak with Jesus secretly. See him through the Lord's eyes. What do you think Jesus felt at the time? Conversely, if you were Nicodemus, what would you have thought of the words Jesus spoke? What would you think about Jesus' words if you had never heard them before? What do these words of Life from Jesus' lips mean to you personally now?

JOURNAL

Ask the Lord if there is anything holding you back from knowing him more. Ask what he thinks, these days, about your relationship with him. Ask him if there is anything he is especially enjoying about you, or desiring to see change. Is there anything that concerns him? Jesus is the same today as yesterday. He listens to our questions and, in many different ways, answers them. Believe that the Lord will meet you in this time of journaling. He delights to have conversations with us, just as he did with Nicodemus. He wants to commune with you. Record your experience—the things you saw during your time of meditation as well as the thoughts the Lord may have given you during this time of dialogue.

13 - A Prophet's Witness

The one who comes from above is above all;
the one who is from the earth belongs to the earth,
and speaks as one from the earth.
The one who comes from heaven is above all.
John 3:31

- John superseded by Jesus (Aenon near Salim): *John 3:22-36*
- Jesus' departure from Judea and John's imprisonment (From Judea, through Samaria, to Galilee): *John 4:1-4, Luke 3:19-20, Matthew 4:12, Mark 1:14a, Luke 4:14a*

A CONTEMPLATIVE VIEW

The wondrous coming of God: witnesses have seen and described it.

Quite a few testified to Jesus' arrival. Archangel Gabriel. Mary and Joseph. Zechariah and Elizabeth. The angels in Bethlehem. The shepherds. Simeon and Anna. The Magi. But it was John the Baptist, Jesus' cousin, who introduced him. However, it wasn't the blood ties to Jesus that made John the fiery, wild prophet that he was. It was the anointing and messages the Holy Spirit gave him.

On the shores of the Old Covenant, John the Baptist pointed to Jesus, who stood, arms wide in welcome, on the shores of the New Covenant. This was the coming of the Kingdom of God.

John, a fisherman and the son of Zebedee, was an eyewitness to the event and testified:

There came a man who was sent from God;
his name was John.
He came as a witness to testify
concerning that light,
so that through him all men might believe.
He himself was not the light;
he came only as a witness to the light.
The true light that gives light to everyone
was coming into the world." John 1:6-9

John also recorded what John the Baptist testified about Jesus:

"I am not the Christ but am sent ahead of him. The bride
belongs to the bridegroom. The friend who attends the bride-
groom waits and listens for him, and is full of joy when he hears
the bridegroom's voice. That joy is mine, and it is now
complete." John 3:28b-29

John the apostle followed Jesus, whom the Baptist pointed out, and became one in the inner circle of Twelve. He walked beside Jesus for three years, looked into his eyes, heard his teachings and saw his miracles. He knew Jesus as an intimate friend. This is his witness of Jesus:

"In the beginning was the Word,
and the Word was with God,
and the Word was God.
He was with God in the beginning.
Through him all things were made;
without him nothing was made that has been made.
In him was life, and that life was the light of men." John 1:1-5

Later in his life, in a letter to established churches, this same John, who became known as the Beloved Apostle, also penned these words about his Friend:

"That which was from the beginning,
which we have heard,
which we have seen with our eyes,
which we have looked at and our hands have touched—
this we proclaim concerning the Word of life.
The life appeared;
we have seen it and testify to it,
and we proclaim to you the eternal life,
which was with the Father and has appeared to us.
We proclaim to you what we have seen and heard,
so that you also may have seen and heard,
so that you also may have fellowship with us.
And our fellowship is with the Father and with his Son, Jesus
Christ.
We write this to make our joy complete." 1 John 1:1-4

These passionate words are full of fervency from a man aflame with love for the One he knew and walked beside. John continued his relationship with Jesus years after his Lord and Friend bodily ascended into heaven. What Jesus had promised John surely took place in his own life: "I will not leave you as orphans. I will come to you . . . I will manifest myself to you . . . I will abide in you, and you in me."

Oh, what Divine love, passion, and joy seized John's heart and life.

Today, witnesses continue to testify concerning the comings of God. The following is from Carlo Carretto, a man known for prayer, who taught others about Jesus' love and Presence, about God's coming to each of us:

"God is always coming, and we, like Adam, hear His footsteps.
God is always coming because He is life,
and life has the unbridled force of creation.
God comes because He is light, and light may not remain hidden.
God comes because He is love, and love needs to give of itself.
God has always been coming:

God is always coming."*

WONDER JUST A LITTLE

God the Father, at the first appearing of his Son in his public ministry, clearly spelled everything out about him through the prophet John the Baptist. Listen to the words of Jesus' forerunner who testified about Jesus' true identity and mission before anyone else knew anything at all about him!

"The one who comes from heaven is above all [Jesus]; the one who is from the earth belongs to the earth, and speaks as one from the earth [anyone else, including himself]. The one who comes from heaven is above all. He testifies to what he has seen and heard, but no one accepts his testimony. [Prediction that Jesus' words will be rejected.] The man who has accepted it has certified that God is truthful. For the one whom God has sent speaks the words of God [Jesus is that one], for God gives the Spirit without limit [Jesus is equal to God in power and authority]. The Father loves the Son and has placed everything in his hands [Jesus is entrusted with everything]. Whoever believes in the Son has eternal life [trusting in Jesus is *Life*], but whoever rejects the Son will not see life, for God's wrath remains on him. [Notice the word 'remains']" John 3:31-36.

In summary, John the Baptist was the Father's eyewitness that Jesus came from heaven, was the Son of God, and possessed God's full authority, power, and words in him. John also predicted that Jesus would be disbelieved. He testified that Jesus is the only way of salvation and that all it takes to have eternal life is to believe in him. All this doctrine was revealed in one breath! And it came to the ears of those who first laid eyes upon Jesus.

Sometimes the words of Scripture become so over-familiar to us that they no longer astound us. Who, at that time, could bear such words? The idea of "the Son of God" was new. The idea that salvation hinged upon a human person—from heaven—and was the only way to obtain eternal life, was radically new. John told people in these few words that God was a trinity. Father, Son and Holy Spirit are all three mentioned as fully resting upon the man before their eyes: the man Jesus, who looked as normal and ordinary as anyone else.

Can you imagine this? It's hard for us to realize the effect the prophet's startling words had on the people of his day. We have been raised with these truths, because we live in the days of the Light of the New Covenant, but the hearers on the shores of the Jordan that day knew none of these things that we take for granted.

WHAT DO YOU SEE?

John is put into prison and Jesus leaves for Galilee. Imagine the scene at the Jordan River just before this happens. Jesus is not baptizing, but he speaks to the people who come to be baptized.

What is John's reaction to the telling news that Jesus and his own disciples are baptizing a little distance away? What is Jesus' reaction to John's being taken prisoner? As these events unfold, do you see God's enemy at work? Can you imagine how Jesus felt when he heard of John's arrest? What decision does Jesus make after receiving that news? These are dramatic events and there is much to learn from them.

Imagine that you are one of the people coming to be baptized. You've heard about the miracles Jesus performed and you've decided to go out and see him. Along with others, you travel from the festival in Jerusalem to the Jordan River. There you hear Jesus and are baptized. You have a private conversation with him. Imagine this. If this could happen, what would you say to him? What do you think he would say to you?

JOURNAL

Record the answers from the above questions and describe what your experience from your time of meditation was like. What was it like to imagine being on the scene at the Jordan River, of being baptized, of being with Jesus?

If you feel inclined, write a poem or prayer to the Lord about your desire for him to come to you more, or about how you rejoice in his presence. Let your heart bubble up in gratefulness for his many comings to you, in the variety of ways he's personally revealed himself and his love to you.

---

* From: *The God Who Comes* by Carlo Carretto, ©Orbis Books, 1974.

14 - Living Water

Everyone who drinks this water will be thirsty again,
but whoever drinks the water I give him will never thirst.
Indeed, the water I give him will become in him a spring of water
welling up to eternal life.
John 4:13-14

- Discussion with a Samaritan woman (Sychar in Samaria): *John 4:5-26*
- Challenge of a spiritual harvest (Sychar in Samaria): *John 4:27-38*
- Evangelization of Sychar (Sychar in Samaria): *John 4:39-42*
- Arrival in Galilee (From Samaria to Galilee): *John 4:43-45*

A CONTEMPLATIVE VIEW

What a scene in the drama of God's Story... At center stage is Jacob's well. This well had, during ancient times, symbolized the covenant God made with Jacob and his descendants. There is no one by the well. Nor is there a bucket with which to draw water.

God himself had given the well to Jacob. It had been a sign of their covenant relationship. From this well God provided everything necessary for life to Jacob and his descendants. For thousands of years, it was the only draw-well in the region. Since the time of Jacob, the chosen people have gone through many changes. At the time of this story, the well belongs to the Samaritans. The covenant relationship this well symbolized is long forgotten, except that is, to Jesus.

As a descendant of Jacob and as the God of Jacob, Jesus enters the scene with his disciples. They see there is nothing left at the well with which to draw up the water. The disciples leave Jesus to rest while they go into town to buy food.

As Jesus settles down beside the well, weary and thirsty, his thoughts are full with the realization of all this well has stood for—and the irony of his predicament. His heart is heavy because he is yearning, thirsting, for the restoration of humankind to God. This means more to him than his physical thirst and hunger.

Within minutes, a woman appears carrying an empty earthen jar. Her burden—the empty vessel—is not unlike herself.

She has come to draw water in the heat of the day. Most women in the land congregate around a well in the mornings or evenings. But this woman avoids those times, since the town does not accept her. She hopes no one will see her, but the one who does see her is her Creator.

It isn't just the Samaritan woman Jesus sees—he sees all of humankind in her. He knows something about the human soul that most people don't know. He knows about thirst. He knows what humans, made in God's image, have been created for.

So, what Jesus saw that day at the well was a woman whose heart was thirsting for life and love.

Jesus saw her heart and his own heart began to beat faster—wanting so much to tell her what he knew. He would have liked to have said, *"My precious, I am the only one who can wholly meet your heart's desires."* But he realized she would have misunderstood him.

And so, Jesus led her through an amazing conversation about herself. He did not point out her failed relationships with men to condemn her or bring her to repentance. But he did point this out to show her that he knew about her needy, thirsty heart.

He did not invite her to stop sinning. Even his motives to turn her life around were not to help her become respectable again in society. He had far more in mind for her. He knew something she didn't know: only God can satisfy a person's truest, deepest needs and desires.

The Samaritan woman, like all humans, had "drunk water from the earth." Her heart, he showed her, was made to enjoy God—to experience "paradise" with him. Only from God could she find all that her heart longed for: acceptance, security, intimacy, meaning, and purpose.

Jesus said to her, "Everyone who drinks this water will be thirsty again, but whoever drinks the water I give him will never thirst. Indeed, the water I give him will become in him a spring of water welling up to eternal life."

At the ancient covenant well, Jesus renewed God's invitation to this woman and to us, in the same way he had spoken ages before through the prophet, Isaiah:

"Come, all you who are thirsty, come to the waters,
and you who have no money, come, buy and eat!
Come, buy wine and milk without money and without cost.
Why spend money on what is not bread, and your labor on what
does not satisfy?
Listen, listen to me, and eat what is good, and your soul will
delight in the richest of fare.
Give ear and come to me; hear me, that your soul may live.
I will make an everlasting covenant with you,
my faithful love promised to David." Isaiah 55:1-3

Less than three years later, when Jesus stood beside the Water Gate during the Tabernacles festival that celebrated "God-abiding-with-us," he called out: "If anyone is thirsty, let him come to me and drink. Whoever believes in me, as the Scripture has said, streams of living water will flow from within him."

Jesus, the Thirst-quencher, came to bring us *Life* in satisfying, extravagant abundance.

WONDER JUST A LITTLE

God thirsts, just as did Jesus in a human body, and yet he is our Thirst-quencher. Can we truly grasp this? Physically, Jesus experienced human need the same as we. This event glows with revelation rich with paradox. We need to open our eyes to see the reality of the situation.

Thirsty, God, in Jesus, comes to the same well he had once given to Jacob as a covenant blessing. But, there is nothing there to help him quench his thirst. This is the Creator who makes the rain, the rivers and fountains, the oceans, and who blesses the earth with all that is necessary for life. He is thirsty. He has come to give true Life to the earth—not physical, but eternal, spiritual *Life*. Jesus has come to bring the life of God to his creatures.

There are other startling things to appreciate about this event at Jacob's well. The gift, the revelation, Jesus gave to this needy, lowly woman was remarkable. He gave to her what he gave to no one else. Jesus never so openly declared being the Messiah to anyone until his trial. She was the first to hear, directly from his lips, that God desired to be worshiped "in spirit and truth," and not through the temple rituals. This was new, blinding revelation. He spoke prophetically to her. Just why did he say so much to her?

We need to appreciate, with deeper understanding, what an isolated, wonderfully endearing moment this was for Jesus and a woman of ill repute. First of all, the woman was not Jewish. God had predetermined to reach the Jews first. Second, she was a woman. In that culture, men did not openly speak to women in public, let alone enter into theological discussions with them. Third, she was a known sinner, which anyone might have guessed because she had come to the well at an odd time of day. More than likely she wore guilt and shame upon her countenance. Speaking with known sinners was also taboo. In many ways, Jesus' conversation with the Samaritan woman went against many norms of the day.

What was it about her that moved Jesus to such openness? He often called himself "the Son of Man," that obscure name from Scripture, which only a few realized was for the Promised One. Usually, Jesus clouded his identity, which is why his enemies repeatedly asked him to tell them who he was. Even his disciples wondered about his true identity and, after a miracle or two, exclaimed, "You are surely the Son of God." Yet they continued to wonder about him until he clearly told them, during the Last Supper, who he was. And then they happily exclaimed, "Now you are speaking clearly without figures of speech."

The Samaritan woman didn't ask him who he was—yet he told her—quite spontaneously. Later, she told the townspeople, "Here is a man who knows everything I ever did." So, even before telling anyone, she had come to realize that Jesus was a prophet, and that was enough for her. But it wasn't enough for Jesus. When she stated, "I know that the Messiah is coming. When he comes, he will explain everything to us," Jesus wanted her to know that he was "explaining everything." The "everything" that was in his heart came pouring out from his own well of love and concern for her, knowing her desires, knowing her pain and empty life, because he couldn't help himself. He was bursting to tell her. To this one soul on the planet who was perhaps the most unlikely one to tell, he disclosed his marvelous, great *secret*: "I who speak to you am he."

WHAT DO YOU SEE?

Imagine the scene at the covenant well. Prayerfully imagine being there. When Jesus' disciples came back and saw him speaking with the woman, imagine their surprise. When the woman left long enough to bring back the whole town, can you see the wonder and joy on Jesus' face? What does it mean to God when we tell others our own testimony of salvation or experiences with Jesus? What other insights do you see from this story? What have you discovered about Jesus' responses and actions? What about this event stirs your heart? Pay attention to those stirrings; God is in them, talking personally through them to you.

JOURNAL

In one way or another, each one of us is like the Samaritan woman. Describe in your journal the first time you discovered your need for God's Living Water that only Jesus gives. Meet him now "at the well"—which is relational prayer. Listen *to* and converse *with* him.

15 - The Good News

The Spirit of the Lord is on me,
because he has anointed me
to preach good news . . .
Luke 4:18a

- Nature of the Galilean ministry (Galilee): *Matthew 4:17;*
  Mark 1:14b-15; Luke 4:14b-15
- Child at Capernaum healed by Jesus while at Cana: *John 4:46-54*
- Ministry and rejection at Nazareth: *Luke 4:16-31a*
- Move to Capernaum (From Nazareth): *Matthew 4:13-16*

A CONTEMPLATIVE VIEW

Home. Rich with meaning, this word carries within itself what
every heart longs for. Ideally, home is a safe, warm, and inviting
place where you can be intimately known and fully accepted—
where you can be yourself, without judgment or prying eyes. It is a
nurturing place. At home, laughter is not phony or forced but is
natural, and tears that have been withheld during a terrible day can
fall freely. Home is a place to rest, to find peace and comfort, to
heal. Home is familiar. Home has a scent all its own. It's your own.
One can talk incessantly or say little or nothing, depending on your
mood. Home feels natural. Home is, well, home.

For most of Jesus' life, home to him was Nazareth. He could find
his way anywhere in the town, even blind-folded. The well-worn path
from his family's carpentry shop to the side door of the house was

exactly fifteen paces west and five paces north. To the well—seven houses down and at the bottom of the hill on the left. He recognized the voice of any neighbor who entered the shop, even before looking up from a project. He could read his sisters' and brothers' moods with one glance, and knew if one of them wanted to be conversational or left alone. He laughed his hardest at home because the funniest things happened there. He did most of his thinking at home while lying on his bed staring at the all-too-familiar ceiling. He enjoyed many late-night conversations with his earthly father, Joseph, while nibbling on a bedtime snack. He attended synagogue regularly, never missing an opportunity to sit with a visiting teacher for group discussions that could last for hours.

Jesus enjoyed his home. But it wasn't his real one. Home here on earth was a temporary place where he stayed for awhile. It is the same for us. Our real home is a place Jesus called "the Kingdom of heaven." We didn't understand this before or while Jesus visited, but now we do. Without his coming, we never would make it to our real *home*.

After Jesus had been gone from Nazareth a few months, he returned. When he went into his beloved synagogue on the Sabbath, the men all wanted to know the truth about the things they'd been hearing about him. They barraged him with questions, which, on the spot, he refrained from answering. And when he sat down in his usual place, the whispers and questions didn't end until the service formally started.

As the opening prayers and chants began, many of the people of Nazareth wondered if Jesus would preach. However, here in his hometown he didn't share any of his engaging stories. Instead, on that Sabbath Day, he opened his heart fully to them and began to reveal his *true* self—his inimitable surprise, his life-long secret. He had always lived his true self while in their midst, but he had never spoken of it. This day in history was a momentous event. He saved this special revelation just for their ears. He hadn't told the rest of the world yet what he wanted to tell them—this was their special blessing because he wanted to give of himself more than he had to any other town.

He was asked to come forward and read from Holy Writ.

The attendant handed him the scroll of Isaiah for the reading that day. Looking lovingly upon their faces, Jesus began to read ancient words he himself had breathed into the prophet's heart. And now, having reached the fulfillment of it, Jesus' heart was full.

He read in a strong, passionate voice, as one with authority: "The Spirit of the Lord is on me, because he has anointed me to preach good news to the poor. He has sent me to proclaim freedom for the prisoners and recovery of sight for the blind, to release the oppressed, to proclaim the year of the Lord's favor." (Isaiah 61:1-2, Luke 4:18-19)

After he finished, many exclaimed at how graciously he had read, and they commented about some of the things they'd been hearing about him. The room buzzed with lowered voices. Everyone's eyes were fastened upon him as he humbly sat down in his place. Looking around at them, now ready to answer their whispered questions, he said, "Today this Scripture is fulfilled in your hearing." How wonderfully he answered all they wanted to know about him! And now his heavenly secret had been revealed.

At first silence reigned. The surprising news had to be digested. All at once, they looked at one another, questioning silently whether they had heard correctly. Only moments passed before most of the congregation shot to their feet and the whole place exploded in uproar.

One of their town's carpenters had just claimed to be the Anointed One—the Messiah; the Promised One; the Ancient of Days; the King of Israel; the royal Son of David; the Lord's great and holy High Priest; the expected Prophet who, like Moses, was prophesied to rise up from among their own. It meant Jesus thought of himself as the Branch, the Tender Shoot, the Hope, and Answer that everyone prayed for.

Rather than rejoice, they were appalled, and turned to one another with the question: *What has happened to Mary's son? Here is the boy, the man, we've always known.* They murmured loudly against him. Even his own brothers, shocked, looked at him, their faces reddened with embarrassment, their heads shaking in disbelief.

Wounded by their rejection, Jesus also rose from his place on the floor. He sadly answered the men's incensed questions and accusing eyes. Jesus, with his voice raised, told the people of Nazareth, that they were like the people in Elijah's day who, during the great famine, could not be helped because of their closed-off hearts. The only one God helped had been a Gentile widow. Jesus predicted that they would soon tell him, "Physician, heal yourself. Do here in your hometown what we heard you did in Capernaum."

Jesus saw a vision of their hate-filled faces from what would be his cross of agony. He stretched out his hands towards heaven and called out, "A prophet is never accepted in his own hometown." And to himself he thought, *but only in Jerusalem must a prophet die.*

His prediction turned the congregation of worshipers into a mob of killers. His lifelong friends and neighbors came physically against him and drove him out of the synagogue to the brow of the hill on which the town was built, with the intention of throwing him off the cliff. With his angels' help, he escaped unharmed.

The new reality then set in. His home in Nazareth was no longer a welcome, safe place to be. Now Jesus knew only too well how temporary and wanting this home on earth was.

After leaving Nazareth, during his three years of public ministry, Jesus managed to turn the world upside down and stand Time on end with his Good News. At the markets, in boats, in synagogues and schools, in fields, along roads, and in every hovel, shop, and house in cities and villages, everywhere, people talked about him. Whenever Jesus passed by, there was left in his wake rumors and tales of strange happenings. And so, when he came into a town, people dared to expect the unexpected. Crowds of people carried their infirm loved ones to him, some on pallets, some in carts, only to return home—joy upon joy—with them whole, walking, skipping, and singing alongside of them.

Here was a man whose love knew no bounds and had no restraints. Everything about him said, "God is here! The Kingdom of heaven has come upon you." He said this through simple yet profound teaching, signs, and miracles. But he said it most clearly through his compassion—and his love was most fully shown at the end of his human life.

The Good News is this: Our God has come to save and heal us, and to bring us home—to him. And, in him, we have security, love, acceptance, and meaning. In him, our heart's true home, we can be, fully, our real selves.

WONDER JUST A LITTLE

Jesus' disciples didn't know it, but while they were with Jesus, they were like God's angels helping him. They carried messages for Jesus, and they helped him in his day-to-day work. Jesus often sent them ahead into towns and villages to prepare the way, proclaiming the good news that he was coming right behind them.

The Gospel's *Good News* isn't a sermon on sanctification—it is a message that brings relief and great joy. Good news sounds like this: "Your tumor is benign." "We're pregnant!" Think about the Good News as something so fantastic and wonderfully new—that people camped out around a man for days on end, hanging onto his every word. To them Jesus was just a man. But he was a man they wanted to be near because he brought God near to them. We are all made for this.

We try to wrap our finite minds around the concept that Jesus was fully God and fully man. There are wonderful hints to this fact that we don't even notice, little things in the Gospel that mean more with a little examination. Jesus acted like God because he was God. Not just with his claims, miracles, and teaching, but in everything he did—including the small things.

For example, when the Holy Spirit drew the crowds of people to the Jordan River to hear the Word of God and be baptized, why did Jesus' disciples do the baptizing and not Jesus?

This is one of those many subtle details of the way in which Jesus always acted like God. At the Jordan River, Jesus preached to people and *received* them. Baptism was an act of commitment and worship, which Jesus received. It still happens the same way today. The Spirit draws us to Jesus and he receives us. When we are baptized, we repent, are immersed, washed clean, and are raised up out of the burial waters of "death to self" to live for and in *him*. Jesus receives this as worship. He receives us into his loving arms.

The stories in the Bible show that the first thing people did after believing the Good News of Jesus was to be baptized. Jesus said,

" . . . Go into the all the world and preach the good news to all creation. Whoever believes and is baptized will be saved, but whoever does not believe will be condemned." When the Good News is accepted, an immediate inner transformation, a whole new way of thinking, a whole new makeup in character takes shape. Suddenly there comes the desire to know and please God. Those who do not believe the Good News will likewise not appreciate the many wonders of Jesus and his love. They will remain separated from him, which is to remain condemned.

Unbelievers who reject Jesus and his Good News cannot appreciate what it means to have gained everything good in life. They cannot know the spontaneous desire to spread the good news that has just set you free and transformed you from the inside out. It's a wonder, really.

WHAT DO YOU SEE?

There were several times when Jesus performed individual miracles only to ask the recipients not to tell anyone what had happened. The reason he did this was because he was having a hard time moving about without being mobbed. But how could one keep such a secret? How many of those people were able to obey him? The Scriptures tell us that most did not keep quiet. I rather doubt that Jesus ever blamed them. Don Francisco's popular song, in about 1980, titled "I've Got to Tell Somebody!" is a delightful retelling of the miracle of the raising of Jairus' twelve-year-old daughter. Jesus presents her alive to her parents along with the simple yet endearing instructions to give her something to eat. As he is leaving them he says, "Don't tell anyone about this." But of course, as the song so expertly and exuberantly points out, obeying that request is just impossible. "I've got to tell somebody!" is having such good news that you will explode without the telling of it. It's just as impossible for any one of us to not tell the Good News once we've experienced Jesus' healing touch and loving embrace.

Find one of your favorite healing Scripture stories in the Gospel and imagine being that person who was healed. Using your senses, imagine the scene, the emotions of Jesus, of those around you, and your own. Let the sense of relief, joy and wonder fill you. This is how Jesus' concern and love is for us. See if you can experience it in prayer. Think about coming home to the One who knows you inside and out, and loves you more than you can imagine.

JOURNAL

Write in your journal the Good News that is bursting from you. Let the words flow as though your pen is screaming, "I've got to tell somebody!" End by thanking Jesus, and let your love flow to his heart. How he loves to receive us in his embrace. He invites us to come home.

16 – Fishers of Men

. . . people . . . came to him from everywhere.
Mark 1:45b

- Call of the four fishermen to discipleship (By the Sea of Galilee, near Capernaum): *Matthew 4:18-22; Mark 1:16-20; Luke 5:1-11*
- Teaching in the synagogue of Capernaum authenticated by healing a demoniac: (Capernaum, in the synagogue): *Mark 1:21-28; Luke 4:31b-37*
- Peter's mother-in-law and others healed (Capernaum, in Peter's home): *Matthew 8:14-17; Mark 1:29-34; Luke 4:38-41*
- Tour of Galilee with Simon and others (Galilee): *Matthew 4:23-25; Mark 1:35-39; Luke 4:42-44*
- Cleansing of a man with leprosy, followed by much publicity (In one of the cities by the Sea of Galilee): *Matthew 8:2-4; Mark 1:40-45; Luke 5:12-16*
- Forgiving and healing of a paralytic (Capernaum): *Matthew 9:1-8; Mark 2:1-12; Luke 5:17-26*

A CONTEMPLATIVE VIEW

Simon Peter, one of Jesus' twelve apostles . . .

Jesus drew souls from everywhere as easily as he attracted boatloads of fish into our nets.

When I first set eyes on him, he was a stranger to me. Yet, apparently, I was no stranger to him. He greeted me by name as though he'd always known me. What surprised me even more was that, in the same breath, he gave me a nickname, by which he called me from then on. He greeted Simon, but named me "Peter," which meant "rock." He didn't explain why until months later.

Of course, being the logical, good judge of people that I am, I was quite skeptical of him. Who wouldn't be?

How did he know me?

How did he know where the fish were?

How did he know my deepest thoughts, my failings, my desires, my fears?

How did he always manage to draw both the best and the worst out of me?

Why, when I repeatedly made a fool of myself, did he seem even warmer towards me than before?

Sometimes I thought he was the most illogical person I'd ever come across. But his wisdom and divine power spurred my faith beyond any doubts about him. Still, he often confused me—only because I couldn't think other than as a man thinks, and not as God thinks, so he told me.

But the biggest question I lived with most of my life? Why did he trust me with *so much*?

I had proven myself utterly unworthy of his love, respect, and trust. Yet, he left the care of his sheep—of his Kingdom—in my hands. My sinful, unworthy, fish-smelling hands.

He made me a fisher of men.

**

John, one of Jesus' twelve apostles . . .

I knew Simon Peter long before he was known as Peter. James and I were sons of Zebedee, who was Peter's fishing partner. Two boats are better than one, and my father's boat and Peter's worked closely together through the long days and nights on Lake Kinneret, also called the Sea of Galilee. We'd known Peter as Simon, a quick-tempered, giant-hearted fisherman of Capernaum. He was hard as rock on the outside, but soft as wet clay on the inside. We were close friends.

Simon Peter, Peter's brother Andrew, and I left our boats and nets for a time and traveled from Capernaum out to the wilderness of Judea to see the prophet, John the Baptist. When we heard the messages God had given him, our hearts were awakened and greatly stirred. We lingered with him for days, unwilling to return home. How could we? Here was a living prophet that we ourselves could see and hear. It had been four hundred silent years, a long wait for Israel, since such passionate, living words of God had come to anyone.

At the Jordan, there was tremendous expectation in the prophet's preaching. This sparked flames of devotion in our dry, ready hearts. We didn't know it until after we'd met him, but Jesus was our reason for being drawn there.

We were unlikely disciples—simple men from Galilee. But we were the first ones to follow Jesus. Just as chicks break from their shells and follow their mother, we were his from the moment we laid eyes on him. We were meant for him. Meant to know him, love him, and share in his work. We were his Kingdom "fishermen," the undeserving men who Jesus turned into messengers of his love. We exchanged our fishing nets of string for nets of his grace. Over our lifetimes, we cast our nets into the sea of perishing souls. God's children, of all ages, were caught alive and whole into that great Kingdom-net of his love.

To think that I saw and heard the Word of God—I saw God's love and light shining from his eyes; saw him still the elements of nature; watched him heal the sick and raise the dead, heard his sighs of pain and cries of agony; and witnessed blood flowing from him. I heard the words of God fall with power and compassion from his lips. More than all this, the memory I treasure most is when I laid my head on his chest and, with my own ears, heard the beating of his heart.

No wonder the symbol for Christianity has quickly become a simple drawing of a fish. We, like fish of the sea, must be caught in that wondrous net of his love. He's out to catch us all.

WONDER JUST A LITTLE

God is full of surprises.

Did anyone realize at the time just what was going on? God comes to live in a small, working-class town and sets up headquarters for world evangelism. He's out to save the whole human race.

So who is it that he enlists to help him? Fishermen. Not the learned theologians or religious leaders. Nor did God call the well-educated into his work, nor the rich who could support his efforts. No, Jesus knew what he was doing. His first followers at the Jordan River were the ones his Father had chosen for him, and he delighted in their friendship. Four of the Twelve were fishermen. When Jesus lovingly said that he would make them "fishers of men," could they have realized the scope?

Yet, these were the ones Jesus called to join him in his Kingdom-building work.

At first, Jesus more than likely walked alone much of the time. For weeks or months, the sight of him coming and going was probably a common one for his neighbors. Perhaps he passed people in the town repeatedly and nodded greetings, maybe he stopped to inquire about their family or business. Before his fame caused him to be mobbed or to be exiled, he was with the people of Capernaum, as he had been with those in Nazareth all his life. He was part of their everyday lives. He became one of them. No doubt, he spent some nights fishing with his friends, engaging in small-talk, and then nodding off to sleep. Yet, in those days, he began to powerfully usher in the kingdom of God.

When Jesus settled in Capernaum, it was summertime and the sun shone brightly in Galilee. He then preached throughout the countryside, up and down the seashore, and along the Jordan as it flowed southward. On foot and by boat, Jesus chased away spiritual darkness with the same message his cousin John had spoken: "Repent! The Kingdom of God is at hand." Jesus opened his heart to all, touching and healing every form of sickness and oppression among the people. He also worked a few wonders just to build faith in the hearts of his disciples.

All this had been prophesied by Isaiah: "Land of Zebulun and land of Naphtali, the way to the sea, along the Jordan, Galilee of the

Gentiles—the people living in darkness have seen a great light; on those living in the land of the shadow of death a light has dawned." (Matthew 4:15-16)

Today we tend to take it all for granted. The stories are so familiar. The fishermen and their boats, and Jesus with them, are part of the fabric of our lives. But, really, God in a fishing boat is an amazing thing to ponder. Imagine: God rolling up his sleeves, calling fish into the net, laughing with and amazing his friends—these are special moments in his life as a man. For what is often overlooked about these events, like the miracle of the catch of fish, is how much Jesus must have enjoyed himself when he let his glory "show" a little. For he certainly let his Light shine in ways nobody would ever have expected.

Can you imagine him turning around to his astonished friend, Peter, and saying to him with a wink—"Don't be afraid; from now on you will catch men."?

Our God is great fun.

WHAT DO YOU SEE?

In this chapter there are a few miracles described in the Scriptures. Using the reading list on the first page, look over the events and choose one to read and meditate upon. Pay attention to the one that most draws you or stirs your heart. After reading that particular Gospel story, close your eyes and imagine it, asking the Lord to show you whatever he would like you to see and learn, keeping in mind the following questions:

If you were there, what would you have thought about Jesus?
Do you think you would have felt drawn to him?
What do others do during this event?
What are the reactions of Jesus' disciples, of his enemies?
Is Jesus laughing, sad, angry?

JOURNAL

In your journal, describe what touched you the most during the time of prayerful meditation. Also, be open to whatever the Lord may wish to teach or reveal to you. Sometimes the best way to end a time of meditation is to write a prayer out to the Lord, allowing your love to be expressed to him on the pages of your journal—like a love letter. Another good practice is to close your journal and sit silently with the Lord, basking in his loving presence.

17 – New Wineskins for New Wine

And no one pours new wine into old wineskins.
If he does, the wine will burst the skins,
and both the wine and the wineskins will be ruined.
No, he pours new wine into new wineskins.
Mark 2:22

- Call of Matthew (Capernaum): *Matthew 9:9; Mark 2:13-14; Luke 5:27-28*
- Banquet at Matthew's house (Capernaum): *Matthew 9:10-13; Mark 2:15-17;Luke 5:29-32*
- Jesus defends his disciples for feasting instead of fasting with three parables (Capernaum): *Matthew 9:14-17; Mark 2:18-22; Luke 5:33-39*
- Jesus heals an invalid on the Sabbath (Jerusalem): *John 5:1-9*
- Effort to kill Jesus for breaking the Sabbath and saying he was equal to God (Jerusalem): *John 5:10-18*
- Discourse demonstrating the Son's equality with the Father (Jerusalem): *John 5:19-47*
- Controversy over disciples' picking grain on the Sabbath (Perhaps Galilee): *Matthew 12:1-8; Mark 2:23-28; Luke 6:1-5*
- Healing of a man's shriveled hand on the Sabbath (In a synagogue in Galilee): *Matthew 12:9-14; Mark 3:1-6; Luke 6:6-11*

A CONTEMPLATIVE VIEW

A disciple of John the Baptist's . . .

The grace Jesus came to pour into our hearts was like a rich new wine that filled us with joy past the boundaries of our religious experience. My reason for existence, as I had always known it, was shattered by him. It was not easy to embrace what seemed the opposite of all I held dear—which I saw as the strict keeping of the laws and traditions of my faith. I was a disciple of the Baptist and, I regret to admit, I had despised the teacher from Nazareth. I thought that he and his disciples had compromised the faith of our fathers and were deceived. It was a decade after I first met Jesus before I met him again, after he had ascended into heaven. I've come to see that my former self, before faith in him, was a self-righteous bag of bones. I've known him in the spirit now for years. I've feasted in his presence and am no longer a lean, empty excuse for a man. Now I am an heir of the Kingdom, and I enjoy his bounteous love moment by moment.

It is with remorse that I tell you how I misjudged him when I saw him in the flesh. I know he's forgiven me, so it is a joy to tell you that I eventually learned the lesson he taught us about spiritual receptivity.

Because of our judgmental attitude, of my fellows and I, we did not *hear* what he said at Matthew's banquet when he spoke of God's mercy and unmerited grace.

"No one sews a patch of unshrunk cloth on an old garment," he said. "If he does, the new piece will pull away from the old, making the tear worse. And no one pours new wine into old wineskins. If he does, the wine will burst the skins, and both the wine and the wineskins will be ruined. No, he pours new wine into new wineskins."

He had said this in reply to my question: "How is it that John's disciples [which included myself] and the disciples of the Pharisees are fasting, and yours are not?"

I had not dared to say what I was thinking—that he was deceiving his disciples, making them unclean, soiling their souls and making a mockery of righteous living.

He saw right through me. He knew that I had no room for God's love and mercy in my heart. I had only the law by which I dutifully lived—as well as expected others to live by. His way of religious expression was opposite mine. Mine was *works*; his was *rest*. Mine was *duty*; his was *desire*. Mine was *self-centered*; his was *self-giving*. Mine was *rigid* and *closed*; his was *graceful* and *inviting*. Like I said, we were opposites.

He had said that God preferred mercy to sacrifice. His statement cut me to the quick. I hated him for it. My life of sacrifice was my identity. At that time, I had no idea how wrong I was—how impossible it was for me to "earn" holiness. I looked at Jesus that day and saw true holiness. Yet I turned from him, thinking I was better than he. I was wrong—so wrong.

His illustration of new wineskins for new wine meant nothing to me that day. It means everything to me now. When I realized that God's true image had come in the form of a gentle, loving teacher and healer who graced everyone he met with the compassion and generosity of God's heart, and that he did nothing but spread joy, wisdom, and compassion to "receptive" people, I was ruined.

Yes, ruined. I had looked God in the face and rejected him. But now, since he's shattered that former, ignorant person I used to be, I am righteous. Not by anything I've done, but by what he's done for me.

His new wine had burst through the hardened skin of my old, unbending self-righteousness. But in the shattering of my former existence, and in the acceptance of a new heart to hold his grace, I became a new man. What had been a heart dead and closed became a heart alive and expanded. Expanded to receive all the passion that God's real life brings. Oh, the joy of Jesus!

WONDER JUST A LITTLE

It is a paradox that the leading Jews did not embrace Jesus. It was easier for some people to believe in him than for others. Take, for example, Matthew, a tax collector, scorned by all. Before Jesus, he was a man without hope. He easily followed Jesus when he called him. Matthew lived "in need of God" every day. He was "poor in spirit"—an empty, open wineskin for Jesus' new wine.

When self-righteous men criticized Jesus for mixing with sinners, he gently replied, "It is not the healthy who need a doctor, but the sick. But go and learn what this means: 'I desire mercy, not sacrifice' (Hosea 6:6). For I have not come to call the righteous, but sinners."

Matthew, to whom Jesus had shown mercy, was called into God's love as well as into an amazing destiny.

Jesus knew everyone needed his doctoring. Those who were full of themselves were left to themselves. They were the ones with their doctrines all neatly sewn up. Jesus ripped their self-righteous religious beliefs to shreds. His teaching was so radical and so central to their sense of worth that they wrote him off as an enemy of their faith. Their pride kept them from recognizing the Messiah.

He showed them that faith and holiness was not "keeping the law"—at least not as they understood it. This convinced most of them that he was a false prophet. The law was all they had. But they missed the purpose of the law, which was to reveal the need for God's love. When Jesus healed on the Sabbath, they accused him of "working"—calling him a sinner. They totally missed the *spirit* of the law of the Sabbath—a day to celebrate God's love with each other and with him. The law was *for* them, not they for the law. Nor did they realize that the law had come *from* Jesus, whom they accused.

Jesus understood why the law existed. For example, the spirit of "Thou shalt not kill" was to love the unlovely, the mean, the unworthy, the "unacceptable" ones. In practical ways, it was to "bless those who curse you—to do good to those who mistreat you." That's why sinners flocked to him.

Jesus knew the law was impossible to keep without his indwelling Spirit. And this is what Jesus meant also by "new wine." The grace he came to give was not only unmerited favor, it was his Spirit, his presence, in them. He would free them from the *letter* of the law, and empower them to live the *spirit* of the law. As Paul said, "It is not I who lives, but Christ in me."

The spirit of "Thou shalt have no other gods before me" was to know and enjoy a close relationship with God—a relationship of mutual trust and devotion. It meant finding one's meaning in life from God alone. It was more than being forbidden to carve idol images and worship them. It was much more than that. Jesus came to write his law of love on hearts of flesh, and to free his children from the curse of the law. Jesus came to capture and rescue every heart. He did not care about anything else. Jesus broke through all the religious preconceived notions of what God was supposed to be like to pour his grace, his new wine, into hearts made new by him.

WHAT DO YOU SEE?

Read Mark 2:18-22. Close your eyes and imagine the scene. During the event, Jesus called himself a bridegroom. What was the underlying message in this image? Can you picture the self-righteous men listening to Jesus' words? Realize that his words were new, unlike any other teaching at the time. Can you sense the Lord's heart in his manner and his tone of voice as he speaks to them? How does this make you feel?

JOURNAL

First record what your meditation time was like, but end by reflecting on what condition you think your own "wineskin" is in. Are you *receptive* to the ways God has been pursuing you? Ask him, in faith, to show you some of the methods with which he's recently been trying to get your attention; ways in which he's tried to draw you closer to himself that, perhaps, you have ignored or not recognized. Often, his wooing of us comes in the form of blessings, surprises, or turns in the road of life. Sometimes it comes through disappointments, or even dead-ends in the road. Sometimes life just gets hard and we need to look for how Jesus is coming to us in the midst of our pain. He's always coming to us, speaking to us, caring about and for us. We just need to look and listen. Receptivity and being reflective are the key elements in recognizing and knowing God.

18 – Establishing the New Order

But I tell you who hear me:
Love your enemies, do good to those who hate you,
bless those who curse you, pray for those who mistreat you.
Luke 6:27-28

- Withdrawal to the Sea of Galilee with large crowds from many places (Sea of Galilee): *Matthew 12:15-21; Mark 3:7-12*
- Twelve apostles chosen (A mountain near the Sea of Galilee): *Mark 3: 13-19; Luke 6:12-16*
- Setting of the Sermon on the Mount (A level place on the mountain): *Matthew 5:1-2; Luke 6:17-19*
- Blessing of those who inherit the kingdom and woe to those who do not (On the mount): *Matthew 5:3-12; Luke 6:20-26*
- Responsibility while awaiting the kingdom (On the mount): *Matthew 5:13-16*
- Law, righteousness, and the kingdom: permanence of the law (On the mount): *Matthew 5:17-20*
- Six contrasts in interpreting the law (On the mount): *Matthew 5:21-48; Luke 6:27-30, 32-36*
- Three hypocritical "acts of righteousness" to be avoided (On the mount): *Matthew 6:1-18*
- Three prohibitions against avarice, harsh judgment, and unwise exposure of sacred things (On the mount): *Matthew 6:19-7:6*
- Application and conclusion (On the mount): *Matthew 7:7-27; Luke 6:31, 43-49*
- Reaction of the crowds (On the mount): *Matthew 7:28-8:1*
- A centurion's faith and the healing of his servant (Capernaum): *Matthew 8:5-13; Luke 7:1-10*

A CONTEMPLATIVE VIEW

Andrew, one of Jesus' twelve apostles . . .

I watched many people come to Jesus. Once when we returned to Capernaum there was a multitude waiting there. They crowded the entire town and the road leading into it, as well as all along the shoreline. Boats of people had come, their vessels crowding the docks. Carts and animals were everywhere.

They had come from the coast of Tyre and Sidon, from Jerusalem, even from as far away as the southern end of Judea.

Before we were near enough to be seen, we saw the crowds from a stretch of the road with a view across a small inlet of water. As we drew near, people spotted Jesus, and many rushed at us. Peter took the lead in creating a wall of protection around the Master. We were afraid the people would crush him.

I think that the sheer numbers overwhelmed him, for he did not minister to anyone there. Rather, he walked up the hillside perpendicular to the road. Everyone followed him, rejoicing when they saw that he was not simply avoiding them, but had signaled an invitation with his hand that all should follow him up the gradual incline. With Peter, John, James, and me walking on either side of him, he sadly said to us, "They are like sheep without a shepherd."

I looked at him. His voice was solemn. His expression showed deep compassion. He remained silent until we reached the place where he stopped. Hands on his hips, he looked around. "It is far better here," he said, eyeing the stand of trees and the level place partially up the mount. He instructed us to have the people spread out and set up camp.

This multitude of men, women, and children—thousands of souls—many suffering from deformities and various ailments, looked at him with anxious eyes. They had followed our Master into a field of grass and flowers. It was bittersweet to watch him walk among them, touching them, blessing them, casting out demons, and encouraging them as he went.

Jesus asked us, his one hundred or so disciples, to set up camp on the hilltop, away from the multitude. At twilight, Jesus, quietly, without a word, walked past our fire and away from us. We did not see him until dawn the next day.

In the morning, he told us that he did not come to heal bodies or souls alone, but that he had come to give people true life—for eternity. He said that we, his disciples, were to be a part of his mission. He said that we would become his hands, feet and mouth, that we would carry on his work, and that he would give us his authority.

Jesus made up his mind that night that it was time to teach us the ways of God's kingdom. He said he needed a small number of us to abide closely with him from then on. And so, he appointed twelve of us, calling us apostles. He placed my brother and I, among his newly appointed Twelve, near him, and he taught God's kingdom ways and truths to us until he no longer had a voice.

It was time to spread abroad the love and wisdom of God. The ways of his kingdom was often the opposite of what we had known and experienced all of our lives. For example, he said, "If a man strikes your cheek, offer him the other also." At first, this did not sit right with us.

"Blessed are you who are the poor, for yours is the kingdom of God." Of course, we had all felt the opposite was true. Looking back on it now, I believe that while we were looking at him, we were seeing the "poorest" among us all—for he had given up everything—of heaven and of this world, and in his heart he carried all of our sorrows.

He preached and preached that day, truths and claims that, within three years, brought him to the cross. But the fullness of time had come that day in Galilee when Jesus began turning a fallen world the right side up. It was a new beginning for all of humanity—the day he began to establish *the new order* on earth.

WONDER JUST A LITTLE

Nowhere else in Scripture do we learn so much in such a short time than from the Sermon on the Mount. What had brought the Lord to teach so much at one time? Maybe he felt the overwhelming burden of the world upon his shoulders.

Nowhere else is there a more fitting "Good Shepherd" scene than this one: Jesus with his flock on the green hills of Galilee.

What had moved him to take the multitude away with him?

Jesus brought the world the kingdom of God that day, in ways we could see and understand. He was a marvelous storyteller, and his words held the power of *creation* in them. Everything he said was true, and would come true.

It is amazing to realize that God's kingdom has spread to all nations. His spiritual revolution has taken root in both the civil law and in hearts all over the planet, especially in Christian countries. But how many people actually live by Jesus' wise teachings? Multitudes choose to do evil and shun the light of God's ways, unwilling to accept his words and live by them. They compromise the spiritual truths Jesus so painfully came to give us. This is tragic.

While on the mount that day, Jesus predicted that few would take him seriously. He knew most of them would not live by his ways, but would choose to go their own ways. Jesus admonished them, saying, "Enter through the narrow gate. For wide is the gate and broad is the road that leads to destruction, and many enter through it. But small is the gate and narrow the road that leads to life, and only a few find it."

If we want to be close to the Good Shepherd, we need to let him lead and guide us. We need to listen to his voice and heed everything he says. He is a faithful God and we can believe in him.

It's easy to see the effects the Sermon on the Mount has had upon our world—and in our lives. It's amazing how powerfully essential his words are for us, even today.

WHAT DO YOU SEE?

This chapter's Scripture verses are many because of all the Lord said and did on that small mount near Capernaum. Today, this mount is still a serene pastoral place. The world has named it "The Mount of Beatitudes." And there is a play on words—"Be Attitudes" or "Beautiful Attitudes"—that works for the English language.

In your time of meditation, imagine being on that mount as a modern day visitor. It's quiet there. The breeze is gentle and warm. You have a wonderful view of the Sea of Galilee from this vantage point. Wildflowers mix in with the green carpeting of grass. An easy slope reaches down to the seashore. Can you sense the Lord's love of the place? Here he revealed his heart to multitudes of people. Here he spent many hours with his Father and with his disciples.

Today the hill has a church upon it commemorating where Jesus taught. It's a beautiful church, with an open and arched hallway encircling the outside. You can walk all around the high, open colonnade and look down over the rolling Galilean countryside. The lawn on the mount's level area is just as it might have been long ago. It's peaceful, pastoral, and grassy. A banana grove tended by a local farmer grows down the hill in the direction of Capernaum. Most of the tourist buses approach from the opposite side of the hill, leaving the gently sloping side, facing the lake, uninhabited. The mount remains similar to the way it must have been in Biblical times.

This was one of Jesus' favorite places. He often returned here to pray and teach. He made a point to come here after his death and resurrection, meeting with at least five hundred who saw him here. And it was upon this same mount that he appeared to his eleven apostles and other close followers and commissioned them to go out into all the world to preach the Good News and to baptize and make disciples of all nations. It's a wonderful place—just to *be*. "Heavenly" best describes it.

Can you imagine it? Can you sense the Lord's fondness of this mount, for the times and experiences he had here? Close your eyes and imagine being there with him now.

JOURNAL

It's hard to imagine Jesus having his own special memories and places. But he is a real person. So often we think of him as that mystical figure out there in the beyond, somewhere up past the clouds and sky. But Jesus is as real a person as you are. In your journal, write what you think regarding some of the things Jesus did and said on the mount. Of all the Beatitudes, which one rings most true in your heart? Or which of the lessons Jesus taught there is the most meaningful to you? Why is this? Journal about why that particular lesson or beatitude is meaningful to you. End by enjoying simply being with the Lord for a while, without any particular thing to do or think about. Waste time with him. You'll find our "upside down" ways will apply in that regard. Doing nothing but simply "being" with him is one of the most beneficial investments you can make of your time.

19 – Kingdom Love in Action

When the Lord saw her, his heart went out to her and he said,
"Don't cry."
. . . the dead man sat up and began to talk, and Jesus gave him
back to his mother.
Luke 7:13, 15

Simon, I have something to tell you . . .
Do you see this woman? . . .
from the time I entered,
[she] has not stopped kissing my feet.
Luke 7:40b-45

- A widow's son raised (In Nain, a town in Galilee): *Luke 7:11-17*
- John the Baptist's relationship to the kingdom (Galilee): *Matthew 11:2-19; Luke 7:18-35*
- Woes upon Korazin and Bethsaida for failure to repent (Galilee): *Matthew 11:20-30*
- Jesus' feet anointed with tears and perfume by a sinful but contrite woman (Galilee, in the house of Simon the Pharisee): *Luke 7:36-50*
- A tour with the Twelve and other followers (Galilee): *Luke 8:1-3*

A CONTEMPLATIVE VIEW

Mary Magdalene, a devoted follower of Jesus . . .

<u>*Jesus* –</u>

Jesus – they say you gave a dead boy another chance
And that you made a lame man leap and dance
The people here in town all say
You are the one to take our fears away

Jesus – they say you have a gentle, loving face
And that your words are full of truth and grace
Yet to a storm you shout, commanding peace
Stilling waves, and making wind to cease

Jesus – they say you sang a joyful song
to an old deaf-mute who sang along
Your love, they say, had found a way
To end his silent, lonely days

Jesus – they say you call the sinners and the meek
And that your arms are opened wide to those who seek
I have never known a man to love for free
And so, I hope that what they say is true for me

Jesus – they say you've come to Magdala today
To heal the sick and cast our sorrows far away
I hear your voice . . . to me you're coming straightaway
As though you know how much I've waited for this day

Mary Magdalene . . .

For months, I had heard stories about Jesus, the healer from
Nazareth. All of Israel talked about him. I knew a crippled boy
Jesus had healed.

And, I wondered, what could he do for a person like me?
But I was afraid to meet him. I was quite certain a man like him

would hate a woman like me. And everyone in town talked about what a good man he was. I'd never met a good man. I was sure there weren't any. Men took what they wanted from me or else they treated me like I had leprosy. It was one way or the other.

When Jesus of Nazareth came to Magdala, I thought perhaps he was the first man I might be able to trust. I saw this in his eyes, in his caring, in the way he walked, touched, spoke . . . in the way he . . . loved. I watched him an entire week and listened to him teach by the lake. I watched his hands heal. Saw his joy.

I found myself, every day, wanting to be near him. If he was gone somewhere, I missed him. He made me feel good. He made me feel good to be alive. For the first time in my life, I felt like I was meant to be alive.

When we met each another face-to-face, it was an awful scene for me. He saw me on the road in town. I flirted with him. What did I know? I was drawn to him . . . had seen how kind he was. I knew no other way. Giving myself to him was all I wanted to do! The only way I knew how to love a man was to . . .

I soon found out, he wanted nothing to do with my body or my charm.

He looked at me and knew at once—my charm was not really me. Within moments, he named the hurts and sins of my scarred existence, calling my demons out by name. Seven had found their home in me. Jesus cast them all away.

Afterwards, he took my trembling hand and said, "My daughter, you are free."

And I knew by the way he said it and how he looked at me, he surely cared for me, the real me!

When he turned and walked away, I heard him say: "Rejoice! Truly, a daughter of Israel has come home."

It was from that moment on that I would forever follow him—all the way home to heaven.

WONDER JUST A LITTLE

Jesus cast seven demons out of a woman named Mary, a known sinner of Magdala, a town along the Sea of Galilee. She was a striking and memorable Gospel figure, known mostly for her passionate devotion to Jesus.

Jesus was a man of *love-in-action*. Mary returned his love— love for love—by her actions. He transformed her life and deeply touched her soul with his love and mercy. She, in turn, wholly adored him. Right after he set her free, she found him and showed him the extent of her gratefulness. She came to see Jesus as he reclined at a supper with the religious men of her town. Surprising everyone, she anointed the feet of Jesus with perfumed oil and tears—in heartfelt worship.

At the table, Pharisee Simon sat in judgment of both the woman and Jesus, so Jesus gave him an earful of a lesson. "Who loves more?" Jesus asked Simon, "the one who is forgiven little or the one who has been forgiven much?"

Her display of affection captivated Jesus. Paying careful attention to the next verses of Scripture in Luke's telling of this Gospel story, we see that Mary immediately became one of Jesus' inner circle. We can read in between the lines to see that Jesus and Mary wanted to be close to each other from then on!

"After this, Jesus traveled about from one town and village to another, proclaiming the good news of the kingdom of God. The Twelve were with him, and also some women who had been cured of evil spirits and diseases: Mary (called Magdalene) from whom seven demons had come out . . ." Luke 8:1-3.

Mary showed Jesus her love when she anointed his feet with perfume, mixed also with her tears, and wiped them with her hair. To say the least, this was a worshipful, humbling, adoring expression in body language. Such a dramatic display is rather hard for us, in our culture, to even imagine. Perhaps she had intended to anoint him only with her fragrant ointment but, upon seeing him, broke down in tears.

Why the tears? Did she feel remorse for her sins? Was she extremely relieved over something? Gratefully unfettered at being in Jesus' presence? Was it deep joy because she had found freedom and received forgiveness from him? Was it worshipful love? Most likely, it was all of these things. What we know for certain is that Jesus responded positively to her actions. He accepted her display of affection and he said so.

There is a lesson to be learned here and it is not one we can easily wrap our intellectual minds around. We must let go of our logic just enough to let our hearts have the binoculars for a minute.

We see this event from a "distanced" viewpoint. It happened a long time ago in an ancient culture. Can you imagine someone kissing the feet of anyone in our day? Who's to say that it was something their culture was used to? The second time it happened, with Mary of Bethany, could have been due to Mary Magdalene's influence. We don't know whether it was an expression typical of that day or not. Even if it was, think about what an amazing, dramatic experience this was for Jesus and for Mary Magdalene. The soul at the feet of Jesus was a woman, but what if she had been a man? This was not a sexual encounter. It was a "spiritual" one. Mary truly adored Jesus. And Jesus loved her much more than she could have known.

The religious leaders at the dinner gathering must have been terribly shocked. The woman snuck into their gathering from "the streets." She came in, uninvited, and made a dramatic display of affection towards a dinner guest, the notorious preacher, whose reputation was already in question with them.

No wonder Simon thought it wrong and strange. Anyone would have. But he had no idea where Mary was really coming from. It's where we all come from when we come to Jesus.

In our spiritual lives, what this woman did is exactly what our souls most long to do. We want to kneel and kiss his feet. We want to cry and tell him how much we love him. It is a natural response to someone who has discovered the real Jesus. He is the Divine Bridegroom who is in love with us—and his love is like a flame that jumps from his heart to ours. Just like that. It is *Love in action.* After the discovery of Jesus' personal and tremendous love, all we want is to be with him, and all he wants is the same. That is what it means to "abide in the Lord," and have "the Lord abide in us." It is experiencing loving union with him. Mary showed us the way.

WHAT DO YOU SEE?

Choose one of the Gospel scenes from this chapter's Scripture readings to meditate upon. Use it as a springboard into prayer.

Imagine being there. What would you think of Jesus after witnessing the things he does? Imagine Jesus coming to you; you see him and you have a chance to ask him for something, or to tell him something, or to do something for him.

It's okay to imagine more than the exact recorded happening of the event. Let God and his love draw and lead you during this time of reflection. Jesus longs to manifest himself to you in ways you may have never seen before. This will be a special, spiritual "place" to be with him. It's all right to be creative with your prayer. Jesus loves it.

JOURNAL

Write about your thoughts and experiences with the Lord. Returning love-for-love can take many forms and ways. The prayer of love, of adoration, is just one way. But it is one of the ways Jesus truly delights in. Be like Mary.

20 – "Who Are My Mother and Brothers?"

Pointing to his disciples, he said,
"Here are my mother and my brothers.
For whoever does the will of my Father in heaven
is my brother and sister and mother."
Matthew 12:49-50

- Blasphemous accusation by the teachers of the law and Pharisees (Galilee): *Matthew 12:22-37; Mark 3:20-30*
- Request for a sign refused (Galilee): *Matthew 12:38-45*
- Announcement of new spiritual kinship (Galilee): *Matthew 12:46-50; Mark 3:31-35; Luke 8:19-21*
- Secrets about the kingdom given in parables (To the crowds by the Sea of Galilee):

    The setting of the parables—*Matthew 13:1-3a; Mark 4:1-2; Luke 8:4*

    The parable of the soils—*Matthew 13:3b-23; Mark 4:3-25; Luke 8:5*-18

    The parable of the seed's spontaneous growth—*Mark 4:26-29*

    The parable of the weeds—*Matthew 13:24-30*

    The parable of the mustard tree—*Matthew 13:31-32; Mark 4:30-32*

    The parable of the leavened loaf—*Matthew 13:33-35; Mark 4:33-34*

A CONTEMPLATIVE VIEW

What's Happened to Our Brother?

We stood outside the door, waiting for Jesus to come out.

Crowds pressed together inside and outside the fisherman's house.

We could hardly breathe for the people and the smell of fish.

We saw that the reports about him were true.

We thought he had lost his mind.

He had made enemies of respectable men, but friends of sinners and beggars.

We've heard impossible things he has said.

He's made a fool of himself, of our town, and of us.

What's happened to our brother?

**

About Jesus, there were diverse reactions in all of Israel—from his own home to the Sanhedrin. The question foremost in every mind was the question of his identity.

It was hard enough to have the religious men doubt and question him, but when the doubts and questions came from the sons of Joseph, his own half-brothers, it cast a shadow over Jesus' life, heaping more sorrow upon him.

On one eventful day, the religious leaders verbally attacked Jesus, telling the people that he did wonders by the power of the devil. Later the same day, his brothers came to him because of the reports they'd heard. They, along with their mother, ". . . went to take charge of him, for they said, 'He is out of his mind.'" (Mark 3:30b)

Jesus knew what was in their hearts before he heard why they had come. His response was surprising. He indirectly disclosed his true identity by showing his "followers" theirs, saying, "Who are my mother and brothers?" Pointing to his disciples, he said, "Here are my mother and my brothers! Whoever does God's will is my brother and sister and mother." Mark 3:34b-35

His physical family was not doing God's will. But they were

afraid Jesus was insane and wanted to stop him from what he was doing. We hope that his mother was innocent of criticism and unbelief, caught in the middle, but we don't know. His brothers sincerely cared for him. At this time, however, they did not believe in him. Knowing their motives, Jesus seized the occasion to teach a lesson, an important one in God's heart and mind: Spiritual relationships are true family ones, as well as eternal.

Jesus did nothing at that time to encourage his half-brothers to believe in him. Nor did he give in to them or defend himself. In fact, Scripture tells us that he worked even harder than before. Upon hearing of his family's visit, he went out of the house, got into a boat along the seashore and taught the people by speaking in parables.

From this time on, Jesus embraced a new teaching style. He had spoken in illustrations before, but not in parables. The stories enabled his spiritual brothers and sisters, his disciples, to learn his kingdom principles and truths, but gave his enemies no opportunity to catch him in his words. Parables hid spiritual truths while, at the same time, revealed them. Prophecy had predicted that the Messiah would teach through parables.

In the morning of the same day Jesus' family came to get him, a few Pharisees had confronted Jesus when they brought to him a demon-possessed man who was blind and mute. After Jesus healed him, the man could both talk and see. All the people were astonished and said, "Could this be the Son of David?" But the Pharisees said that Jesus had healed by the power of the prince of demons.

Jesus explained to them that a kingdom, a city, and a family, each divided against itself, would be ruined and not stand. He asked them why Satan would drive out Satan, for it would mean he was divided against himself. He concluded, "But if I drive out demons by the Spirit of God, then the kingdom of God has come upon you."

Jesus explained further, "He who is not with me is against me, and he who does not gather with me scatters . . . For by your words you will be acquitted, and by your words you will be condemned." Matthew 12:30-37

In one eventful day, Jesus was judged by "Israel," represented by her respected rulers, to be possessed by demons and empowered by the devil, and by his family, to be insane. Jesus clearly drew a line. Believers are on the kingdom side; non-believers are on the other. Jesus' own physical family, at least at this point, was divided against itself. Jesus proclaimed that his true *relatives* were the ones who knew and obeyed God.

WONDER JUST A LITTLE

Jesus is God, down here on earth, a servant, made in human likeness, coming to us as a man. The incarnation brings us the Servant King who has come to touch us and let us touch him. He comes to tell us the truth about himself and about those who believe in him.

"Who is my family?" Jesus asks. To those who believe in him, the answer is wonderful. Jesus goes on to tell them parables about themselves.

Members of his family "hear the word and produce a crop." They "light a lamp, put it on a stand and light up the dark." They "plant tiny mustard seeds of God-given faith, which grow into giant trees with large shady branches." They "find a great treasure and sell all to own the field in which it is buried." They "discover a fine pearl of great value and sell everything else they own to buy it."

They will be the ones "reaped during harvest time by the angels, having grown into wheat, whereas the weeds which were sown by God's enemies will be thrown out and burned."

They "will be good fish caught in the angel's fishing nets from the sea, but the bad fish will be thrown away."

Jesus used a phrase that became a prevalent one for him: "He who has ears, let him hear." And to those of his true family, he said, "Blessed are your eyes because they see, and your ears because they hear. For I tell you the truth, many prophets and righteous men longed to see what you see but did not see it, and to hear what you hear and did not hear it."

WHAT DO YOU SEE?

Can you imagine the events of that day in Jesus' life when so much happened that caused him to reveal the life in the Spirit—of the kingdom of God? Read the Scriptures provided for this chapter that most draw you. Imagine being there that day in Capernaum in the crowded house, or along the sea. Watch Jesus as he climbs into a fishing boat, pushes off from shore a little, and addresses the multitude. Listen to his words as though for the first time. Notice Jesus' tone of voice as he speaks. Watch his expressions, his enthusiasm, and let the blessing of his presence and words find their way into your heart.

JOURNAL

What is it like to be a member of God's family? Have you experienced the struggles or the hardships of unbelieving family members? Express these sorrows to the Lord; let him comfort you—for truly, he has experienced this himself. Of all the parables or words of Jesus found in this chapter, which ones minister the most to you at this time? Share these thoughts with the Lord in your journal.

21 – What Kind of Man is This?

They were terrified and asked each other,
"Who is this? Even the wind and the waves obey him!"
Mark 4:41

- Secrets about the kingdom given in parables, *Continued* (Galilee)—To the disciples in the house:
    The parable of the weeds explained—*Matthew 13:36-43*
    The parable of the hidden treasure—*Matthew 13:44*
    The parable of the valuable pearl—*Matthew 13:45-46*
    The parable of the net—*Matthew 13:47-50*
    The parable of the house owner—*Matthew 13:51-53*

- Crossing the lake and calming the storm (On the Sea of Galilee): *Matthew 8:18, 23-27; Mark 4:35-41; Luke 8:22-25*
- Healing the Gerasene demoniacs and resultant opposition (Gerasa): *Matthew 8:28-34; Mark 5:1-20; Luke 8:26-39*
- Return to Galilee, healing of a woman who touched Jesus' garment, and the raising of Jairus' daughter (Galilee, by the lake): *Matthew 9:18-26; Mark 5:21-43; Luke 8:40-56*

A CONTEMPLATIVE VIEW

Matthew, one of the apostles of Jesus . . .

My rabbi had exhausted himself. The morning held harassing confrontations from the local Pharisees and other rabbis, and the

middle of the day brought his mother and brothers. They were critical of him and wanted to take him back home with them. Their
coming had weighed heavily on him, but had greatly angered me,
for I was a tax collector and had lived a sinner's life longer than the
other disciples. A quick judge of people, I saw how his brothers
looked at him with disdain. I was relieved to see them leave us.

The rest of the day Jesus had tirelessly preached to the pressing
crowds in a new method of his which he, from then on, used to
mystify his accusers but to teach those with "ears to hear"—as he
put it. We listened carefully, but even we, his own disciples, found it
necessary that he explain the meaning of his stories to us.

Later that day, when we were alone with him in the house, he
explained to us the meaning of his parables, so that we could learn
from him and one day teach others. Immediately following this,
Jesus said that he must take us away to a solitary place for some
rest. And so, leaving the people behind, we set out in our boat to
cross the lake to an area where there would be very few Jews. The
eastern shore was not as inhabited as our western side and was
peopled by those who were not Jewish. This, then, would be a place
of refuge and relief to our rabbi—and us.

But as we were crossing the lake late that afternoon, a violent
tempest arose against us and we were terrified. Because of his
trying day, Jesus had fallen asleep on a cushion in the stern of the
boat and knew nothing of our plight until we woke him.

I will never forget the sight of him. He had been sound asleep,
without a care in the world, as though his Father had rocked him to
sleep. But how he could continue undisturbed through the tumult of
thunder and lightning, the boat heaving and being tossed about, not
to mention our cries to one another, I cannot guess. When he finally
heard us call his name, crying for him to save us, he awoke with a
start and, seeing the situation, came quickly to his feet. At once, he
raised his hand and rebuked the waves, telling them to be still and
the wind to cease. They obeyed him as quickly as he said the words
and we found ourselves sitting in a vessel upon a sea as calm and
smooth as glass. He turned to us with a look of disappointment,
telling us that we should not have been so afraid, rebuking us for
having such little faith.

But we would surely have perished without him.

Afterwards, in a low voice, one of us voiced all of our thoughts for us: "What kind of man is this? Even the winds and the waves obey him."

Those of us who lived with him and walked beside him, we who witnessed the miraculous things he did, never grew accustomed to him. We feared him and loved him equally. He sometimes terrified us by his goodness. We knew he was a man just like us, but he was also very much unlike us. He walked in such wisdom and authority, we never knew what to expect. He had God's power in his finger-tips, in his words, and in his breath. For surely, we began to believe in him not just as our rabbi, or a prophet, or the Messiah, but as the only Son of God. We became men who would do anything for him, even die for him. We knew how dangerous it was to be with him, for he had many strong enemies who were out to kill him. Yet, for the most part, we felt safe with him. After all, if he could command the elements of nature and the powers of evil, who or what could stand against him, and us with him? We learned to live by faith with this amazing man, my rabbi, the Lord Jesus.

WONDER JUST A LITTLE

Jesus illustrated the power of God when he turned a wild storm into peaceful sailing. A hush of awe fell upon the hearts of his men.

During the storm, notice how Jesus is compared to the others in the boat. He is asleep. They are terrified. We see that Jesus was unaware of the situation, so he is not afraid. Do you think that Jesus, even for a moment, would have been afraid?

He had power over the forces of nature. Also, he knew where, when, and just how he would die—it would not be at sea.

But is there a part of you that feels Jesus was a little unreasonable to think that his disciples shouldn't have been afraid? Faith is one thing, but having the good sense of self-preservation is another. Why was Jesus so disappointed in their fear, in their lack of faith? Surely, he must have considered that their reactions were normal. If Jesus was disappointed in his disciples, it is easy to ask the question about ourselves. How often do we disappoint him with our lack of faith? Where does natural, common-sense leave off and faith take over?

In truth, faith should always take over. No matter what.

Jesus had the right idea, resting in faith, calm as a sleeping babe in his Father's arms. Nothing can happen to us without God's knowledge and care.

God can still the storms of our lives, or be with us as we ride them out. Either way, Jesus will be with us. If he hadn't awakened to quiet the storm, do you think he and the disciples would have drowned? The answer to that question is what Jesus knew and had wished the disciples had believed. The same goes for us.

WHAT DO YOU SEE?

If you read all the Scripture references for this chapter, you will see that Jesus worked many wonders one after another, in very short order. Can you imagine what it was like to be around Jesus when these things happened? What of all the events of this chapter is the most significant to you? Enter into that particular Gospel scene and ask the Lord to show you what he wants you to see.

Perhaps your life right now feels stormy. Can you transfer your present circumstances to the wind-tossed Sea of Galilee and imagine Jesus in your boat with you? Perhaps you are battling a sickness and feel more like the woman who stretched her hand out to touch the fringe of Jesus' clothing. Maybe your children are in need of Jesus to bring them to Life. As you read and meditate, let the images flow freely and allow yourself to play an imaginative part in the events of the Gospel to let these truths penetrate the inside of you.

JOURNAL

What things are significant from your reading and time of meditation? Have you been able to see the real, human Jesus a little more clearly? We know the Lord more truly when we get to know what he was like as a human being. That is why he came. He wanted to make himself touchable and real to us. Listen for his voice. This same Jesus is with you at this moment. He communicates himself to us within our hearts. Sometimes it is with words, images, or thoughts. Sometimes it is a sense of peace from his presence. After you've finished journaling, stay quiet and share a time of closeness with him.

22 – "Do as You Have Seen Me Do"

When Jesus had called the Twelve together,
he gave them power and authority to drive out all demons
and to cure diseases, and he sent them out
to preach the kingdom of God and to heal the sick.
Luke 9:1-5

- Three miracles of healing and another blasphemous accusation (Galilee): *Matthew 9:27-34*
- Final visit to unbelieving Nazareth: *Matthew 13:54-58; Mark 6:1-6a*
- Final Galilean Campaign—shortage of workers (Traveling in Galilee): *Matthew 9:35-38; Mark 6:6b*
- Commissioning of the Twelve (Galilee): *Matthew 10:1-42; Mark 6:7-11; Luke 9:1-5*
- Workers sent out (Traveling in Galilee): *Matthew 11:1; Mark 6:12-13; Luke 9:6*
- Antipas' mistaken identification of Jesus: *Matthew 14:1-2; Mark 6:14-16; Luke 9:7-9*
- Imprisonment and beheading of John the Baptist (Probably Tiberias): *Matthew 14:3-12; Mark 6:17-29*
- Return of the workers (Galilee): *Mark 6:30; Luke 9:10a*
- Withdrawal from Galilee (Galilee to Bethsaida, near Julias): *Matthew 14:13-14; Mark 6:31-34; Luke 9:10b-11; John 6:1-3*
- Feeding the five thousand (Bethsaida): *Matthew 14:15-21; Mark 6:35-44; Luke 9:12-17; John 6:4-13*
- A premature attempt to make Jesus king blocked (Alone on a mountain): *Matthew 14:22-23; Mark 6:45-46; John 6:14-15*

- Walking on the water during a storm on the lake (On the Sea of Galilee): *Matthew 14:24-33; Mark 6:47-52; John 6:16-21*
- Healings at Gennesaret: *Matthew 14:34-36; Mark 6:53-56*

A CONTEMPLATIVE VIEW

Simon Peter, the "rock" . . .

Among many things I've come to love about Lord Jesus, the most endearing one is his trust in me. One of my favorite memories is the time I briefly walked on water.

You might think that my walking on water had nothing to do with his trust in me, but rather was a sign of my trust in him. Yet here, beloved of the Lord, lies the puzzling truth. You see, it took trust on *his* part to receive me onto those dangerous waves. His faith in me was strong enough for him to know that I could, like him, walk on water. That, I tell you, amazes me. You see, my faith in him often failed me. As everyone knows, I sank after a few steps only because I stopped believing I could do it.

When I saw him coming to us on the waves, I was thrilled. I called out to him, full of faith, asking that if it were he on the waves, that he bid me to come to him. And, to my own amazement, he called back, "Come!"

I will never forget his look of delight in me before I began to sink. Even though my walk lasted only briefly, I have never felt more exhilarated in my life.

The others in the boat could not understand what caused the preposterous thought to come into my head. Although such a fool-hardy idea as climbing out of the boat seemed sudden, let me explain how it gradually came about.

Prior to my walking on the water, Jesus told us we were ready to minister to people in his name. This is what he said on the mount in Galilee, as he touched each one of us: "I give you authority to heal the sick, cast out demons, and proclaim God's kingdom. Do as you have seen me do." Then he immediately sent us out, two-by-two. According to his word, we did signs and wonders, and returned to him full of excitement, and with testimonies of having done all he said we could do.

Shortly after, Herod beheaded John the Baptist. After learning of this tragedy, Jesus wanted to be alone. But the crowds watched him where he went in his boat, and ran ahead to meet him when he landed. The twelve of us, seeing this, also joined him.

Jesus had compassion on the crowds and healed and taught them until it grew late that day. He miraculously fed all of us with five loaves of bread and two fish. We gathered up twelve basketfuls of leftovers after he had fed five thousand people. Next, he sent us off in our boat to cross the lake; he sent the crowds home, with their stomachs full. He wanted to have time alone with his Father while we put out to sea. In the middle of the night, seeing that we were struggling against the wind and waves, he came to us, walking on the water.

He could do anything. The fact that he had no boat was not a problem for him, we soon discovered.

Because of Jesus, I had faith to do impossible things. If he told me I could heal the sick, I could, and did. If he told me I could preach the kingdom in his name, I did so. If he said I could walk on water with him . . . Well, why not?

Since then, I've had countless occasions to "walk on water." I still have the boldness to do the things he's done or asks me to do—and I've learned to keep my eyes on him all the time. Otherwise, I sink. And I did something worse than sink. It nearly destroyed me when I betrayed him. But, as it was on the water, he reached down to me and pulled me up out of the threatening depth that could have taken my life. I've learned from these experiences. He trusts me to trust in him.

"Do as you have seen me do," Jesus said to us. He says it still.

WONDER JUST A LITTLE

Jesus had found, in Peter, a man willing to believe and do the impossible for, and with, him. In Peter's letter to the churches in 64 A.D., he wrote, "As you come to him, the living Stone—rejected by men but chosen by God and precious to him—you also, like living stones, are being built into a spiritual house to be a holy priesthood, offering spiritual sacrifices acceptable to God through Jesus Christ."

Peter saw himself and every believer as *a living stone.* Considering Jesus' nickname for him, the Rock, Peter was certainly that. He became a foundational stone placed directly upon the chief Cornerstone. It was his faith that earned Peter a key place in the Lord's heart and in his Spiritual House—the Church.

What was it about Peter's faith and personality that so endeared him to the Lord?

Let's look closely. Peter, spontaneous and emotional Peter, was honest, authentic, and full of devotion to Jesus. What did Jesus look for in the man to whom he would hand over the "keys to the kingdom?" He looked for a person who had bold faith.

Peter was always outspoken about his feelings toward Jesus. He was the first to proclaim that Jesus was "the Son of God." He was the first to preach Jesus publicly, only minutes after the Holy Spirit fell upon the believers during Pentecost. Peter was a man of faith-in-action, and his action was based on one thing: his devotion to Jesus.

Bold faith is doing the works of Jesus, and trusting your God-given gifts, with your eyes on the one who enables you to "walk on water."

WHAT DO YOU SEE?

What has God been calling you to do in, and for, him? His gifting or calling may take many forms. He begins giving you desires, but sometimes we don't realize those are the very callings he has for us. Maybe you feel inadequate or doubtful about something you've dreamed of doing, not knowing whether it's his will or not.

Meet Jesus during a time of meditative prayer. Is there anything you desire to do for him? Maybe you're not sure if it's the Lord. Imagine being Peter. Ask him, "Lord, is it you?" Find out what he says about it.

JOURNAL

Describe what thoughts you've had during this chapter. Perhaps from the Scripture reading you've gained new personal insights. What was your time of imaginative meditation like? Did you sense Jesus calling you to have the faith to do something for him? Or did you sense his pleasure in you for having already taken faithful steps towards him on the water? Record your experiences and give Jesus your assurance that you will be faithful and believe in yourself— because he does. Ask him to keep you aware of the times we live in, and that you will be obedient to his voice.

23 – Hard Words

"You do not want to leave too, do you?" Jesus asked the Twelve.
Simon Peter answered him, "Lord, to whom shall we go?
You have the words of eternal life.
We believe and know that you are the Holy One of God."
John 6:67-69

- Discourse on the true bread of life (Capernaum): *John 6:22-59*
- Defection among the disciples (Capernaum): *John 6:60-71*
- Conflict over the tradition of ceremonial uncleanness (Galilee, perhaps Capernaum): *Matthew 15:1-3a, 7-9, 3b-6, 10-20; Mark 7:1-23; John 7:1*
- Ministry to a believing Greek woman (The vicinity of Tyre and Sidon): *Matthew 15:21-28; Mark 7:24-30*
- Healings in Decapolis (From Tyre to the region of the Decapolis near the Sea of Galilee): *Matthew 15:29-31; Mark 7:31-37*
- Feeding the four thousand in Decapolis (The region of Decapolis): *Matthew 15:32-38; Mark 8:1-9a*
- Return to Galilee and encounter with the Pharisees and Sadducees (From the Decapolis to Magadan/Dalmanutha): *Matthew 15:39-16:4; Mark 8:9b-12*
- Warning about the error of the Pharisees, Sadducees, and Herodians (Crossing to the east side of the Sea of Galilee): *Matthew 16:5-12; Mark 8:13-21*
- Healing a blind man at Bethsaida: *Mark 8:22-26*

A CONTEMPLATIVE VIEW

Jairus, the ruler of the synagogue in Capernaum . . .

Jesus snatched my daughter away from the angel of death and returned her to my arms, alive, healed, and full of kisses for me.

Since the days I first met the carpenter from Nazareth, I have been like the wind, changing with the seasons. I've mistrusted him, admired him, praised him, and now I cannot allow him to set foot in our synagogue again.

What is the truth? I now beseech the God of Israel.

How can Jesus tell us he is living bread come down from heaven?

Oh, I know, he is a man of imagery and illustration, using stories to teach. This is his particular method. And so, I've tried to understand him. But he's gone too far. He says that unless a man eats the flesh of the Son of Man and drinks his blood, that man will have no life in him. He said it three times to be sure we heard him. Furthermore, he claims that he will raise to life, on the last day, only those who do so.

I had come to think of Jesus as the wisest, most compassionate, generous man I'd ever known—until now. As the ruler of Capernaum's synagogue, I have, before God, the responsibility to protect the congregation from deceivers.

People hold differing opinions of the Nazarene. Some say he is crazy, and has power that comes from his madness. Others think he is possessed by the devil and intends to destroy our faith—and us. And there are a few who still hold that he is the Messiah. But if he is, how can he claim such things, or use such a gruesome riddle? Such words seem devilish. What madness is this that falls from his lips?

Some of the officials from Jerusalem are staying in my house. They have enough evidence to bring him to trial. And when they do, they will kill him.

What do I do about a man whose claims are intolerable, yet who seemed to have come to us straight from heaven? For, if I search the bottom of my heart, I find that I want to believe in him. How could anyone bring my daughter back from the dead, unless he was from

God? I pray, then, for this man if he is of God, for I cannot tell for certain.

God have mercy on us and give us wisdom.

Judas from Kerioth, one of Jesus' twelve apostles . . .

I was excited when certain important Jews came into the synagogue in Capernaum, having journeyed directly to us from Jerusalem.

I carry our money, and Jesus trusts me with many of the details of our group's itinerant life: what we eat, where we stay, helping the poor, caring for the needs around us. He confides in me. I told him recently that he needs to gain the approval of the Sanhedrin. He answered me with a thoughtful but doubtful look. The second time I mentioned it, he said, "Things are not what you think, Judas."

I had hoped that he would soon come into his destiny and take his place of leadership in Jerusalem. I wondered if he would overthrow Herod or the High Priest, or try to get their support. Being the kind of man he is, I thought he would want the support of Israel's religious rulers.

I can't imagine him fighting anyone for a throne. Of course, many men would fight *for* him. All he needs to do is ask and thousands would come from all around, multitudes, and they would crown him king. Perhaps there will be no battles at all. With the sheer numbers behind him, he could take his place as Israel's righteous ruler, the Messiah. He's the Son of David, never denying it whenever someone calls him by that name.

Often, I've imagined Jesus coming into his kingdom reign. When he is in power, life for us, his disciples, will be much different.

When the Jewish leaders from Jerusalem came, Jesus purposefully made enemies of them with one short speech. I realize now that he would more likely start a revolution than try to gain their approval. However, we cannot compare ourselves to Gideon's army, for we who are left are so few. It is only the twelve of us now. Things are volatile. I cannot tell what the future will bring; but, for now, I will stay.

Simon Peter, one of Jesus' twelve apostles . . .

I am the man who walked on water, ever so briefly, but long enough to know that my Master has the power of God in him. I will ride out this storm, this storm of tossing thoughts, for the things my rabbi has said to us are unreasonable.

I mentioned to the others that he must be teaching us another parable. Surely, he doesn't intend for us to eat his flesh and drink his blood. In saying that he is the living bread from heaven, this must certainly be the key to the parable's meaning.

Usually, Jesus takes us aside and explains his parables to us. But this time he did not.

All we had to go on, which was his only explanation, were his words: "My words are spiritual and they are life."

Perhaps that is his only meaning! It is enough for me. Whatever he says I know is true, whether or not I understand him now.

WONDER JUST A LITTLE

"'Whoever eats my flesh and drinks my blood remains in me, and I in him. Just as the living Father sent me and I live because of the Father, so the one who feeds on me will live because of me. This is the bread that came down from heaven. Your forefathers ate manna, but he who feeds on this bread will live forever.' He said this while teaching in the synagogue in Capernaum." John 6:56-59

In the mind of Jesus, the most needful thing of the hour was to bring spiritual life to those who looked to him for the wrong reasons. After the miracle of the loaves and fishes, some of the men wanted to make Jesus king. They hoped he would meet their earthly needs, which may have included freedom from Roman oppression. The hard words Jesus spoke were directed to them and to those who came to spy on him from Jerusalem. The delegation from the Sanhedrin came for spiritual reasons. They believed Jesus to be a false prophet.

Jesus also spoke his hard lesson for the sake of his disciples, knowing his words would shake their belief in him to the core.

He was right. Many of his disciples left him, saying, "This is a hard teaching, who can accept it?"

Scripture records: "Aware that his disciples were grumbling about this, Jesus said to them, 'Does this offend you? What if you see the Son of Man ascend to where he was before? The Spirit gives life; the flesh counts for nothing. The words I have spoken to you are spirit and they are life . . . This is why I told you that no one can come to me unless the Father has enabled him."

Jesus sifted their hearts. Many turned away from him. It was even hard for his Twelve to stay. Seeing many of them go, Jesus said to his chosen apostles, "You do not want to leave too, do you?" (Refer to John 6:60-70.)

Jesus was experiencing heartache. Truly and deeply. It is a wonder that he risked so much at this juncture. Would his apostles remain steadfast in faith? Who would remain through the painful sifting, emotionally painful to Jesus? Only pure faith would survive this sifting. He had to try them, had to purify them, had to turn their faith into gold. He knew that what lay ahead would be even harder for them.

Today, we have the benefit of knowing what his words meant. Although they were shocking at the time, we can appreciate the layers of wondrous theology in them. We see the symbol of the Lord's Supper—Holy Communion—God's new covenant with us through the body and blood of Jesus' sacrifice. We understand that Jesus himself is our "spiritual food"— because he comes within and gives us his *Life* moment by moment. We are in communion with him; abiding in him, and he in us; walking in the Spirit. He is, just as he said, the "true bread that came down from heaven."

We must embrace this mystery. The words Jesus spoke that day in the synagogue in Capernaum became words of life to those of us who believe. It is a wonder, yet we who have tasted this *Bread* know—what he said is absolutely, gloriously true.

WHAT DO YOU SEE?

We are so accustomed to what Jesus said, we don't realize how strange it was to his first listeners. Can you imagine hearing those words, spoken by Jesus for the very first time, that day in the synagogue? We have the benefit of knowing about Jesus' sacrifice on the cross, and they, at that time, did not. To better appreciate this event in Jesus' life, imagine yourself there with the disciples.

Watch the faces of the men while Jesus tells them to eat his flesh and drink his blood. How does Jesus look when he says this? What does his voice sound like? Is he pacing his words as he speaks? What happens after he is finished? What does he do when he is alone with his disciples? How is Jesus feeling? How are they? What do you suppose happened that made Jesus blurt out that there was a "devil" among them? Can you imagine this event in all its dramatic, emotional details? You can better know your Lord by this kind of "seeing"—be open to the Spirit's revelations. Jesus wants us to intimately know him through the many details, and things to ponder, about his life on earth.

JOURNAL

After your meditation, journal about the things you felt and learned. What do you feel now towards Jesus after having seen this event in a prayerful, meditative way? If you wish to express your love and gratefulness—and your faith—you may wish to end by sitting in silence with him. Simply be still and know his heart now and let him fill you with his peace and love.

24 – With the Cross in View

From that time on Jesus
began to explain to his disciples that he
must go to Jerusalem and suffer many things
at the hands of the elders,
chief priests and teachers of the law,
and that he must be killed
and on the last day be raised to life.
Matthew 16:21

- Peter's identification of Jesus as the Christ and first prophecy of the church (The region of Caesarea-Philippi): *Matthew 16:13-20; Mark 8:27-30; Luke 9:18-21*
- First direct prediction of the rejection, crucifixion, and resurrection (Near Caesarea Philippi): *Mark 16:21-26; Mark 8:31-37; Luke 9:22-25*
- Coming of the Son of Man and judgment (Near Caesarea Philippi): *Matthew 16:27-28; Mark 8:38-9:1; Luke 9:26-27*
- Transfiguration of Jesus (High mountain, perhaps Mount Hermon): *Matthew 17:1-8; Mark 9:2-8; Luke 9:28-36a*
- Discussion of resurrection, Elijah, and John the Baptist (Coming down the mountain): *Matthew 17:9-13; Mark 9:9-13; Luke 9:36b*
- Healing the demoniac boy and unbelief rebuked (Near the mount of transfiguration): *Matthew 17:14-20; Mark 9:14-29; Luke 9:37-43a*
- Second prediction of Jesus' death and resurrection (Traveling in Galilee): *Matthew 17:22-23; Mark 9:30-32; Luke 9:43b-45*
- Payment of the temple tax (Capernaum): *Matthew 17:24-27*

- Rivalry over greatness in the kingdom (Capernaum): *Matthew 18:1-5; Mark 9:33-37; Luke 9:46-48*
- Warning against causing believers to sin (Capernaum): *Matthew 18:6-14; Mark 9:38-50; Luke 9:49-50*

A CONTEMPLATIVE VIEW

James, son of Zebedee, one of Jesus' twelve apostles . . .

"Who do people say I am?" Jesus asked us.

His question was unlike him. We looked around at one another, wondering how to answer or who might speak first. My brother John and I were usually not timid. We'd say anything and everything that was on our minds. "Sons of thunder," Jesus had nicknamed us.

We said our minds, no matter how spontaneous or impulsive our ideas were. The twelve of us talked with him often and openly—while traveling on foot, by boat, when camping, or staying in houses. When you spend as much time together as we did, you see every side of a person: one's habits, mannerisms; you know how the other will react to something; you can know one's thoughts. That's how it was with us. Although, we had a harder time knowing what was on our Rabbi's mind than how quickly he knew what was on ours. And we couldn't guess what he might do next. But he knew us, and the twelve of us knew one another.

When the Master took us into the northern part of Galilee, a mostly heathen region full of idol-worshippers, he told us it was because we needed time away from the crowds and spies for a while. He wanted time just with us, he said.

We were sitting beside the rapids near the headwaters of the Jordan River when we had a conversation with him that we will always remember. We had been walking for days. Even though we had been among non-Jews, there were still many people who recognized our rabbi. He healed some people in the villages, and a few others living near Tyre and Sidon—both evil, pagan cities. Finally, we went far enough north that we were in an isolated area, and we stopped to rest.

He asked us that surprising question: "Who do people say that I am?"

No one answered him at first. Truly, the question seemed strange on his lips. Then someone said, "Some say John the Baptist."

Jesus pinched his eyebrows together with a doubtful look.

The Baptist and Jesus had been seen together. And some of us had actually been disciples of the Baptist when we met Jesus. Someone else said, "Elijah." And another added, "Jeremiah, or one of the prophets."

Then, with that penetrating expression of his, he asked, "But what about you? Who do *you* say I am?"

After only a few moments of silence, Simon Peter, who up to this point hadn't said anything, stood to his feet. And, in a full voice, he said to Jesus, "You are the Messiah, the Son of the living God."

Moved by Peter's proclamation, the Master also stood, took several steps to Peter, and embraced him. In a hushed, loving voice, but loud enough that we heard him, the Master said, "Blessed are you, Simon son of Jonah, for this was not revealed to you by man, but by my Father in heaven. And I tell you that you are Peter, and on this rock I will build my church, and the gates of Hades will not overcome it."

Peter was beside himself. Never had I seen him so stunned. Tears welled up in his eyes.

Jesus wrapped his right arm around the top of Peter's shoulders, pulling him close to himself. Then the two of them stood side by side, facing us. Jesus, looking proudly at Peter, said, "I will give you the keys of the kingdom of heaven; whatever you bind on earth will be bound in heaven, and whatever you loose on earth will be loosed in heaven."

Immediately after this, Jesus strictly warned us not to tell anyone that he was the Messiah.

We were terribly excited. But it wasn't long before he revealed something else to us, something we could not understand, could not accept, could not think about. He told us that he must go to Jerusalem and suffer at the hands of the elders, chief priests and teachers of the law, be killed, and on the third day he would be raised to life.

A few days after the time he admitted to us that he was the Messiah, he repeated that he would suffer and die in Jerusalem. Peter raised his voice to Jesus, saying, "Never, Lord! No! This will never happen to you!"

The Master rebuked Peter, telling him the devil had spoken through him.

Oh, things were happening too fast for us. We were in turmoil. The Master told us we would all have to take up our crosses and follow him, and that we would have to die to save our lives.

Jesus told us over and over that he would suffer many things and be rejected and killed. But he always ended by saying he would be raised on the third day. It didn't matter how many times he told us, we blocked it out. It was as though our ears couldn't bear the words.

It wasn't long after Jesus had rebuked Peter that the Master took three of us—Peter, my brother, and me—up a high mountain to pray. While Jesus prayed, he changed into a radiant man in front of us—with the whitest white clothing. He shone like the sun. Then, a cloud enveloped him. Two figures also bathed in light stood and talked with him. We could hear their conversation. It was Moses and Elijah with him! The holy men of old encouraged Jesus and spoke of his departure, which he was about to bring to fulfillment in Jerusalem. Then a voice sounded in the cloud, and it spoke to the three of us frightened men, saying, "This is my Son, whom I love; with him I am well pleased. Listen to him!"

And, so, for whatever reasons Jesus brought us up there, as I am his witness, he was a determined man coming back down that mountain. And, we—we were in awe of him.

WONDER JUST A LITTLE

The end of Jesus' earthly life draws near and he takes time to be alone with his disciples. No doubt his heart is heavy, knowing what lies ahead of him—and them. Can you sense this? Look closely at his steps, the things he says, and how he says them.

Because we go from Gospel to Gospel, often reading the events out of order, we don't truly appreciate the unfolding of Jesus' days. But his gracious humanity is never more wondrously realized than during these days as he begins his final steps toward the cross. For the first time, Jesus affirms his identity as the Messiah. But, even more shocking to his men, he tells them that he will suffer, die, and rise again. This grave news is a shock to them. They can't understand it or believe it.

Is there a sense of relief when Jesus reveals his two-fold secret (his true identity, and his mission), a secret he has kept to himself all of his life?

In the isolated hills of upper Galilee, away from the world, Jesus takes his twelve disciples away for a time of respite. But it is more than a break from the mobs and endless demands; it is a time of great revelation. Here he reveals himself to them, more than he has to anyone.

What tremendous love this is—the love that faces the cross, yet goes about daily life with his friends, preparing and teaching them, loving them, just being with them. On the sunset of his life, Jesus embraces the inevitable, knowing it is his main purpose for coming. He also begins to prepare them, saying, "If anyone would come after me, he must deny himself and take up his cross daily and follow me. For whoever wants to save his life will lose it, but whoever loses his life for me will save it."

Jesus' words fall upon ears that cannot understand. Not yet. But he knows that one day, they will.

Jesus takes three of his disciples up a high mountain and is transfigured before them. It is a moment in Time that transcends physical time and space. Jesus is seen, resembling his former glory, and meets with two faithful followers—great prophets from the past. This event is such a mystery, the reality cannot be fully comprehended.

There are things we can ponder: Moses, when he lived on earth, had talked with God on a mountain, his face aglow after these encounters. This time, Jesus' face is aglow. Two old friends transcend time and space, and meet with the Lord. Elijah, who had closely "walked with" God during his earthly days, comes to speak with his Friend once again. A true wonder, there is so much to ponder about this event.

It was part of the preparation of Jesus and his men for what lay ahead. Jesus faced the cross, ready to embrace his mission: the blame, the shame, the pain, the full weight of what it would take to save humanity.

WHAT DO YOU SEE?

Read about the time Jesus asked his disciples, "Who do you say that I am?" When you pray, imagine what it must have been like when Jesus asked his disciples that meaningful question.

Then close your Bible and your eyes. You are, in prayer, just as present to Jesus as were his disciples that day during their travels. He is with you now. It is a typical day in your life's journey with him, and here you are, alone with him, and he has your full attention. He's taken you aside for a time, like he did his disciples that day.

Jesus looks into your eyes and asks you, "Who am I to you?"

The wording is a little different from the question he asked his disciples. We already know his identity—that he is the Messiah, the Son of God.

How do you treat him? What do you think of him? What is your favorite image of God? Tell the Lord why you think of him as you do. Is your image of him as your brother, lover, parent, healer, provider, shepherd, or king?

Who is Jesus to you? What does knowing him mean to you? Tell him.

Have you heard him call you by a nickname—a name that maybe only he has for you? Listen closely, what is his own special name for you? You see, he also wants *you* to know *who you are to him*. "Listen to him."

JOURNAL

In your journal, record this chapter's thoughts and reflections. Record your dialogue with the Lord, if there is one. End with what your favorite image of God is, and why. What answer did you give Jesus regarding who he is to you? What does he say about you?

25 – The Feast of Tabernacles

On the last and greatest day of the Feast,
Jesus stood and said in a loud voice,
"If anyone is thirsty, let him come to me and drink.
Whoever believes in me, as the Scripture has said,
streams of living water will flow from within him."
John 7:37-38

- Ridicule by Jesus' half-brothers (Galilee): *John 7:2-9*
- Journey through Samaria (Start of journey to Jerusalem): *Luke 9:51-56; John 7:10*
- Mixed reaction to Jesus' teaching and miracles (Jerusalem, in the temple): *John 7:11-31*
- Frustrated attempt to arrest Jesus (Jerusalem): *John 7:32-52*

A CONTEMPLATIVE VIEW

Jesus' life was the journey God took when he once again tabernacled (dwelt) with his people, Israel. Jesus' steps in his pilgrimage on earth brought him to the Feast of Tabernacles in Jerusalem. But first, he returned home to Nazareth, alone, for a final visit there.

It was his secret goodbye, because of course, his family didn't know that he was there for the last time.

His half-brothers were upset with him. They could not accept the person Jesus had become; and when they saw him, they said, "You ought to leave here and go to Judea, so that your disciples may see the miracles you do. No one who wants to become a public

151

figure acts in secret. Since you are doing these things, show yourself to the world."

Perhaps their disbelief was because they were afraid or ashamed of him. Whatever they felt, they most certainly did not know who he really was.

Jesus planned to go to the Tabernacles Feast secretly. Too many of his enemies wanted him dead, and he had to be careful. The time had not yet come for him to die. His death was destined for the Passover Feast, five months later.

When Jesus arrived in Jerusalem midway through the Feast, he certainly did "show himself." This feast was one of the hardest, most grueling times he endured during his public ministry. The confrontations in Jerusalem brought Jesus to proclaim truths the leaders could not bear. He revealed himself to them, holding nothing back.

This particular Feast was a fulfillment, although sadly tragic, of the Feast of Tabernacles itself.

One of the boldest things Jesus said and did was to stand outside the Water Gate, during the symbolic ritual service of water-pouring and branch-waving, and utter for all to hear: "If anyone is thirsty, let him come to me and drink. Whoever believes in me, as the Scripture has said, streams of living water will flow from within him."

God had come to them. But Sin blinded them.

WONDER JUST A LITTLE

Wonderful treasures can be uncovered by looking closely at the origins of the Feast of Tabernacles, which fell late in the harvest time of the year. During the days of the temple, it was mandatory for all able-bodied men of Israel to attend the feast in Jerusalem. Even today, among Jews and Christians, Tabernacles holds great significance. And the Scriptures predict that, during the Messianic Age, the kings of the nations will stream to Jerusalem on this feast to worship the Lord.

What is the importance of this feast? Perhaps a deeper look will bring us the appreciation for what Jesus said and did on that last

Feast of Tabernacles he celebrated on earth.

After saving the children of Israel from slavery and the oppression of Egypt, God wanted to bring them directly back to their own land of "milk and honey." But because of fear and unbelief, they refused to reclaim the land God had given them. And so, after all the mighty things the Lord had done to deliver them, they wandered in the Sinai wilderness for forty years.

God had delivered them so that they could be free to worship him. The only reason for the Tabernacle was to avail a living relationship with God.

Not for a moment did he leave them alone. In fact, to that generation of forty years, the Lord revealed himself in ways Israel had never known before. Besides giving them his commandments to live by, God created a way for them to enjoy a covenant relationship with him. Here began to flourish worship practices involving the Tabernacle and God's presence *with* them.

The Tabernacle, also called the *Tent of Meeting*, was meticulously designed by the Lord himself, and was rich with symbolic meaning. Everything about the Tabernacle pointed to the new covenant Jesus would bring.

The portable Tabernacle in the wilderness was a tent, later replaced by the Temple in Jerusalem, which used the same design, activities, and furnishings. Of course, the Temple was magnificently built, and rebuilt, of materials that Israel used to bring glory to God.

But it was God's Presence, his *Shekinah*, which brought true glory into the Tabernacle, or Temple, God's dwelling place.

To better appreciate the meaning and beauty of the Tabernacle, we must consider the effect it had on God and his people. Here is where God came to reveal himself. He certainly didn't need a place to rest his head, for he held the entire universe in place. The Tabernacle was a physical place in which his people could come to *seek his face*, could pray and commune with him, and could express their love for him.

The Tabernacle itself was a symbol of Heaven, and was enclosed, with one central gate. The entire enclosed area was divided into three sections, moving from the gate inwardly to the place where God dwelt: the outer court, the Holy Place, and the

Most Holy Place.

Just inside the gate was the brazen altar, the meeting place between God and man, and foreshadowing the cross. It represents substitutionary atonement. Only a perfect life can atone for sin—a sinner's life cannot. Jesus was the only one worthy to die for the remission for sin. The sacrificing of lambs—innocent lives for others—was a foreshadowing of the coming of the Lamb of God, who would be worthy to take away sins once for all. *Life* for life. Symbolically, the brazen altar accepts Jesus' life-blood poured out. Therefore, faith in the Blood of the Lamb is the only remission for sin—not by works or by any other means is anyone given this gift of *Life*.

Moving further inside is the Laver. This represents the washing of the Word as Jesus, the Priest, who cleanses us by his ongoing forgiveness.

Going further inside, we come to the Holy Place and see the Golden Candlestick—the Menorah. Made of pure gold, its seven branches represent the seven Spirits of God. Its top, central flame is the Lord of Lords, the King of Kings—the true Light of the world. The Messiah, Jesus.

The light from the Menorah never goes out. It is an eternal flame. This is what illumines our relationship with God. It is the only light in the Most Holy Place.

Moving deeper into the Tabernacle is the table of Shewbread, which literally is "Bread of his Presence." This represents eating the bread that has come down from heaven. This is our fellowship, our relationship, with the Lord. This represents "manna" from heaven; and Jesus, the "Bread of Life."

Also, just before the Veil of Separation that leads into the Most Holy Place, is the golden Altar of Incense. This represents adoration. A burning desire for intimacy with God—for God himself—will rise up like a fragrant burning of incense to Heaven. Beyond the thick veil of curtains, we pass into the Holy of Holies. But only through the Blood of the Lamb, and intimacy with him, can we enter. His sacrifice tears the veil from top to bottom so that we can pass through.

Inside the Holy of Holies is the Ark of the Covenant; the tablets of the Law are kept within. Here is the Mercy Seat. Everything thus far brings us to this. This is God's ultimate and eternal plan: Mercy. Here grace abounds. This is intimate union with his Presence. There is no light inside the Holy of Holies. It is dark here and represents experiencing the "cloud of unknowing"—which is the Mystery of God. Here the worshipper experiences intimate union with God.

Jesus, the Lord, became a man, humbling himself, and dwelt with us in a body (a tabernacle). He knew he would be rejected and hated so that he could die for us, shedding his blood for the forgiveness of sin. He preached that whosoever believed in him would cross over from death to life—and would enjoy that unfathomable, eternal love and union with him.

WHAT DO YOU SEE?

What "tabernacle" have you experienced lately? It could be in your prayer closet or in a retreat room. Perhaps the celebration of a church service is where you meet most powerfully with God. There are all kinds of ways God *tabernacles* with us.

Close your eyes and imagine the Temple or the Tent of Meeting. Jesus said he is the Gate. You won't even be able to enter the "tabernacle experience" unless you believe in Jesus as your Lord.

Can you see the altar? Can you imagine blood poured out upon it? Red, real blood? Picture the cross. Blood is running down the face and arms of Jesus. Blood is dripping from the nails, the wounds, falling into small red pools upon the clay earth. As you kneel there, a drop falls upon your head.

You are back at the brazen altar and you realize that Jesus is calling you to give your life to him. He wants you to live for him. You realize something. This is what you truly want now.

You move on from this place. At the Laver, you encounter the cleansing waters as Jesus washes you with his Word, forgives your sins, and renews your mind. The Word of God recreates in you the truths you want to live by.

Jesus, with a nod of his head, tells you he wants you to move into the Holy Place. Just inside, your eyes see the Golden Candlestick. Everything is softly bathed in its light, for you are inside a sanctuary now and have left the outer court. Your entire life now is about Jesus. You want him to guide you in daily life. He is very near you, and he has become the Light of your life.

Jesus takes you by the hand. He brings you to the Table of Bread. He gives you this bread to eat. Imagine him placing a piece of the bread with his own fingers into your mouth. "Eat this bread, for this is my body," he says to you. "These words are spirit, and they are life," he whispers in your ear.

You smile, knowing how wonderful it is knowing him. Now you've come to the altar of incense. Here you desire Jesus only. You desire him for himself alone—not for what he can do for you, not even for what you can do for him. You desire just to be with him; you adore him. You long to see his face.

Jesus puts his arm around you. He parts the curtain and the two of you walk into the Holy of Holies. This is the throne room in Heaven. You are caught up in the glory of God. You lose yourself in him. He becomes everything. You are one with him.

JOURNAL

What are your thoughts about this chapter? What was your meditation like? Listen to what Jesus wants to tell you. Or simply sit quietly in his presence and bask in his wonderful love. This is your "tabernacle" time.

26 - Hear, O Israel!

Why is my language not clear to you?
Because you are unable to hear what I say.
John 8:43

- Jesus' forgiveness of a woman caught in adultery (Jerusalem, in the temple): *John 7:53-8:11*
- Conflict over Jesus' claim to be the light of the world (Jerusalem, in the temple): *John 8:12-20*
- Jesus' relationship to God the Father (Jerusalem, in the temple): *John 8:21-30*
- Jesus' relationship to Abraham and attempted stoning (Jerusalem, in the temple): *John 8:31-59*

A CONTEMPLATIVE VIEW

To understand the loving passion Jesus felt for his people, Israel, one must consider their history, which is also ours. It is the history of God's love and faithfulness—his selfless, eternal, unrelenting love for the world. One must look at the days of Jesus' visitation to Israel as one would look at a scene in a dramatic love story. One particular act in that scene takes place in Jerusalem between Jesus and the rulers of Israel. It was a pivotal moment.

God and *Israel* stood facing each other. In the eyes of the Jewish leaders, Jesus' audacity and self-proclaimed authority angered them—so much so that they wanted to kill him. They saw him as a threat to everything they called sacred.

What a paradox.

He was their savior, the Holy One of Israel, the Most High come to them in person. He was their longed-for Messiah. But he wasn't who they expected, nor did he come the way that they expected, so they didn't recognize him.

But really, how should their Messiah act? What had they expected? What blinded them?

The Jewish leaders clung to their pride. They saw Jesus through faithless eyes, because their hearts were as hard as rock.

Because we know the beginning from the end, and see things from this side of Jesus' earthly life, we know what this confrontation with Israel's leaders was all about. We wish it could have been different. Now, we see the Savior's glory and walk in the light of his goodness. But the people on that stage in Jerusalem did not.

In the middle of heated dialogue, Jesus said to them, "I am going away, and you will look for me, and you will die in your sin. Where I go, you cannot come." When Jesus said this, he looked into eyes darkened with hatred. His words were heartbreaking ones for him to say. We can sense his longing and disappointment.

It's difficult for us to understand the religious rulers' hatred. We'd give anything to have been there, to have heard Jesus' voice and to have seen him. We want so much to see his face—to look into his loving eyes. We pity those who missed seeing him when he came to them. We who never saw him are the ones who are blessed (as Jesus said we would be). We are the ones who know him and have "seen" him.

Today, we see the nation of Israel. We know that most of them still do not recognize their Messiah. Not yet. With Jesus, our hearts long for their blindness to fall away, for them to believe in their Lord. With Jesus, we say, "Hear, O Israel, the Lord our God, the Lord is one. And you shall love the Lord your God with all your heart, with all your soul, and with all your might."

Yes, hear, O, Israel!

Wonder Just a Little

A sinful woman faces her accusers and their stones. Her

accusers—the religious leaders—want to see "justice" done, so they take their pitiful victim to Jesus, whom they hope to bring to justice in much the same way. They hope to trap him. But who traps whom?

What a wonder! The shaking, hopeless sinner looks into the eyes of her Judge and finds only tenderness and love. The "religious" men stand before the same Judge with not only stones in their hands, but stones for hearts. These are the ones Jesus judges.

Knowing the condition of every heart, Jesus asks a question within his own heart: *How will these men ever know the same forgiveness as she?* And so, later that day he tells his accusers: "I told you that you would die in your sins; if you do not believe that I am the one I claim to be, you will indeed die in your sins. You are ready to kill me, because you have no room for my word. I am telling you what I have seen in the Father's presence, and you do what you have heard from your father."

There is tremendous pain in Jesus' next words, for he longed for his enemies to receive from him what only he could give them: "If God were your Father, you would love me, for I came from God and now am here. I have not come on my own; but he sent me. Why is my language not clear to you? It is because you are unable to hear what I say. You belong to your father, the devil, and you want to carry out your father's desire."

Can you sense the depth of wisdom and sorrow he has for their souls? He is fighting for their lives, knowing their eternal enemy holds them tightly in the grip of death and sin. Jesus passionately tells them what he knows, saying: "He [the devil] was a murderer from the beginning, not holding to the truth, for there is no truth in him. When he lies, he speaks his native language, for he is a liar and the father of lies. Yet because I tell the truth, you do not believe me!"

How tragic is the irony of the moment as Jesus reasons with them, trying to open their eyes: "Can any of you prove me guilty of sin? If I am telling the truth, why don't you believe me?"

Listen, as he pronounces what will save them and kill him, ". . . I honor my Father and you dishonor me. I am not seeking glory for myself; but there is one who seeks it, and he is the judge. I tell you the truth, if anyone keeps my word, he will never see death."

And, hearing him, they ask, "Are you greater than Abraham?

Who do you think you are?"

When Jesus answers their rebuttal that they claim to be "sons of Abraham," with his claim, "Before Abraham was born, I am!" they pick up stones to kill him.

We read the ending act of this scene: "Jesus hid himself, slipping away from the temple grounds."

This was tragic and, in a way, it is still true today. Yet, Jesus continues to reveal himself to his people. As the loving husband in an unrelenting search for his wayward wife, he will never stop, for he has pledged himself to her forever.

WHAT DO YOU SEE?

Once again, Jesus clearly speaks to those who await the coming of the Messiah, though they refuse to accept him as such. They hear the One we've come to know as *The Word* of God say, *"Why is my language not clear to you?"*

Can you feel Jesus' heartache in these words? Can you sense the floods of love beneath them? Imagine the elders of Israel surrounding Jesus in the temple court. The misguided religious rulers are badgering him even as Jesus is teaching the pilgrims, those who have come to the Feast of Tabernacles in Jerusalem to celebrate the Feast of "God-with-us." Jesus is speaking to the pilgrims about the kingdom of heaven.

The Feast of Tabernacles celebrated God's coming to dwell with his people, Israel, during their journey between Egypt and the Promised Land. In the form of a cloud by day and a pillar of fire by night, the Lord God guided them, cared for them, and kept them safe. What a tragically symbolic coincidence that Jesus should be rejected by Israel's leaders during this Feast.

How is it that the elders do not listen to him? Jesus is the God of Israel who had, during their sojourn in the desert, tabernacled with them. Here, now, he's come in a different form—a much more personal form to again be their guide, and helper, and protector. He's come to guide them into salvation and truth, to heal and deliver them from sickness and oppression, and to save them from their enemies—sin and death. He's come to show them the way back to intimacy and a relationship with *him*.

But instead of welcoming him, they confront and drill him, looking to trick him into saying something for which their warped justice can kill him.

Let this scene of Jesus' confrontation with the Jewish leaders in the temple play out in your imagination. Then snap a picture in your mind's eye. What images do you see? If you can see faces in your picture, whose are they and what do they express? Is Jesus in your snapshot? How does he look?

Does Jesus, in this scene, show you more about the heart of God than you knew before? Can you relate more closely to a God who has feelings and desires, even disappointments, like we do? Doesn't this draw you to have a deeper understanding of Jesus, knowing of his hurt and rejection?

We know that he came to lay down his life for "his friends." Do you only see Jesus as hurling harsh words at these men? Aren't they, rather, words borne from the deeply loving heart of a friend? Or of a rejected God in love with his people?

God's love extends to the entire world. His unrequited love, just like in this scene, is repeated over and over every day. Jesus longs for all the souls of the world to come to know him.

JOURNAL

Describe in your journal the snapshot you have of Jesus during this confrontation. Maybe your heart was moved by the incident with the woman caught in adultery and pardoned by Jesus. Invite the Lord to come into your time of journaling. Be sensitive to his voice. What, in your readings, has stirred your heart? Be sensitive to these things: let them "steep" in your inward being. What inspirational thoughts come to you? God's voice is so often subtle, a drawing or urge; sometimes it is much more. Maybe dialogue will come between the Lord and you. Listening to God with a prayer journal can be wonderfully life changing. After all, he says, "Do you hear me? . . . Listen, . . . Those who have ears to hear, hear what the Spirit says . . ." He's never stopped speaking and asking us to listen. This is one way, in faith, that we can hear him.

27 – Blessed Eyes that See and Gaze

Then he turned to his disciples and said privately,
"Blessed are the eyes that see what you see.
For I tell you that many prophets and kings
wanted to see what you see but did not see it,
and to hear what you hear but did not hear it."
Luke 10:23-24

- Healing of a man born blind (Jerusalem): *John 9:1-7*
- Response of the blind man's neighbors (Jerusalem): *John 9:8-12*
- Examination and excommunication of the blind man by the Pharisees (Jerusalem): *John 9:13-34*
- Jesus' identification of himself to the blind man (Jerusalem): *John 9:35-38*
- Spiritual blindness of the Pharisees (Jerusalem): *John 9:39-41*
- Allegory of the good shepherd and the thief (Jerusalem): *John 10:1-18*
- Further division among the Jews (Jerusalem): *John 10:19-21*
- Commissioning of the seventy (Probably in Judea): *Luke 10:1-18*
- Return of the seventy (Probably in Judea): *Luke 10:17-24*
- Story of the good Samaritan (Probably in Judea): *Luke 10:25-37*
- Jesus' visit with Mary and Martha (Bethany, near Jerusalem): *Luke 10:38-42*

A CONTEMPLATIVE VIEW

Martha from Bethany . . .

People from all walks of life followed our friend around like he was God or something. I could see the look on their faces when they listened to him. It bothered me a lot. Here was a man we'd known for years, going about the whole country performing signs and teaching great crowds of people. Then he would come to our house to rest. But if we had Jesus staying at our house in Bethany, a short walk to Jerusalem, we'd also get at least twenty more guests with him. I didn't let on to him that it sometimes bothered me that our home became too public for my liking; well, I guess, to be honest, sometimes I actually enjoyed it. I have always liked having guests over and cooking, so it wasn't too much trouble. But we sometimes lost all our privacy for days on end. It was hard to find any peace and quiet when Jesus came to stay with us. I think that is why, when the weather permitted, he took his disciples off to some cave to sleep, on the Jerusalem side of our Mount of Olives.

I liked Jesus right away when Lazarus first brought him home after the two of them met in Jerusalem, years before all the excitement. Our younger sister, Mary, thought an awful lot of him, too. She always looked up to him and he gave her that big-brother kind of attention.

Jesus was kind, gentle, and open. He was an approachable man, yet not forward in any improper way; in fact, he was more respectful towards women than any man I'd ever known, including my brother.

Jesus made us laugh and was, from the day I met him, fascinating to talk to. We enjoyed him every time he came to visit.

During the days of Jesus' popularity, he continued to visit us when he came to Jerusalem. Always, he had followers and disciples along. Once when he was here, talking in our house at the time of the Feast of Tabernacles, Mary sat with the others and completely ignored the fact that I was left to cook and serve all by myself. A few times I went into the room and intentionally made noise, shuffling about and clattering bowls and cups to get attention—hoping, at least, that Jesus would realize I was working alone. He didn't

164

even see me, he was so engrossed in whatever it was he was talking about. And Mary was just as absorbed; she didn't notice me either.

Well, I complained.

I will never forget his look and words to me, when, at last, I had his full attention.

First of all, his eyes nearly broke my heart—I'd never seen that look on anyone's face before—it was penetrating love, disappointment, and compassion all at once. And it was intense!

He said that I was worried about too many things and that there was only one thing necessary. Looking at Mary at his feet, he said to me, "Mary has chosen the better part and it will not be taken from her."

In that instant, I understood his disappointment in me—and it changed me. It was an amazing experience. He had unveiled his heart to me. I sensed his love and what he desired for me. Suddenly, he was more, much more, than a popular rabbi-friend of my brother's. I wanted to know him. I needed to find out—who was this man to say such a thing, and to make me feel this way?

I, too, wanted nothing but to sit and gaze at him, to listen and to soak up, like a sponge, every sound that fell from his lips. And now I understand. Jesus *was* God walking around. The many cares of the world, and my preoccupation with myself, had blinded me. I am so thankful he let me see his heart—he let me see his great and real love for *me*.

WONDER JUST A LITTLE

Jesus loves his sheep. He goes to great lengths to save and bring each of his lambs close to himself. He calls them and leads them like a true shepherd. The Good Shepherd of David's Psalms is Jesus.

What Martha, Mary, and the many others who followed Jesus had the chance to see was . . . the face of God. They heard the Word of God in person.

Things today haven't changed all that much. We, too, can "see" Jesus and we can enjoy a vital, intimate relationship with him. Yet, even as believers, we so often become preoccupied with this life—

sometimes even with what we do *for* him. The heart of Jesus has not changed. He prefers our presence, our devotion and our *listening* attention, to our serving him.

We can also be just like the Pharisees. The leaders knew that Jesus healed a blind man, yet they found fault with him. We ask ourselves, how can they be so stupid? What's wrong with them?

But we often miss his miracles too. If we only realized the many signs and wonders Jesus performs just for us, we'd be astounded. We just don't believe in them. We think they are coincidences, or natural, explainable events. We need eyes to see and ears to hear!

One way we can be more aware and faithful in this regard is to become a "reflective" person. Looking for God and his doings should be a moment-by-moment experience in our relationship with him. There are windows into heaven, windows of our souls, with which we can gaze upon our Lord and see him and his doings.

WHAT DO YOU SEE?

Read John 10:1-18. Here Jesus calls himself the good shepherd. As you read of Jesus' claims about himself, pay attention to whatever stirs your heart the most. For example, if the words that most draw you are: "I am the good shepherd; I know my sheep and my sheep know me . . ." Or, only "my sheep know me," be sure to focus on just the part that seems the most meaningful. With your eyes closed, repeat those few words to yourself.

During this prayer time, ask yourself what is he saying to you through these words of Scripture you've felt stirred by? What else does he want you to know?

Do you see and hear Jesus with eyes of faith? Do you sense that same person who walked the earth and spoke these words of Scripture is really with you? Do you believe that he is speaking to you right now?

The one speaking to you is the Good Shepherd of your soul. He is blessing you with eyes to see and gaze upon him. You, who have never really "seen" him, but believe in him, can truly know him, can hear his voice—in the now.

This is the reason he came—so that we might really know him.

If our spiritual ears and eyes are open, through faith, we will hear his voice and experience his own personal love for us.

JOURNAL

Describe in your journal what you've learned from this portion of Scripture. What were the special words Jesus spoke into your prayer time just now? What does this mean to you—to him? Write in your journal, to him, about what you are feeling. Ask him what he thinks or feels about this time with you.

28 – Tell Us Plainly

I and the Father are one.
John 10:30

- Lesson on how to pray and parable of the bold friend (Probably in Judea): *Luke 11:1-13*
- A third blasphemous accusation and a second debate (Probably in Judea): *Luke 11:14-36*
- Woes against the Pharisees and the teachers of the law while eating with a Pharisee (Probably in Judea): *Luke 11:37-54*
- Warning the disciples about hypocrisy (Probably in Judea): *Luke 12:1-12*
- Warning about greed and trust in wealth (Probably in Judea): *Luke 12:13-34*
- Warning against being unprepared for the Son of Man's coming (Probably in Judea): *Luke 12:35-48*
- Warning about the coming division (Probably in Judea): *Luke 12:49-53*
- Warning against failing to discern the present time (Probably in Judea): *Luke 12:54-59*
- Two alternatives—repent or perish (Probably in Judea): *Luke 13:1-9*
- Opposition from a synagogue ruler for healing a woman on the Sabbath (Probably in Judea): *Luke 13:10-21*
- Another attempt to stone or arrest Jesus for blasphemy at the Feast of Dedication (Jerusalem): *John 10:22-39*

A CONTEMPLATIVE VIEW

Jesus . . .

Father, where are the little children, the sheep of our flock? I have searched for them and have found so very few.

These men refuse to listen. Father, my heart is heavy. My accusers—everywhere I turn, they surround me. They burden me with sorrow upon sorrow. I feel such grief for them. Father, I have seen their faces. They are cold and hard—dead men. They go about pretending to know you. I grieve, my Father.

They seek me out, only to trap me. My words and miracles do nothing to open their eyes and hearts. If only they would listen to me without pride and fear.

Father, they refuse to believe and are afraid to love. They are trapped like dead men in tombs, wrapped tightly in grave cloths. Their eyes are unseeing; their ears are deaf.

I can only weep prayers for them, Father. Hear my prayers.

Father, forgive them for trying to kill me today. I know you helped me escape their stones. When they closed in around me, I saw Satan and the evil spirits with these religious men—and you saw, through my eyes, our enemies' faces.

Even now, I see their faces.

They wanted to kill me even before they stopped to speak to me. I felt their hatred as I approached them. They had been waiting to trap me. Of all places, it was in the temple.

Their words flew at me through the icy wind, "How long will you keep us in suspense? If you are the Messiah, tell us plainly."

There was no hint of greeting, no pretense of kindness, only contempt. They have eagerly awaited the coming of the Messiah every day, day after day, year after year after year—and here I am, and they want to kill me. Satan has blinded them so . . .

Father, I told them that the miracles I do in your name speak for me. I told them that my sheep listen to my voice, your voice, Father. I told them that I know my sheep and they follow me, and that I will give them eternal life—and these sheep of mine will never perish. I told them that no one can snatch them out of my hand. I said these words, not just to these men, but to their demons with them, and I said them to Satan. Surely, it was his hatred in the hearts of the men.

I told the men that they do not believe in me, so they are not my sheep. Father, there is still time for them. I pray for them to come into the sheepfold. Every one of them. Father, do you see their faces?

Father, when I told them that we are one, they tried to kill me, believing that I, a mere man, blasphemed because I claim to be God. I had answered their question truthfully. I plainly told them who I am. They refuse to believe in me. Satan has hold of them, and they are still dead.

Father, I tried to help them to see—through Scripture—hoping to give them light. They believe in the Scriptures, yet they refuse to see that they point to me. I had hoped to put water on the fire of their hatred—for surely they would listen to the truth of Holy Writ—which they say they live by.

I said to them, "Is it not written in your Law, 'I have said you are gods'?" I explained to them that you, Father, called them 'gods' in the Scriptures. And I asked them, "If God calls you 'gods', to whom the Word of God came—and the Scripture cannot be broken—what about the one whom the Father set apart as his very own and sent into the world?" My words cannot be any plainer, can they, Father? I told them you are my Father and that I am your very own, and that you sent me here.

Father, I want them to believe in me and live. They just cannot accept that I have come to fulfill their longing, their emptiness. Face to face, we stood apart, and I looked into dead men's eyes.

Father, when I said, "Why then do you accuse me of blasphemy because I said, 'I am God's Son'?" their faces vanished completely from me—all I could see, instead, were the faces of demons. It was as though the men disappeared inside the hatred of our enemies.

Hoping the men's hearts could still hear me, I told them not to believe me unless I do what my Father does—that they should at least believe that the miracles speak for me. I told them that that is how they may know and understand that you are in me, and that I am in you.

Father, I know that words of *Life* can penetrate the enemy's hold on them, and that is why I said, "I and the Father are one." But when I did so, the men and their demons tried to seize me—to do away with me.

Besides the cross, my Father, what more can I do before I leave this world? What more can I say? Today I have spoken plainly to them, as they asked me to do. I pray, now, that my blood will cover their sins in due time. Do you see their faces? I know you can see each one, my Father, and I pray for each one. Amen.

WONDER JUST A LITTLE

One wintry day in the temple courts, as Jesus walked in Solomon's Colonnade, the religious rulers demanded that he plainly identify himself. His response, given in clear language, was that he was the Son of God, and was one with God. They refused to believe him. All they saw was a man who claimed to be equal to God. And they were right about that. At that moment, they were speaking to God face to face. Think what awe and joy it could have been if they'd believed him. But they met only a man, a man they hated.

When Jesus presented them with Psalm 82:6, it was more than his defense at calling himself "God's Son." He reasoned further that he was "the one whom the Father set apart as his very own son and sent into the world." First of all, Jesus clearly explained that the Most High *sent* him to them.

Second, he claimed to be God's very own, only, Son.

Third, Jesus boldly said that not only was he *in the Father*, but the *Father was in him*, and that he was *one with God*.

Fourth, he had stated in the beginning of their dialogue, that he, Jesus, gives "eternal life."

Could Jesus have spoken any plainer?

What kind of Messiah were these men waiting for? What did they think the Promised One would look or act like? What blinded them? He worked miracles and taught more profoundly than any of their prophets or teachers or rabbis. What was it that some believed in him and others could not? He gave them overwhelming evidence, not only to satisfy their eyes and ears and minds, but their hearts as well. Why does faith elude so many? What is that key to the doors of faith?

The answer is wonderfully simple. Listen to these gentle, inviting, endearing words of Jesus: "So I say to you: Ask and it will be given to you; seek and you will find; knock and the door will be opened to you. For everyone who asks receives; he who seeks finds; and to him who knocks, the door will be opened.

"Which of you fathers, if your son asks for a fish, will give him a snake instead? Or if he asks for an egg, will give him a scorpion? If you, then, though you are evil, know how to give good gifts to your children, how much more will your Father in heaven give the Holy Spirit to those who ask him!"

Is it that easy? If we wish to know God, or the truth about his Son, all we need to do is ask him?

These Jewish rulers asked him. So why did faith elude them?

The key to faith is hidden within Jesus' words of Scripture when he told us about the Father's generous heart. Notice *the way* Jesus teaches this truth about *asking and seeking.* Isn't his tone and manner rather like how a father would speak to his children, even while he is using that as his illustration?

Jesus says here that we don't need any formulas to get our prayers answered. No "steps" or conditions. Just ask and believe our "daddy" wants to give us, his children, good things. He especially wants to give us the Holy Spirit.

Here is Jesus speaking for his Father, to his children on earth. We will only hear if we listen with an open, trusting, humble heart. Like children do.

The Pharisees and men of the law could not believe in Jesus because of their pride and closed hearts. We must become like little children.

WHAT DO YOU SEE?

Jesus had a way of reading motives and hearts. He could turn a sinner into a saint with a compassionate glance. He could turn a hypocrite on his head with one remark. He had an uncanny way of bringing the proud low, and the lowly to blessedness.

He didn't use charm or flattery to win people. Nor did he "chase" after people to get them to believe in him. And yet, paradoxically, he is the great "Hound of Heaven." Jesus' coming to earth is part of God's fervent, unrelenting pursuit of us. And God continues to come to us in many ways and through amazing methods.

Praying with Scripture is just one way. There are a number of wonderful illustrations in this chapter's Scripture readings that capture the Lord's passion and heart for us.

Choose from the list of Scriptures at the beginning of the chapter, paying attention to what draws you. Enter into the scene in prayerful meditation. In this sanctified imagination, try to see what the Lord would like to reveal to you about himself—or about you. Notice how he speaks to people, what his tone of voice is. Can you see his body language? Let him reveal his heart to you in ways that only your heart can see.

JOURNAL

During this time in the Lord's life, he is nearing the cross and has begun to reveal himself more boldly. But because we are so familiar with the story, we are usually too numb to appreciate what we read. Ask the Lord to help you feel the sense of awe at the things he says and does. What specific part of this story does the Lord wish you to ponder, to sit with? The Lord desires to reveal himself to you more and more. He desires to show you the heart he has for you. Record in your journal your thoughts and meditations. What have you learned and seen in these Scriptures? What stands out as the most meaningful? Express your love to the Lord and give him the opportunity, by being quietly present to him, to do the same.

29 – "I Am the Resurrection and the Life"

I am the resurrection and the life.
He who believes in me will live, even though he dies;
and whoever lives and believes in me will never die.
Do you believe this?
John 11:25-26

- From Jerusalem to Perea: *John 10:40-42*
- Question about salvation and entering the kingdom (Traveling toward Jerusalem while in Perea): *Luke 13:22-30*
- Anticipation of Jesus' coming death and his sorrow over Jerusalem (Traveling toward Jerusalem while in Perea): *Luke 13:31-35*
- Healing of a man with dropsy while eating with a prominent Pharisee on the Sabbath, and three parables suggested by the occasion (Probably in Perea): *Luke 14:1-24*
- Cost of discipleship (Probably in Perea): *Luke 14:25-35*
- Parables in defense of association with sinners (Probably in Perea): *Luke 15:1-32*
- Parable to teach the proper use of money (Probably in Perea): *Luke 16:1-13*
- Story to teach the danger of wealth (Probably in Perea): *Luke 16:14-31*
- Four lessons on discipleship (Probably in Perea): *Luke 17:1-10*
- Sickness and death of Lazarus (From Perea to Bethany, near Jerusalem): *John 11:1-16*

- Lazarus raised from the dead (Bethany, near Jerusalem): *John 11:17-44*
- Decision of the Sanhedrin to put Jesus to death (Jerusalem): *John 11:45-53*

A CONTEMPLATIVE VIEW

Lazarus from Bethany . . .

I had fallen sick during the wintertime. No matter how much bedding Martha and Mary heaped on me, I spent long, wasted hours shivering in my bed. Whatever food I managed to keep down passed through me within hours. This went on for days. My business partners came daily to see me and I could read by their faces how terrible I looked. I heard my sisters weeping in the evenings, and the doctors came and went without hope or answers.

I slipped into unconsciousness, or maybe it was sleep. I awoke off and on, but for shorter and shorter periods of time. The last time I awoke I saw Martha, sitting solemnly beside my bed, busy with sewing in her lap. When I stirred, she looked up and our eyes met.

"Lazarus!" She was excited to see me awake. I knew by her reaction that I was dying. She shouted for Mary, and Mary appeared by my side within moments.

"Lazarus, don't leave us. Jesus is coming. He should be here soon." Both of them spoke at once.

"How long have I been asleep?"

They looked at each other, neither of them willing to tell me.

"Two days," Mary finally admitted.

"That's what you said last time I asked." I tried to smile.

Mary lifted my head and pressed a cup of water to my mouth and told me to swallow.

"We sent for Jesus," Martha said. "Josiah went to find him and will bring him back to us. He should be here any time."

Oh, to see Jesus. Surely he would bring me out of this misery and the relentless, bone-chilling cold I felt. I fell asleep again after those few words with my sisters.

The next thing I knew, I was floating above my bed looking

down at my own sleeping form. It was early morning and still quite dim in the room. Just as I realized I must have died, two beings in light appeared and greeted me by name, telling me not to be afraid. They took me to a warm, comfortable place and told me to rest and wait, saying that Adonai, my Lord and theirs, would come for me shortly.

I knew then that my dear friend, Jesus, was Adonai! The well-being and peace I felt wrapped around me was *his* love. Like a young, weaned child, content and peacefully resting in his mother's arms, I wanted nothing. I realized that the beings of light who had been with me were *his* angels. I was unaware of the passing of time until I heard the voice of my Friend calling me: "Lazarus, come out!"

Although I was a little disoriented, I tried at once to do what he asked. I wasn't shivering as I had been when I was ill, but I felt cold. What was I lying on that was so hard? And when I tried to move I realized that my limbs were bound together. I was awfully stiff, and then I realized there was cloth over my face.

I struggled to get up. By the time I was on my feet, having managed to loosen whatever I was wearing enough to walk, I realized I had been called from that "resting place" back into the world.

I was grateful not to be shivering. I felt fine. I wasn't even weak. But it was slow-going as I shuffled towards the light. I could barely see through the woven fabric wrapped around my head. I finally managed to pull it off. I groped my way along the edge of a rough wall which snagged my wrappings until I finally stepped out into the open daylight.

As I stepped outside, I heard multiple gasps and, sounding clearly over them, the voice of my Friend. I couldn't see him, for I had shut my eyes to the glaring sunlight.

"Take off his grave clothes and let him go."

Within moments Jesus was in front of me along with my sisters. When I looked at them, we all began to cry. I will always remember how it felt to see his face at that moment. His love. His joy—he was as happy as I was. I would worship him from that moment on.

It's an odd thing. I lived to tell what it was like to be resurrected by him. Now I'm waiting to see him again after I die, for I will leave these bones behind some day. I like to remember the words

Jesus said to my sister, Martha, just before he raised me: "I am the resurrection and the life. He who believes in me will live, even though he dies; and whoever lives and believes in me will never die. Do you believe this?"

I *know* it is true. I am a man to be resurrected twice—to wake up to Jesus, twice. Once on earth, next time in heaven. Now I have a good idea of what to expect. It's like waking up. And to open my eyes to see Jesus' glorious face in heaven will be unspeakably worth living and dying for twice, of that I am convinced.

WONDER JUST A LITTLE

We have come to the central, most pivotal message that Jesus came to give us. Actually, it is much more than truth. It is a promise. " . . . Whoever lives and believes in me will never die."

From the moment we are born, we journey towards death. It is inevitable.

But Jesus *showed* us that he is the Resurrection and the Life. In him, death has no power over us. It is not our final destination. We will merely pass through it. It will be like falling asleep and waking up. Jesus is the author and keeper of our lives, and when we believe in him, we will hear him call our names from the grave.

There is so much to ponder in this story about Lazarus. Through this wonderful miracle, our Savior has given us tremendous hope. What would life be for us if we didn't have this example, these powerful words from Jesus? How hard would it be for us to say goodbye to our loved ones if we didn't have this event to remember and comfort us? This is the hope, the glory, of the Gospel.

Upon hearing the news of his friend's illness, Jesus said, "This sickness will not end in death. No, it is for God's glory so that God's Son may be glorified through it."

When Lazarus fell sick and died, Jesus was marching courageously towards the end of his earthly life. He knew that this was part of the unveiling of his glory.

Lazarus' death was a preview of his own soon to come. At his own death, Jesus would entrust himself to his Father, to be raised up on the third day. Perhaps God the Father used this powerful event for his own Son's sake. Certainly, it helped Jesus prepare himself for what lay ahead of him. He must have thought about the death and burial that was swiftly drawing near.

It is so tragic to think that this profound miracle proved beyond any shadow of doubt that Jesus had the power of God in him, yet was, at the same time, the impetus that brought about the agreement of the Sanhedrin to "take his life."

Jesus had, and still has, the power *to give life*. The men of that day had the power *to take his*.

But the Lord actually let them have that power to take his life—so that he could give his life to anyone who would believe in him. He knew we would die without him, because without his death and resurrection, we would certainly perish.

Immediately after Jesus raised Lazarus, the Sanhedrin, a mixture of Pharisees and Sadducees, convened to determine what should be done. The more powerful members, including the chief priests, were Sadducean and did not believe in the resurrection of the dead. This miracle of the raising of Lazarus posed a significant threat to them, and they took the lead over the Pharisees to do away with Jesus. The Scriptures record some of what was said during that meeting:

"'If we let him go on like this, everyone will believe in him, and then the Romans will come and take away both our place [temple] and our nation.'

"Then one of them, named Caiaphas, who was high priest that year, spoke up, 'You know nothing at all! You do not realize that it is better for you that one man die for the people than the whole nation perish.' He did not say this on his own, but as high priest that year he prophesied that Jesus would die for the Jewish nation, and not only for that nation but also for the scattered children of God, to bring them together and make them one. So from that day on they plotted to take his life." John 11:48-53

Isn't that amazing? The Jewish rulers were convinced that God wanted them to kill Jesus—and they were right. But, they did not realize why or what all the implications were. No, they did not.

This is the wonder of it—the majesty of what Jesus came to do. Everything was coming together to bring about Salvation.

WHAT DO YOU SEE?

There is so much to ponder in this leg of our journey with Jesus. We need to allow these happenings of his life to penetrate into the deep places of our hearts. What would you like to see more clearly, to understand more fully?

Can you imagine being with Jesus when he received the news about Lazarus? What might he have been feeling at that time? Do you think it was hard for him to wait the two days before setting off to his dear friend, knowing he would die while he tarried? What does this teach us about God's perfect timing, no matter how terrible or impossible things look?

What was it like for Mary and Martha, who felt abandoned by Jesus when he didn't come to them on time? Have you ever felt Jesus look the other way when you desperately needed him?

Imagine being with Jesus that day after Lazarus was resurrected—what might that household have been like then? If you were Mary, Martha, Lazarus, or anyone who witnessed the miracle—what would you think about Jesus after that? What would you say to him? These are some of the things to consider as you open your heart to see "the glory of God's Son" by meditating upon this incredible miracle.

Imagine being there. Feel the glory of it.

JOURNAL

Record in your journal what you experienced during your reading and meditation time, and reflect upon what this miracle and the words of Jesus mean to you. Be open to any other thoughts or truths the Lord may want to show you at this time. Allow the power of the hope of your own resurrection, of seeing Jesus, to fill you.

30 – "Next Time in Jerusalem"

The kingdom of God does not come
with your careful observation, nor will people say,
"Here it is," or "There it is," because the kingdom of God
is within you.
Luke 17:20b-21

- Jesus no longer moves publicly among the Jewish leaders (From Jerusalem to Ephraim, a remote city in the northern district of Perea): *John 11:54*

The following events likely happened during Jesus' traveling from Ephraim to meet the pilgrims who are traveling south through the district between or within the borders of Samaria and Galilee on their way to Jerusalem for Passover.

- Healing of ten lepers (Samaria in Galilee): Luke 17:11-21
- Instructions regarding the Son of Man's coming (Exact location unknown; probably along the border of Samaria): *Luke 17:22-37*
- Two parables on prayer: the persistent widow, and the Pharisee and the tax collector (Traveling toward Jerusalem for Passover): *Luke 18:1-14*
- Conflict with Pharisaic teaching on divorce (Perea): *Matthew 19:1-12; Mark 10:1-12*
- Example of little children in relation to the kingdom (Perea): *Matthew 19:13-15; Mark 10:13-16; Luke 18:15-17*
- Riches and the kingdom (Perea): *Matthew 19:16-30; Mark 10:17-31; Luke 18:18-30*
- Parable of landowner's sovereignty (Perea): *Matthew 20:1-16*

A CONTEMPLATIVE VIEW

Lazarus from Bethany . . .

The day of my resurrection had grown late and dark. I was a new man, with new eyes, and a heart that was in awe of Jesus. I could hardly bear being alone with him because I now knew who he was. How could I hold a normal conversation with this Man? Yet, I had to remember that he was still my friend, whom I'd loved and known for years.

When I returned to the living, I knew who he was, and so I didn't ask him how he had raised me from the dead. But I asked him why. Was it because of my sisters? Or did he have something he still wished me to do in this life? I asked him these questions when we first sat down together in our garden courtyard.

He explained that the story of my resurrection—obediently walking out of the tomb when he called me—would bring comfort to and increase faith of a great many people.

After he embraced me sideways across my shoulders with his left arm, and then released me again, he told me there would be plenty for me to do, but not right now. Then he did not speak for some time. Nor did I. I didn't know what to say. I was in awe of him; my nerves were jittery with excitement. I was all ears. I loved and adored Jesus, who was sitting calmly and quietly beside me.

From where we sat, we could hear all the voices and noises from inside the house; there was much laughter and lightheartedness.

But Jesus was quiet. Finally, he broke the silence between us.

"Lazarus, I have something to tell you."

"What is it, Lord?" I asked.

"The next time I return to Jerusalem will be Passover." He drew in a deep breath and slowly exhaled. "There is something that I have not kept from my disciples, nor do I wish to keep it from you."

I looked at him and wondered what this could be, for his face was solemn, as was his voice.

"I will be handed over to the Romans by the Sanhedrin. They have decided this today."

My face must have told him what I felt—alarm and anger—for

he quickly added, "It was my decision first, not theirs—a decision I made at the foundation of this world."

Many of us had feared something like this, and now he was telling me what would happen. Someone came outside just then; we could both hear movements on the other side of the lattice wall behind us, but we couldn't see who it was.

"Master?" the person asked.

"Yes, Andrew, I am here."

"Two men from Jerusalem have come to see you."

"Thank them for coming. Tell them I will go away until Passover and will see them then," Jesus answered.

My Lord looked at me, and with a quiet voice, said, "Nothing will happen to me until Passover."

I was sick at heart. I couldn't bear the thought of him being imprisoned by the authorities.

"We will raise an army for you, Lord. We will not let what happened to our dear Prophet John happen to you. You are meant to reign on David's throne."

He looked at me with his head slightly bowed, but with his eyes peering up at me from beneath his brows. His nostrils flared and his eyes began to water.

"Truly, I will forever reign on the throne of my kingdom, but it is not of this world. Lazarus, now you know more than the others."

Jesus stood and took the three or four steps to the waist-high stone wall that served as a planter, which, in other seasons, held an array of flowers. At this time, it was empty. He leaned against it, with his hands beside him on both sides, resting elbows on top of the low wall. His eyes were upon me. There was a lantern's flame flickering a golden light onto his face.

"I will suffer and die a terrible death. But I will rise from the grave on the third day."

I was stunned. I could not imagine him suffering and dying.

I groaned, and straightened up.

"As surely as you have risen from the dead, so will I," he assured me.

"Lord, how can this be? Why?"

"I will live again."

"Do you *want* this happen to you?" I asked him. I couldn't

understand—nor imagine it.

"You will understand soon enough, my friend. What I am telling you is not evil tidings. It is good news, news of salvation. One day you will agree, I promise."

Afterwards, he drew me to my feet, took me by my arm, and led me inside the house, saying, "Do not tell anyone what I have told you."

"Where will you go now?" I asked.

"Ephraim," he answered.

During inclement weather, Ephraim is not an easy place to live, nor is it easy to get to. Located in mountainous, rough terrain that eventually leads down to the Jordan Valley, it's a small village in the northern part of Judea. The winter rains and mud make the journey a challenge, and those who live there must make do with the supplies on hand for weeks.

"I will go with you."

"No," he answered. "Surely, your sisters would never forgive me if I took you away so soon after they have just received you back into their arms."

He was right, of course.

But I didn't want Jesus to leave us. But he had powerful enemies in Jerusalem, making it unsafe for him to be with us when the crowds weren't around. Most thought I was unsafe as well. But death no longer frightened me.

With a heart both heavy and light, I watched my dear Friend leave the next morning.

WONDER JUST A LITTLE

Jesus repeatedly told his disciples of his upcoming ordeal, so it is more than likely that he told his beloved friend, Lazarus. These are the days when Jesus bides his time, readying his men and himself for his final ordeal. We can see from the Scriptures that Jesus sought refuge in the remote area of northern Judea. Eventually, he made his way a little north as the time of Passover drew near, meeting many pilgrims along the borders of Samaria and Galilee as they traveled towards Jerusalem for the feast. That area was like a "no man's" district and Jesus was able to minister to many people. He met caravans of pilgrims when it was time for the Passover, without having to travel about. Here, Jesus taught many things and performed miracles. Many of his recorded teachings come to us from this time.

He spoke more specifically and openly about the kingdom of God and its future, speaking of aspects of the kingdom that went against the commonly accepted teachings. Nowhere in any of Jesus' teachings or words did he refer to a future for himself on earth beyond the upcoming Passover. In fact, during these final days, Jesus openly taught about a spiritual kingdom, that would be "within you" as well as "to come." About himself, he said, "The time is coming when you will long to see one of the days of the Son of Man, but you will not see it. Men will tell you, 'There he is!' or 'Here he is!' Do not go running off after them. For the Son of Man in his day will be like the lightning, which flashes and lights up the sky from one end to the other. But first he must suffer many things and be rejected by this generation. Just as it was in the days of Noah, so also will it be in the days of the Son of Man. . . ." Luke 17:22-26

What must he have felt during this bittersweet, awe-inspiring time? These are the closing days of his life among us as a human being.

What did his disciples think of what Jesus told them about his upcoming ordeal? They seemed to be in denial about it, and we have to wonder why. What was it like to be around Jesus at this time? We know that his popularity had risen very high after the Feast of Tabernacles, and again after he raised Lazarus from the dead. Long forgotten were his strange claims and the difficult words that made people think he was crazy or of the devil.

Paying attention to the focus of Jesus' teachings during this time, we can see he was lovingly conferring the kingdom into the hands of his followers: "Peter said to him, 'We have left all we had to follow you!'" Luke 18:28

And Jesus answered him, "'I tell you the truth, no one who has left home or wife or brothers or parents or children for the sake of the kingdom of God will fail to receive many times as much in this age and, in the age to come, eternal life.'" Luke 18:29-30

WHAT DO YOU SEE?

John, in his Gospel, made a point of saying that Jesus "withdrew to a region near the desert, to a village called Ephraim, where he stayed with his disciples." It is likely that the area was inhospitable and remote. Therefore, the women who normally followed Jesus were probably not with him. Can you imagine Jesus and his men, cold and hungry, pressing on to their destination, seeking shelter? Unable to stay warm and dry as they journeyed, Jesus and his men were certainly soaked, and chilled to the bone when the rains, typical for that season, came. Where did they sleep? What did they eat and drink? Can you imagine Jesus and his men, gathered around a fire, camping, perhaps, in a cave?

Imagine being in a cave with Jesus and his men. It is cold and raining. They are trying to dry their clothes, and at the same time stay warm. How do you start a fire when everything is soaking wet, and all you have is flint to start a spark? Jesus was obedient with his power, so it is probable that he and the disciples struggled to start their fire just as anyone else would. Can you see them sleeping close to one another for warmth? By now they are well accustomed to each other's snoring. What might it have been like to share those days of trial and discomfort with the Lord of Glory? Most likely, Jesus continued to teach, for these were days of intense closeness, and time was short. He must have often encouraged them in the trials of their situation, perhaps making things humorously bearable. Maybe he expressed his gratitude to them for all they had shared together over the three years. Perhaps they talked among themselves about their past, their families, their hopes and dreams—about everything and anything that came to mind.

And later, in early spring, when Passover drew near, how good it must have felt to them to walk about the countryside in the sun again. Yet, for Jesus, with spring came Passover, and with it, his destiny.

You may wish to prayerfully imagine the time when Jesus met the rich young ruler. Contrast this man's situation—a man who is materially rich but spiritually poor—to Jesus' present situation, in discomfort and hardship. Notice the disappointment and love on the Lord's face when the man walks away from him. His Twelve have shared many months of "being poor" with Jesus—yet, look at how richly favored they were when being with Jesus was the center of their lives.

Imagine Jesus, on his way to Jerusalem, as he takes the Twelve aside to tell them, yet another time, what lies ahead of him: "We are going up to Jerusalem, and the Son of Man will be betrayed to the chief priests and teachers of the law . . ." What is Jesus feeling when he takes his men aside? What are they feeling? What is the Lord's tone of voice? What does his face and body language express? How do you see the men respond to him? How does this make you feel?

Ask the Lord to give you a special awareness to sense the deeper things that can be seen and felt from this special period of time in his life. Ask him to reveal his heart to you, to show you the treasures of his love as depicted in his actions and teachings during those days. Be sensitive to the gentle movements of the Holy Spirit and ask for eyes to see and ears to hear.

JOURNAL

After you are finished with your sanctified, imaginative meditation, reflect upon just one thing that Jesus said or did that especially touched you. What is it that so stirred your heart? Write about this in your journal.

31 – Salvation's First Coming

Rejoice greatly, O Daughter of Zion!
Shout, Daughter of Jerusalem!
See, your king comes to you,
Righteous and having salvation,
Gentle and riding on a donkey,
On a colt, the foal of a donkey.
Zechariah 9:9 and Matthew 21:5

- Another prediction of Jesus' death and resurrection (On the road up to Jerusalem): *Matthew 20:17-19; Mark 10:32-34; Luke 18:31-34*
- Warning against ambitious pride (On the road up to Jerusalem): *Matthew 20:20-28; Mark 10:35-45*
- Healing of blind Bartimaeus and his companion (Jericho): *Matthew 20:29-34; Mark 10:46-52; Luke 18:35-43*
- Salvation of Zaccheus (Jericho): *Luke 19:1-10*
- Parable to teach responsibility while the kingdom is delayed (Jericho and the final trip up to Jerusalem): *Luke 19:11-28*
- Arrival at Bethany (Near Jerusalem): *John 11:55-12:1, 9-11*
- Triumphal entry into Jerusalem (From Bethany to Jerusalem to Bethany): *Matthew 21:1-3, 6-7, 8-11, 14-17; Mark 11:1-11; Luke 19:29-44; John 12:12-19*

A CONTEMPLATIVE VIEW

Gentle and Riding on a Donkey

The Lamb is perfect and all is right
When our Savior-King rides into sight
Adoring cries, such a tumult is raised
And so the stones keep silent of praise

The Passover Victim he knows he will be
For us he has come to win and redeem
To shed his own blood is the reason he's come
The only one worthy is God's holy Son

Listen, Adam, have you heard the news?
Your redeeming Seed has come from the Jews
The son of your loins by God's holy plan
For he is the promised "Son of Man"

Sinners and children, do you hear?
To God the Father the Son draws us near
His Life for ours he is willing to give
So that in him we forever will live

The Lord of Hosts on a donkey's foal
Is the rider, Almighty, in his Servant role
He's the Lamb to be slain, just as foretold
Whose coming was pledged in Eden of old

Hosannah! Hosannah! Blessed be He!
The Son of David will set captives free
Desire of Nations, his name we lift high
Comes gently and kingly, ready to die.

**

Matthew, one of Jesus' twelve apostles . . .

I witnessed firsthand the fulfillment of Zechariah's prophecy concerning my Master's entrance into Jerusalem, for Jesus was ". . . righteous and having salvation, gentle and riding on a donkey, on a colt, the foal of a donkey." (Zechariah 9:9)

I, along with Philip, fetched the donkey and her colt after Jesus sent us to the next village beyond Bethany on the Mount of Olives. When we untied them, their owners asked us what we were doing. We told the men the Lord needed them and would send them back shortly, and they consented to let us take them. Amazing us, everything happened exactly as Jesus had predicted.

The procession was not planned by us, or by the crowds. It was spontaneous. The excitement over our Master coming to Jerusalem for Passover had begun to kindle long before our trek there. Also, our Master had intentionally made himself available to the caravans of pilgrims traveling south from upper Israel. Word spread like wildfire among them to the towns he would pass through on his way to the Passover Feast.

The belief that he was the Messiah had taken root in the hearts of many. And there was no other town more excited to see him than Jericho. We could hardly walk through the pressing, shouting crowd there. We found refuge from the overzealous people and ate and rested in the house of a rich man, whom our Master had found delight in.

As we made our way slowly to Jerusalem, Jesus was more and more being hailed as the "Son of David." This title for him enflamed everyone's hearts, for it meant so much to our weary souls and eyes—long awaiting relief from our oppressors. At last, the whole world seemed to know that our Master was the Promised One! We disciples were nearly out of our minds with joy and excitement by the time we came to the outskirts of Jerusalem.

When we brought the donkeys to Jesus, it was the most fitting honor we could do for him, because, unlike every other king, Jesus was gentle and approachable—and he was one of our own! He did not come into Jerusalem on a mighty horse, riding in as a conqueror. Rather, he was more truly known as a gentle and humble liberator. He freed people from disease, evil spirits, sinful lives, and even death. And many people wanted to make him king.

When the crowd of pilgrims traveling with us arrived in Bethany, we were met by another one that came up from Jerusalem. Everyone hoped that Jesus would accept this open and zealous expression of heartfelt acclaim for him. And, Heaven be praised and the earth be filled with God's glory—he did! We were over-joyed! I, and everyone else with me, gave our hearts to him.

Oh, the noise of that pressing, ecstatic crowd! Such a tumult of jubilation! Shouting and singing, the waving of palms, the throwing of cloaks—it was a celebration of hope.

We led the donkey ahead of her colt, upon which Jesus sat. Since the foal had never borne a rider before, he was more at ease trotting behind his mother. John and Andrew led the donkeys care-fully down the path of strewn cloaks and foliage. The crowd parted before us, waving palm branches in the air, shouting acclamations of joy. His coming was like a new king or friendly conqueror being received in joy and hope; or like a Greek athlete welcomed home from the games, triumphant in his victories won. But we knew that Jesus, our own beloved Master, was more than any of these: he was the Promised Messiah, the Son of David.

Here was the champion of all we had longed and prayed for, sitting upon that small, young beast. Our Messiah had officially come! I will always treasure the sight. He looked more like a priest or prophet than a king, humbly wrapped in his prayer shawl. Many people reached out to touch him as he passed by. With his hands outspread in blessing, our Master accepted the crowd's acclaim. And I, I did not shout or praise him out loud, for I was too overcome by joy to even speak. I could only beam at him the whole time, soaking in the befitting and wonderful sight of him riding into Jerusalem.

At long last, we all expressed how we felt to him. The many whom he had healed or set free, or who had heard his comforting wisdom, or benefited from his uplifting instruction—those who had seen his power and goodness—shouted their praises to him. We knew what we were doing! We were welcoming and celebrating the coming of our long-awaited Son of David, our Messiah, the King of Israel! I knew deep in my soul that day that seeing my Master ushered into Jerusalem in such a fitting way was how things were truly meant to be.

WONDER JUST A LITTLE

> "Lift up your heads, O you gates;
> Be lifted up, you ancient doors,
> that the King of Glory shall come in.
> Who is the King of glory?
> The Lord strong and mighty,
> the Lord mighty in battle."
> Psalm 24:9-10

This Messianic Psalm could be for one person only: Jesus—the Savior. During the triumphal entry, he entered through Jerusalem's eastern gate as Israel's long-awaited Messianic king. A gentle, humble king, he came to usher in Salvation, which only he could bring. This was his first coming.

Since then, his coming is ongoing because, as he said, his kingdom on earth is "within you."
And so the Psalm is also for us:

> Lift up your heads – [only people have heads],
> you everlasting gates!
> Open the gates of your heart,
> and the Lord of Glory will come in!

One future day, when the fullness of time comes, Jesus will return and fully establish his kingdom on earth. As he promised, he will come again in triumph and glory. The King of Kings and the Lord of Lords will take his rightful place on David's throne. He will reign forever.

Jesus the Messiah, the Son of God, is the Son of David and the Lord of David. He is the King of Israel and King of the Universe. He is the only One who can bring peace to the world. Out of Jerusalem, as prophecy predicts, will the one true Light of the world shine forth to the ends of the earth. And the Prince of Peace will finish the work he's begun. The government of the world will rest on his shoulders.

Until then, we cry, "Maranatha! Lord, come!"

WHAT DO YOU SEE?

After reading the following words, close your eyes and try to imagine the sights and, especially, the sounds of that procession. Imagine the tumult, the excitement. Imagine what the Lord may have looked like, or how he reacted to the experience. What might his disciples have been doing during this event? Can you see the faces of the Lord's accusers?

The following quotes are taken from the Scriptures, combining some of the words found in all four gospel accounts. Prayerfully imagine the dramatic procession as Jesus rode into Jerusalem on the donkey's colt. But first, just listen to the words of that prophetic hour, the day Jesus came in submissive power . . .

"Blessed is the king who comes in the name of the Lord!"
"Peace in heaven and glory in the highest!"
"Hosanna to the Son of David!"
*"If you, even you, had only known what would bring you peace—
but now it is hidden from your eyes."*
"Blessed is the King of Israel!"
"Hosanna! Hosanna!"
"Blessed is the King of Israel!"
"Hosanna to the Son of David!"
"Blessed is the coming kingdom of our father David!"
"Who is this?"
"This is Jesus, the prophet from Nazareth in Galilee."
"Hosanna to the Son of David!"
"Blessed is the King, the Son of David!"
"Hosanna!
See, this is getting us nowhere."
"Look how the whole world has gone after him!"
"Hosanna! Hosanna!"
"Teacher, rebuke your disciples!"
"I tell you, if they keep quiet, the stones will cry out."
"Blessed is he who comes in the name of the Lord!"
"Hosanna, Hosanna, Hosanna!"
"Do you hear what these children are saying?"

"Yes, have you never read,
'From the lips of children and infants you have ordained praise'?"

JOURNAL

Ask the Lord to help you soak in the reality of what his *triumphal entry* meant—not just to Israel, to the men of that day, to the world, to you—but to *him*. Be open to the Lord's revelation of what it may have felt like for him to taste praise as our king, even knowing what would happen to him in a matter of days. Be open to what the Lord desires to show you and record in your journal the reflections and thoughts you experience.

32 – The Barren Fig Tree

When he had finished speaking,
Jesus left and hid himself from them.
Even after Jesus had done all these miraculous
signs in their presence,
they still would not believe in him.
This was to fulfill the word of Isaiah the prophet:
"Lord, who has believed our message
and to whom has the arm of the Lord been revealed?"
John 12:36b-38 and Isaiah 53:1

- Cursing the fig tree having leaves but no figs (From Bethany to Jerusalem): *Matthew 21:18-19a; Mark 11:12-14*
- Second cleansing of the temple (Jerusalem, in the temple): *Matthew 21:12-13; Mark 11:15-18; Luke 19:45-48*
- Request of some Greeks to see Jesus and necessity of the Son of Man's being lifted up (Jerusalem): *John 12:20-36a*
- Different responses to Jesus and Jesus' response to the crowds (Jerusalem): *John 12:36b-50*
- Withered fig tree and the lesson on faith (Back to Bethany and return to Jerusalem): *Matthew 21:19b-22; Mark 11:19-25; Luke 21:37-38*

A CONTEMPLATIVE VIEW

Simon Peter . . .

Early in the morning, on our way from Bethany to Jerusalem, Jesus approached a fig tree in leaf. He pulled on its branches, and peered this way and that, searching for fruit. We were all hungry. But, here was Jesus, looking for figs out of season. But what amazed us more was that he said to the tree, "May no one ever eat fruit from you again."

It seemed so unlike him. But on the other hand, we never knew what he might say or do at any given moment. He was as unpredictable as the wind. And, after all, it was only a tree, so we thought little of it at the time.

The next morning, when we passed the tree again on our way to the temple, I saw it had lost its leaves and looked pitiful. Remembering what Jesus had said to it, I exclaimed, "Rabbi, look! The fig tree you cursed has withered!"

He kept walking with only a glance in its direction. "Yes, Simon, it has."

We, on the other hand, went over to examine it more closely. It had withered from the roots up.

When we caught up to Jesus, Philip asked him, "How did the fig tree wither so quickly?"

Because of our surprised reactions, Jesus said, "Have faith in God. I tell you the truth, if anyone says to this mountain, 'Go, throw yourself into the sea,' and does not doubt in his heart but believes that what he says will happen, it will be done. If you believe, you will receive whatever you ask."

Did he mean the Mount of Olives? I wondered.

He taught us a lesson on prayer and faith that morning, when he cursed a beautiful, full fig tree. For many years, I puzzled over that event. First of all, Jesus knew, as we all knew, it wasn't the time for figs. Why had he looked for them? Why did he curse the tree when he found none? It had been a healthy tree. Surely, at the right time, it would have produced plenty of figs. What was the real meaning of what had happened? Was the reason Jesus looked for figs that day simply because he was so hungry? As a man of great faith, had he hoped there would be fruit on that tree for him? And so, in finding nothing, had the tree disappointed its own Maker? Or, did Jesus want to teach us a lesson on prayer and "mountain moving" faith—and that only?

Jesus could have produced fruit from that tree by speaking it into existence. I had seen his creative power firsthand on many occasions. He had turned water into wine and multiplied bread and fish. He could create or change anything he wanted. So, what was it about that fig tree? Why did its barren condition bring about such a strong reaction in him?

I have begun to see a broader perspective of what happened. For one thing, it wasn't only the fig tree that Jesus judged with his words that last week of his earthly life. Immediately after cursing the fig tree, he drove out from the temple, once again, the marketplace buyers and sellers, and then blocked the way of anyone trying to bring merchandise into the temple. He followed that up, throughout that day and the next, with scathing parables and words of judgment against the religious leaders.

Another puzzling thing happened the day the fig tree withered. In the temple, Greeks came to see Jesus, which brought another strong reaction in him. The effect of their coming caused him to say, "The hour has come for the Son of Man to be glorified. I tell you the truth, unless a kernel of wheat falls to the ground and dies, it remains only a single seed. But if it dies, it produces many seeds. The man who loves his life will lose it, while the man who hates his life in this world will keep it for eternal life."

He was upset, saying, "Now my heart is troubled, and what shall I say? 'Father, save me from this hour?' No, it was for this very reason I came to this hour. Father, glorify your name!"

Then a voice sounded from heaven in response to him. Some thought it was thunder. But clearly, the words were: "I have glorified it and will glorify it again."

I have asked these questions over and over: What caused such emotion to arise in Jesus when the Greeks came to see him? I know now what his prayer and the reply from his Father were about. And, evidently, the Greeks were a sign to him. Did it mean that the climax of his ministry had come?

The cursing of the fig tree and the coming of the Greeks. What was going on in our Lord's heart and mind then? We all knew he carried things inside of him that only he could bear. Were these signs to help us better understand in the future? And, were these two symbols or signs about the same thing? The Jews officially refused him, but the Gentiles had come searching for him. Was the cursing of the fig tree a sign or symbol?

If the beautiful, leafy fig tree resembled our Jewish system of religion on that day, Jesus found no pleasure in it, found it out of season, and entirely without fruit. It had nothing but leaves. It drew the eye, but had nothing to offer its Maker. And, our God was hungry—hungry for true, spiritual fruit.

WONDER JUST A LITTLE

In the temple, Jesus warns those who are lost in their own religious trappings, using strong, powerful imagery and language. There are layers of meaning in Jesus' words and actions during his last public days of ministry. But let's stop and examine what happened, because, in the fabric of Time, these final hours of Jesus before his death give us wonderful things to ponder about the heart and love of God.

On the surface, we see our Savior speaking and teaching lessons of faith, as well as giving warnings and signs. But what about the deeper things that are happening—within the heart of the Savior?

First, Jesus curses the fig tree. Is this about his spiritual hunger?

Next, he purges the temple's marketplace again. Is this about his desires too?

Then the Greeks come to see him and he immediately connects this with the necessity of his being lifted up on the cross. If this is about his dread, than this is also a glimpse at the extent of his sacrificial love. Jesus' prayer becomes verbal communion with the Father. What a way for us to see their union and love revealed.

Next, Jesus hides himself. Doesn't this show us his pain at being rejected? And, doesn't this also show us his deep love? Is the Lord experiencing pain for those who refuse to believe in him, because without faith in him they will remain lost?

Jesus cries out to unbelievers in an effort to show them the consequences of their rejection, as well as what the consequences of faith in him could bring. Is this his last-ditch effort to open their hearts, so that he can save them?

Last, using the illustration of the withered fig tree, Jesus teaches a lesson to his disciples about faith and spiritual power. Are these not the words of a heart full of love and promise? He is physically about to leave them and so he wants them to learn to live in powerful, mountain-moving faith.

WHAT DO YOU SEE?

Let's ponder a particular event that happened during the critical, revealing last days in Jesus' life.

Jesus is emotionally moved when some Greeks come to see him. Why was he so affected by this? What was going on deep in the Lord's heart? What caused him to say and do what he did?

At that time, a crowd in the temple surrounded Jesus when some Greeks came to see him. Read John 12:20-36, then close your eyes and try to picture the scene. The foreigners approach Philip and ask to see their rabbi. Philip tells Andrew, and the two of them tell Jesus.

Picking up at this point in the story, prayerfully imagine being there. Using your inner eye to see, watch closely how the men interact with one another. We don't know why the Greeks have come to the temple, perhaps they had embraced the Jewish faith. We don't know why they wished to see Jesus. Do you think they ever got to speak with him? Watch as Jesus reacts when he hears of their request from his two disciples. Follow the story through to when Jesus abruptly leaves the scene. What is the last thing he says before he leaves them? Is there meaning in the actions that follow his words? Follow Jesus and imagine him somewhere in solitude. Is he alone in the city? How does he hide himself? What do you see? How is he feeling? How does all this make you feel towards him? Tell him. Allow your love to flow to his heart. After all, *you* are his reward—the joy he set before himself during his trials and pain.

JOURNAL

Record in your journal what the love of Jesus means to you at this moment. Record your experiences of this chapter. Worship the Lord with pen and paper in your journal. Be open to whatever more the Lord may wish to show you as you pray and write.

33 – Final Words

"O Jerusalem, Jerusalem,
you who kill the prophets . . .
Look, your house is left to you desolate.
For I tell you, you will not see me again until you say,
'Blessed is he who comes in the name of the Lord.'"
Matthew 23:37a, 38-39

- Questioning of Jesus' authority by the chief priests, teachers of the law, and elders (Jerusalem, in the temple): *Matthew 21:23-27; Mark 11:27-33; Luke 20:1-8*
- Jesus' response with his own question and three parables (Jerusalem, in the temple): *Matthew 21:28-22:14; Mark 12:1-12; Luke 20:9-19*
- Attempts by Pharisees and Herodians to trap Jesus with a question about paying taxes to Caesar (Jerusalem, probably in the temple): *Matthew 22:15-22; Mark 12:13-17; Luke 20:20-26*
- Sadducees' puzzling question about the resurrection (Jerusalem, probably in temple): *Matthew 22:23-33; Mark 12:18-27; Luke 20:27-40*
- A Pharisee's legal question (Jerusalem, probably in the temple): *Matthew 22:34-40; Mark 12:28-34*
- Christ's relationship to David as son and Lord (Jerusalem, in the temple): *Matthew 22:41-46; Mark 12:35-37; Luke 20:41-44*
- Seven woes against the teachers of the law and Pharisees (Jerusalem, in the temple): *Matthew 23:1-36; Mark 12:38-40; Luke 20:45-47*
- Jesus' sorrow over Jerusalem (Jerusalem, in the temple): *Matthew*

23:37-39

• A poor widow's gift of all she had (Jerusalem, in the temple): *Mark 12:41-44;Luke 21:1-4*

A CONTEMPLATIVE VIEW

Nicodemus, a leading Pharisee and member of the Sanhedrin . . .

I was more than a Pharisee interested in Rabbi Jesus, son of Joseph. I was one of the few elders who knew he was a prophet. I'd come to that conclusion long before he came to Jerusalem that last Passover.

If there is anything worthy of my opinion to pass along to you, I must tell you of the time he took my breath away. I'd seen him do miracles. I'd heard him preach. But never was I as deeply overcome by him than the time I witnessed Jesus unveil God's outraged heart in the temple.

Some would justly say that he gave us leaders a scathing piece of his mind. It was more than that. He was under holy anointing, or should I say, he was turned inside out. The Spirit of God's passion and love—the deepest understanding of God's desires towards us—became, as it were, fire from his mouth. Yes, he was a fiery prophet without compare. He was a living paradox. In anger, his ardent love engulfed, as fire consumes a house, all of us within God's house that day.

I was *undone* by him.

His uplifted voice echoed, silencing everyone and everything in that court. His tirade went on and on, getting louder and louder, his face turning redder and redder. These were his final words to us— the last I heard him speak.

Listen, if you will to those words he left us . . .

"Woe to you, teachers of the law and Pharisees, you hypocrites! You travel over land and sea to win a single convert, and when he becomes one, you make him twice as much a son of hell as you are.

"Woe to you, teachers of the law and Pharisees, you hypocrites! You shut the kingdom of heaven in men's faces. You yourselves do not enter, nor will you let those enter who are trying to.

"Woe to you, blind guides! You say, 'If anyone swears by the temple, it means nothing; but if anyone swears by the gold on the temple, he is bound by his oath.' You blind fools! Which is greater: the gold, or the temple that makes the gold sacred? You say, 'If anyone swears by the altar, it means nothing; but if anyone swears by the gift on it, he is bound by his oath.' You blind men! Which is greater: the gift, or the altar that makes the gift sacred?

"Therefore, he who swears by the altar swears by it and by everything on it. And he who swears by the temple swears by it and by the one who dwells in it. And he who swears by heaven swears by God's throne and by the one who sits on it.

"Woe to you, teachers of the law and Pharisees, you hypocrites! You give a tenth of your spices—mint, dill, and cumin. But you have neglected the more important matters of the law—justice, mercy and faithfulness. You should have practiced the latter, without neglecting the former. You blind guides! You strain out a gnat and swallow a camel.

"Woe to you, teachers of the law and Pharisees, you hypocrites! You clean the outside of the cup and dish, but inside they are full of greed and self-indulgence.

"Blind Pharisee! First clean the inside of the cup and dish, and then the outside also will be clean.

"Woe to you, teachers of the law and Pharisees, you hypocrites! You are like whitewashed tombs, which look beautiful on the outside but on the inside are full of dead men's bones and everything unclean. In the same way, on the outside you appear to people as righteous but on the inside you are full of hypocrisy and wickedness.

"Woe to you, teachers of the law and Pharisees, you hypocrites! You build tombs for the prophets and decorate the graves of the righteous. And you say, 'If we had lived in the days of our forefathers, we would not have taken part with them in shedding the blood of the prophets.' So you testify against yourselves that you are the descendants of those who murdered the prophets.

"Fill up then!—the measure of the sin of your forefathers! You snakes! You brood of vipers! How will you escape being condemned to hell?

"Therefore, I am sending you prophets and wise men and teachers. Some of them you will kill and crucify; others you will flog in your synagogues and pursue from town to town.

"And so upon you will come all the righteous blood that has been shed on earth, from the blood of righteous Abel to the blood of Zechariah son of Berekiah, whom you murdered between the temple and the altar.

"I tell you the truth, all this will come upon this generation. . . .

"O Jerusalem, Jerusalem, you who kill the prophets and stone those sent to you, how often I have longed to gather your children together, as a hen gathers her chicks under her wings, but you were not willing.

"Look, your house is left to you desolate. For I tell you, you will not see me again until you say, 'Blessed is he who comes in the name of the Lord.'"

With a long, last, hard look at the inside of the temple, Jesus walked out from our sight.

Let me tell you something. I've been a married man for three decades. I love my wife, but she frustrates and disappoints me sometimes. That's why, when Jesus hurled insulting, angry words of judgment our way, I saw God in him. I saw God-in-love with us. Prophet Hosea saw a ray of that light. But, Jesus, he was the Sun!

Oh, to see and hear his voice so full of passion and heartache— shouting, with all of his heart and soul, that angry love so unwilling to let go. Yet, he had to.

But he said that he would return—after we would learn to say, "Blessed is he who comes in the name of the Lord."

When he left us alone in the temple that day, I was as a statue of salt left behind. I had looked upon God's judgment, that consuming love, and was frozen in my place.

You know how angry you can be towards the people you love most? You want things to be different. You want them to know and understand you. You want more, much more, and you fight your beloved with all your heart and all your might. Indifference is nowhere to be found. You fight madly because you love madly. That is what I saw. God's love through the angry young man named Jesus loved *me* that much!

Just as Jesus predicted, when he left the temple that afternoon, I saw him no more. He ended all public appearances. The next time I saw his body, I helped bury it. Truly, he had left us. With aching remorse and shattered faith, I mourned his death. But that is not the end of my story. Weeks later, the Spirit of God came revealing Jesus' presence to me in a whole new way. I have become, along with many of his followers, his new temple. It is with a grateful heart I know and worship him today, the Son of God, Adonai Jesus.

WONDER JUST A LITTLE

What is beneath Jesus' final, angry words in the temple? This is an amazing glimpse into the extent of love that knew no bounds, knew the cost of his words, and yet held nothing back. The biblical scholars or critics who see this explosion of words as a flaw in Jesus' character—who see only a man with a temper—have missed the outrageously wonderful meaning beneath Jesus' actions and words. They have utterly misjudged the heart of God.

In the temple, a *Husband* lets his *beloved* have it. He's fed up with her empty lip service, her hypocrisy, her self-righteousness, her cold shoulder. Religion had become a hierarchy of social status, a cultural group of unbending traditionalists, an impossible list of dos and don'ts that actually kept sincere, God-seeking people away, rather than near, God. And, it was a business, as well.

God offers his beloved his dying love and forgiveness, but she wants nothing to do with him. In fact, she abhors his goodness. She'd rather be with abusive lovers. She's turning away from the only One who will ever accept her and help her become truly happy and whole.

Her husband holds out a gentlemen's hand, and he invites her home. But she refuses him. She wants nothing to do with him, or with their home.

In this last week of Jesus' life, he knows that he is fighting a losing battle. But he also knows that in the end he will win the war. He knows that the Jewish people, his bride, will remember the words he said—and that one day his bride will love him.

He will give her all that he has to give—even though she wants nothing from him. In fact, she will kill him—that's how much she hates him.

The words and actions of Jesus in the temple are those of a brokenhearted God. At last all that has been stored up inside his heart is unleashed in a love-storm of words. He leaves his beloved until she will learn to say, "Blessed is he who comes in the name of the Lord."

One day, the City of the Great King will recognize and know her glorious Messiah. She will see that her savior, her Husband, is Jesus, the One whom she rejected and killed. And she will see that he wears love-scars on his body. One day she will mourn for the One [she] pierced.

As the prophet Zechariah said, "If someone asks him, 'What are these wounds on your body?' he will answer, 'The wounds I was given at the house of my friends'" Zechariah 13:6.

"For it is written, 'And I will pour out on the house of David and the inhabitants of Jerusalem a spirit of grace and supplication. They will look on me, the one they have pierced, and they will mourn for him as one mourns for an only child, and grieve bitterly for him as one grieves for a firstborn son. On that day the weeping in Jerusalem will be great...'" Zechariah 12:10-11a.

WHAT DO YOU SEE?

Find a place next to one of the columns in the temple and listen and watch Jesus as he says his final public words there. How does this make you feel? What does his voice sound like as it echoes? How are his words affecting those around you? Is Jesus standing in place, or do you see him moving as he speaks? What are his gestures? How does he look when he sorrowfully laments about his feelings for Jerusalem? Is he still angry? Is he near tears? Is he on his knees, or is he standing? When he leaves, follow him out of the temple court. Call to him, "Blessed is he who comes in the name of the Lord!" He turns to see you. You approach him. It's just the two of you now. The rest of the world fades away. It's just you and him. Tell him what is on your heart. What are his words in reply?

JOURNAL

What passed between you and the Lord? Record this time in your journal.

Sometimes we are no different than the ones who refused to believe in Jesus two thousand years ago. We become stuck in our ways so much that we miss God's reaching out to us, inviting us to know him more. Ask Jesus to reveal to you the "more" he longs for you to experience in your relationship with him. Sometimes it is our image of God that he wants to shatter. Or, perhaps you cling to an understanding of him that you've outgrown, or that simply is not true. Let him have his way with you and be open to whatever he wants. Ask him to show or give you what he longs for you to know or have. He'll answer this prayer with something more—no matter where you are in your faith journey—perhaps in ways you might never have dreamed. He's the lover of your soul. He's the same One you just witnessed in the temple courts—wanting so much more for his beloved. He loves you that way. In your prayer journal, or without it, let that love flow between you and your Lord.

34 – Things to Come

Be careful, or your hearts will be weighed down
with dissipation, drunkenness and the anxieties of life,
and that day will close on you unexpectedly like a trap.
For it will come upon all those who live on the face of the whole
earth. Be always on the watch and pray . . .
Luke 21:34-36a

At that time men will see the Son of Man coming
in clouds with great power and glory.
Mark 13:26 and Daniel 7:13

- Setting of the Olivet Discourse for when Jesus speaks prophetically about the temple and his own second coming (From the temple to the Mount of Olives): *Matthew 24:1-3; Mark 13:1-4; Luke 21:5-7*
- Beginning of birth pangs (Mount of Olives): *Matthew 24:4-14; Mark 13:5-13; Luke 21:8-19*
- Abomination of desolation and subsequent distress (Mount of Olives): *Matthew 24:15-28; Mark 13:14-23; Luke 21:20-24*
- Coming of the Son of Man (Mount of Olives): *Matthew 24:29-31; Mark 13:24-27; Luke 21:25-27*
- Signs of nearness but unknown time (Mount of Olives): *Matthew 24:32-41; Mark 13:28-32; Luke 21:28-33*
- Five parables to teach watchfulness and faithfulness (Mount of Olives): *Matthew 24:42-25:30; Mark 13:33-37; Luke 21:34-36*
- Judgment at the Son of Man's coming (Mount of Olives): *Matthew 25:31-46*
- Plot by the Sanhedrin to arrest and kill Jesus (Mount of Olives

and the palace of the high priest): *Matthew 26:1-5; Mark 14:1-2; Luke 21:37-38; 22:1-2*

A CONTEMPLATIVE VIEW

**"A God too large to walk in
human shoes
Has outgrown every hope of
human use.
And heavy skeptics weighted down
with doubt
Can never rise to find what
God's about."***

Andrew, one of Jesus' apostles . . .

As one of his closest men, Jesus confided in me. I don't know how I earned his trust, I didn't do anything out of the ordinary for him—not like my brother Peter, for example, who made bold, spontaneous leaps and bounds for him on countless occasions.

As a reflective man, I was the opposite of Peter. I let my thoughts settle and steep inside of me. I pondered things I observed and heard—especially when it involved our Rabbi. About Jesus and the things I learned or witnessed, I usually kept them—whether a treasure or a doubt—to myself. But I believe Jesus knew my heart and mind. Perhaps that is why he so often took me aside privately to talk.

I was terribly unsettled as we trudged up the Mount of Olives behind our Master the afternoon he last went into the temple. We left Jerusalem with heavy hearts. Jesus had just unleashed a torrent of scorching words there, ending with what sounded to my ears like a promise that he'd not return.

Our beloved Rabbi, in a matter of minutes, had dashed to pieces all my hopes and dreams in and for him. Here we were, it seemed, following him away from everything I believed in.

The temple was the central hub in the wheel of Jewish faith. And now, my faith in Jesus' identity was in question once again. How could he possibly fulfill the prophecies about the Messiah and yet not set foot in the temple until his enemies there believed in him? How would they ever know him? They certainly would execute him now. Since, at the same time, Jesus insisted that he would suffer and die, I could finally see his predictions coming true.

Nothing made sense anymore, not to my way of thinking. Why would our long-awaited Messiah die? Who was this man to whom I was giving my life?

We disciples were understandably distraught as we tagged along behind him. I tried to get Jesus to open up to us while we walked away from Jerusalem. I did this indirectly by asking him to look at what he was leaving behind. Truly, my words to him meant more than what was on the surface, for we all knew how much he loved the temple—"Look, Rabbi!" I said, while waving my hand across the panoramic view falling behind us, "What magnificent buildings!"

"Do you see all these things?" he asked, first looking at me, then at the view. He continued, with a stern look, "I tell you the truth, not one stone will be left on another; every one will be thrown down."

At this, my heart nearly stopped. He continued up the steep road.

When we came to the place on the mount where Jesus liked to pray, we left him alone, realizing he needed the solitude. We sat apart from him and talked among ourselves. We didn't know what to think. Our hearts were in turmoil. Finally, four of us went to him and asked him more about his prediction regarding his return which he said would happen after the rulers recognized him as "coming in the name of the Lord." This is what troubled us. We couldn't imagine them ever believing in him in that way. His face brightened when we approached him with our concerns. He invited me to sit beside him. I asked, "Tell us when will this happen, and what will be the sign of your coming and of the end of the age?"

And so, on that occasion, he told us about many things to come.

WONDER JUST A LITTLE

Jesus gave important, parting words to his disciples about what to expect after he was gone. He told them he was leaving his

Kingdom in their hands and that it would grow until it covered the entire earth—and that that would happen before his return.

Seated on the mount, on that spring day during the week of Passover, Jesus told them many things that would come to pass. First, he spoke of the destruction of the temple (which would happen in 70 A.D). He also warned them about persecution and how they should respond.

The recurring Messianic theme in the Old Testament Scriptures was the deliverance and hope of Israel. Likewise, Jesus revealed specific warnings regarding the last days concerning Israel.

He gave signs for his second coming and said that they would be like "birth pangs" leading up to the climax when he would return. *Beloved reader, many of these signs are escalating to that climax right now.*

About his Jewish nation, he said, "There will be great distress in the land and wrath against this people. They will fall by the sword and will be taken as prisoners to all the nations. Jerusalem will be trampled on by the Gentiles until the times of the Gentiles are fulfilled." Luke 21:20-24

The Jews have always been hated, because Satan hates what is precious to God. God's people are the brunt of the enemy's most gruesome deeds; it's been this way all throughout Jewish and Christian history. When Hitler's terror ended, the Jews began to return to their land. This became the beginning of the end of the times of the Gentiles. Only one or two of Jesus' signs have not yet happened: "The sun will be darkened, and the moon will not give its light; the stars will fall." Mark 12:24-27

And, the sign concerning Israel regarding "Jacob's troubles" could be happening right now. Jesus said, "There will be great distress, unequaled from the beginning of the world until now— never to be equaled again." Matthew 24:21

One day there will be national deliverance of Israel but probably not until the second coming of the Son of Man. About that day, Jesus said, "For as lightning that comes from the east is visible even in the west, so will be the coming of the Son of Man." Matthew 24:27

What is obvious in these signs of Scripture, given to us by God, is that Israel is at the center of end-time events. She is also at the center of our daily news. Jesus wants us to be alert and on guard, and not weighed down. He wants us ready. He said we would know the times . . . "When you see the fig tree sprout its leaves . . ." This could be the sign of prophecy being fulfilled in our generation. The nations that are gathered around her in hate, is another sign. We need to be well aware of these things, just as Jesus told us to be.

As his bride we long for him, sober in faith, ready in hope. We are his beloved, waiting for him on tiptoe, straining our eyes and hearts for that wondrous glimpse of him. We have "oil in jars along with our lamps"—and we are prepared. He's been gone a long time, his return has been delayed—just as his parable said it would be. But we want to be ready when he comes. "At midnight the cry will ring out, 'Here's the bridegroom! Come and meet him!'"

Today, we look forward to his glorious return. He comes to us through his Spirit and readies us for that wonderful day when we will see him at long last.

WHAT DO YOU SEE?

How amazing it would have been to have heard, for the first time, Jesus' words, "When the Son of Man comes in his glory, and all the angels with him, he will sit on his throne in heavenly glory. All the nations will be gathered before him, and he will separate the people one from another as a shepherd separates the sheep from the goats." Matthew 25:31-32

How the disciple's hearts must have burned to hear such things. Surely the Lord lifted their doubting, troubled hearts at that time. The "throne" Jesus spoke of was the Throne of David, in Jerusalem, on earth. He clearly said that he would sit in heavenly glory upon that throne. He was that holy, eternal heir—the one to bring harmony and restoration to earth, bind up Satan, and renew God's creation. His glory would fill the entire earth. Surely, their doubts lifted upon the hearing of his powerful, promising words!

His kingdom would be heaven on earth, not the earthly kingdom Jesus' disciples imagined at that time. As Jesus sat with his men that day on the Mount of Olives, when he looked into their eyes and gave them words of hope and warning, it was also for us.

At that time, Jesus knew his time to leave was approaching swiftly. He had outgrown his time to stay with us as a man.

Prayerfully imagine how Jesus might have felt after he delivered his impassioned, final words in the temple and during his walk away from there, up the Mount of Olives. Watch him as he finds a place to sit and pray on the mount. What is his expression as he gazes down upon that spectacular view he loved of Jerusalem? What do you suppose his prayer was? What do you think it was like for his disciples to be with him during that time? Read the things he said to them and try to see and hear him. What was his tone of voice? What was his body language?

Ask the Lord to reveal what his predictions mean today. Be open to what is on his heart concerning world events these days. What is he saying to you personally that he wants you to be aware of, or do, during these turbulent times?

JOURNAL

It is by no accident that Jesus' beloved Israel has survived and is a nation today, still awaiting the deliverance of her Messiah. Christians are grafted into that tree. Israel's eyes are blinded and it is our eyes that are opened. Can you sense the love Jesus has for his Jewish people? What message, sign, or words of advice meant the most to you in this chapter? Describe in your journal your feelings, or what has been revealed to you. Is there anything you wish to ask Jesus now? Record in your journal what the Lord wants you to know—about his love for you, or the times you live in.

---

35 – Love's Anointing

She has done a beautiful thing to me.
Matthew 26:10b

So they counted out for him thirty silver coins.
From then on Judas watched
for an opportunity to hand him over.
Matthew 26:15b-16

- Mary's anointing of Jesus for burial (Bethany, in the home of Simon the Leper): *Matthew 26:6-13; Mark 14:3-9; John 12:2-8*
- Judas' agreement to betray Jesus (Jerusalem): *Matthew 26:14-16; Mark 14:10-11; Luke 22:3-6*

A CONTEMPLATIVE VIEW

Mary, from Bethany . . .

I trembled most of the evening with my plan to anoint the Messiah as he reclined at a banqueting table at Simon the Leper's house. Of all the houses in Bethany, Simon's villa had the largest capacity for the crowd of people who came from Jerusalem, Bethany, and Galilee to honor Rabbi Jesus from Nazareth. Tables were laden with food for dozens of guests, and I was supposed to be seated with Martha in another room. Simon's dinner became a spirited celebration. While Lazarus was someone everyone wanted to see and touch, most of the excitement came on the heels of Jesus' kingly entry into Jerusalem for the week of Passover.

Most of us were convinced that Jesus was King David's heir to the throne—Israel's eternal King, without beginnings, come to us at last. I knew, since Jesus raised Lazarus from the dead, that Jesus was much more than a prophet. He astounded Martha and me, in the hour of our deepest grief, by saying that he was the "Resurrection and the Life," and then proved it, bringing Lazarus back after four days in the grave. Oh, yes, our Messiah had come from God in heaven. And he is the Giver of life—our good friend, Jesus.

I nervously watched while he reclined in the place of honor beside my brother.

I tried to imagine how I would approach him and how he might react to my anointing him. But this gave me such nerves that I decided not to plan out my exact course of action, but simply wait for the right moment and let my heart show me the way.

There were three tables of Jesus' closest followers and guests in the largest room. Hidden from view, I stood beside a tall planter filled with meandering vines near an archway. Even my green-colored clothing, by happenstance, helped me remain unnoticed. From here I could watch Master Jesus at his table, his back towards me. He turned my way a couple of times, probably because he could feel my gaze upon him. But if he saw me, he did not let on. I could not stop myself from reveling in the sight of him. He was like water to my thirsty soul.

There was a lot of commotion, musicians playing music, people laughing and talking loudly. People glided past me continually, but no one cared anything about me standing there, except Martha. Once, while walking from one room to another, she stopped to look at me for a moment, long enough to shrug her shoulders. She did not rebuke me, for she knew that my desire was to be near the Teacher. I held the slender alabaster vial tightly and waited, ignoring Martha's unsettling shrug.

My devotion towards the Rabbi had increased daily. I loved him more than life itself. Everything he said to me was fire to my soul. I felt that I was a favorite of his. If I felt that way, then it was *his* doing, not mine. I pondered his sayings long into the nights. It was more than his words. It was his manner too. It was everything about him: his tender strength, his compassion, his strong but gentle love—mostly, his purity and goodness. He lit up a room. He lit up the world. He lit up my life.

I have never known anyone with such wisdom and insight. His miracles proved he was from God. He was full of joy and smiled often. He made people feel accepted and special, no matter who they were. He touched lepers without a thought for himself. He treated women as equals to men. Sinners enjoyed his company and found themselves changed just from being with him. Children adored him. The poor, beggars, even the most odious individuals, were unafraid of him because he treated them like his dearest friends.

Wherever he happened to go, a fragrance of joy and love went with him. I thought that when he stepped into Simon's house. Upon seeing his frame in the doorway, I had thought, *How can I thank him for what he has done for us? How can I show him how I feel? What gift could I possibly give him that would be worthy of him? What do I have worthy for a king—for God's Anointed?*

All at once came the idea to anoint him with my fragrant spikenard. Surely, this would show him how much I valued him. It would be perfect—a symbolic gesture—wouldn't it?

I slipped out of Simon's house and ran to ours to retrieve the keepsake. The idea to anoint him felt like the most wonderful, perfect expression of honor and love I could ever show him. It was valuable too—given to me by my father before he died. It was my dowry, to give to a prospective husband. From Persia, it was very costly perfume.

After eating the meal, the guests lingered at their tables and the musicians put their instruments down. Only the sound of low conversations hung in the rooms. The banquet was nearly over.

Jesus had not taught or shared stories the whole time. He was simply enjoying himself and the company of friends. When he stretched and repositioned himself on his pillows, I suddenly worried that he might get up and leave. The time had come—I must not wait another moment.

With my heart pounding, I left my hiding place and stepped up to where Jesus reclined at the table.

Lazarus looked up at me expectantly. I snapped and broke the seal of the vial. Jesus was caught off-guard, but he slowly turned to see me. My hand shook nervously while I poured out about a pint of perfume on his head. As the beautiful, heady aroma filled the room; everyone stopped talking.

I saw his hands folded . . . his eyes closed . . . his gentle face.

As I poured the perfume on his head, I was surprised that he did not stop me. He sat very still and received this gift of mine. I was so relieved. So glad. I wanted to call him "My King," but instead, I said it only within my heart—over and over: *My King . . . My King . . . My King . . .* all the while slowly pouring the perfume on him.

He looked up at me. His eyes were watery and I wondered if he'd heard my silent praise.

The perfume had begun to run down his forehead, so I wiped a stream away from his eyes. Too much was already in his hair, soaking and dripping down thick, strands, wetting the back and sides of his head and his beard. The stream of perfume droplets soaked the neck, back and shoulders of his tunic. Had I overdone it? I hoped he wouldn't mind that I'd soaked his whole upper body with the heady, fragrant spikenard.

I saw that I still had some left in my jar, so I removed my veil and bowed low to kiss his feet. On them I poured out the remaining pint of nard, wiping the excess off with my hair.

After I emptied the jar of its contents and remained bowed at his feet, I wished the moments could have lasted longer. I did not want to leave him.

He leaned towards me, withdrawing his feet, bending over to me. And then I looked at him. He didn't say a word, but his face surely did.

I had truly blessed him.

Judas, from Kerioth . . .

I am outraged by this thing. How can Jesus sit there and allow such a waste? And in such a manner? This is an indecent show. The perfume could have been sold . . . how many poor might be fed with that much money? What kind of rabbi is he?

I rebuked her for such waste, and him for allowing it.

Lord Jesus . . .

Leave her alone. Why are you bothering her? She has done a beautiful thing to me. The poor you will always have with you. You will not always have me. She did what she could. She poured perfume on my body beforehand to prepare for my burial. I tell you the truth, wherever the gospel is preached throughout the world, what she has done will also be told, in memory of her.

WONDER JUST A LITTLE

One phrase in Jesus' response to Mary's lavish expression of love has affected countless souls throughout the ages. Listen to Jesus' response: "You will not always have me. She did what she could."

Souls in love with Jesus know . . . she did what we wish that we could do. Mary anointed him on behalf of us all.

She expressed to him the love of his Church.

Mary anointed the Anointed One with the love that he died for.

This was only the beginning. Mary led the way, showing others how to love the Lord.

Extravagance deserves extravagance. And, Jesus was the most extravagant giver of all.

No wonder what Mary of Bethany did to Lord Jesus has been told all over the world, for two thousand years.

She expressed her deep love for him on behalf of all God's beloveds! She did it for you. She did it for me!

What a wonderful joy that Providence saw to it that Jesus tasted, at least once during his earthly life, that extravagant anointing of love he so richly deserved. Just as David and other kings of Israel had been anointed as kings, so Jesus was anointed king for his kingdom—the Kingdom of Love.

Mary poured great love upon the Beloved. Her love anointed Jesus for burial. Nothing could have been more appropriate.

WHAT DO YOU SEE?

Two people. Two choices. Night and day. Judas and Mary. After reading the Scriptural account of Mary's anointing of Jesus, close your eyes and imagine the scene. In your prayerful meditation, take part in that banquet and see the two in action. How can two people react so differently? What causes us to love or to hate? What is it about the freedom to choose that cost the Lord so much?

Imagine anointing Jesus. What would you say to him if you could? Try to imagine some of what Mary might have experienced. What did it mean to Jesus? What does it mean in your relationship with him? How can we "anoint" him today?

JOURNAL

What creative new way can you express your devotion to Jesus? Write in your journal what you have learned or experienced from the Scripture reading and your meditation prayer time. Since Jesus is no longer with us in person (in the flesh), is there any other way to lavish one's very best on him? What form(s) might that take?

36 – All Is Made Ready

*Then came the day of Unleavened Bread on which
the Passover Lamb had to be sacrificed.*
Luke 22:7

- Preparation for the Passover meal (Jerusalem): *Matthew 26:17-19; Mark 14:12-16; Luke 22:7-13*
- Beginning of Passover meal (Jerusalem, in the upper room): *Matthew 26:20, Mark 14:17; Luke 22:14-16*

A CONTEMPLATIVE VIEW

God and Man at Table are Sat Down

O, welcome all you noble saints of old
As now before your very eyes unfold
The wonders all so long ago foretold
God and man at table are sat down

Elders, martyrs, all are falling down
Prophets, patriarchs are gath'ring 'round
What angels longed to see now man has found
God and man at table are sat down

Who is this who spreads the vict'ry feast?
Who is this who makes our warring cease?
Jesus, risen Savior, Prince of Peace
God and man at table are sat down

Beggars, lame and harlots also here
Repentant publicans are drawing near
Wayward sons come home without a fear
God and man at table are sat down

Here He gives Himself to us, as bread;
Here, as wine, we drink the blood He shed.
Born to die, we eat and live instead!
God and man at table are sat down.

Worship in the presence of the Lord
With joyful songs and hearts in one accord
And let our Host at table be adored
God and man at table are sat down

When at last this earth shall pass away
When Jesus and His Bride are one to stay
The feast of love is just begun that day
God and man at table are sat down

Dr. Robert J. Stamps, © 1997. Used with permission.

Jesus, before entering the Upper Room . . .

Father, I am about to walk into that room and to a table "prepared before the foundation of the world." This is the beginning of the fulfillment of the hope and vision we have carried for so long. At this moment, my heart overflows with the anticipation of what I am about to do.

All is made ready. Including me.

I have greatly longed to share this time and holy meal with the ones you have given me. I pray not only for these, but for all who will believe and continue to remember the meaning of this night.

What makes this night different than any other night, my Father?

I have come now to the primary reason for my birth. Father, strengthen me for what lies just ahead. This will be an eventful night—of light and of shadows—as I walk through the valley of the shadow of death.

As I open the door to this room, Abba, I pray for not just those here, but for all the hearts that will eternally open and receive that which I have come to give them. I pray that the world will know that you have sent me and that all who will believe in me and in my words will pass over from darkness into light, from death into eternal life. Amen.

WONDER JUST A LITTLE

Who would ever have thought that a single meal could mean so much?

One incredible night mankind sat down at a table with God and, from then on, everything between us became communion.

That supper between Jesus and his disciples became a pivotal moment of transcendence. It began the Day—that Day—which became the climax in God's Story. It became the center of the Universe, a red pinpoint in the mappings of God's Creation. It defined the cross. It defined God's love. It defined us.

That upper room was more than a meeting place. The traditional meal was more than a religious observance and much, much more than food and wine. From that night on, humanity's relationship with God would never be the same.

What was it about that night that changed everything? That special evening closed the book on the Old Covenant, and opened the New. What had been in the mind of God, at the foundation of the world, when he planned that sit-down, sacramental supper? That holy, particular meal with twelve ordinary men was beyond extraordinary. It became the end of the beginning (for those twelve) and the beginning of the end (for their Master).

Over symbolic food and cups of wine, through the spoken words of the Word of God, the unknowable Mystery of the person of God bared himself more than ever before.

The faithful Son of Man stepped into that upper room in Jerusalem, on the eve of his death, and made sense of all the thousands of years God had worked to reveal himself through the traditions of religious worship and expression. No more blood would ever need to be shed to cover sin. The promised *Seed* of Eden had come to be planted in death once and for all.

During that last meal known ever since as The Last Supper, Jesus gave meaning to everything so that we would at last see him, know him, and receive him—as the very image of God-with-us. And by his sacrifice he would help us see the measure of his love.

The Passover was a feast that celebrated, in reality, the giving of *himself*.

He had planned it meticulously way ahead of time. History and tradition paved the way.

What better way could God, who is unseen, make himself so profoundly understood? How else could he continue to be understood after he laid his life down for us?

Yes, God is so very wise. So very gracious. He finds such creative ways to reveal himself and his love. He is forever reaching for us and showing us the way to know him. This night was one such way. It became a beacon of light on a rock in the ocean of our wandering.

God had come to redeem us, and so Jesus entered into the upper room to show us, in both symbol and word, the truth of our salvation: his life freely and wholly given for us.

At this meal we must all learn to let Jesus serve us. We must permit him to wash our feet, stooping low to show us how to love, for without him we would never think of anyone but ourselves. We must take from his hands what he offers us to eat and drink—for it is the reality of his love and life he so freely, so wondrously came to give us.

As now before your very eyes unfold
The wonders all so long ago foretold
God and man at table are sat down

WHAT DO YOU SEE?

To appreciate the impact of these final hours in Jesus' life, it is good to realize that they are his last hours as one of us. At no other time did Jesus disclose himself more fully and clearly to his disciples than during their last evening together as he bared his heart and soul. He prepared his men for what would come in the near future. He spoke his most tender words of love and encouragement to them. His parting words would be remembered and last for their lifetimes, and for ours.

What was the meaning of the Passover meal? What was the meaning of Jesus' words: "Take and eat, this is my body . . . Take and drink, this is my blood . . . Do this in memory of me"?

The disciples later understood the happenings of that night and remembered that John the Baptist had called Jesus "the Lamb of God."

There is a scarlet thread of atonement being pulled through the fabric of time all the way back from the Garden of Eden. The first time sin was covered by blood was when God killed an animal and used the skin to cover Adam and Eve's shame. Eden was a place of paradise, not only for Adam and Eve, but for all the other creatures as well. Before disobedience, creation was in harmony, and full of God's love. There was no "food chain." But on the day God covered Adam and Eve's nakedness, an animal had to die—the first covering for sin was the beginning of the Scarlet Thread.

Why did God kill an animal to cover them? They were no longer innocent and naked before him. Why did God command that animals, perfect ones, be sacrificed for sins up until the day of Jesus? Why was a spotless lamb killed, and its blood applied to the doorposts on the first Passover? The blood on the doorposts of all the Hebrew homes is what God used to deliver them from the angel of death in Egypt. Why, ever after that, did the Jews celebrate Passover each year with a sacrificial lamb and unleavened bread? Why did Jesus die on that very feast day? Why does it take the blood of Jesus to take away our sins when we believe in him? Do you see the Scarlet Thread?

We can see Jesus as the redeemer promised by God in the Garden of Eden. We can see the symbolic, spiritual meaning behind the Hebraic tradition of the Passover. We understand that the Exodus of Israel becomes our "exodus." Their journey to the Promised Land is like ours.

The Lamb of God and the Passover Lamb is Jesus. The unleavened bread is Jesus' body, broken for our redemption. The cups of blessings—Jesus' blood poured out for the atonement of our sins. The Passover meal Jesus had with his disciples was the pivotal moment of God's salvation, and of his revelation to man.

Can you imagine what may have been in the Lord's heart as he neared that climactic hour? Close your eyes and prayerfully imagine Peter and John as they prepare the room and the meal before Jesus and the others enter. Notice the beautiful table full of elements and symbols where Jesus will so poignantly reveal himself and where he will break bread and drink wine with his own. Watch Jesus as he steps up to the upper room, as he prays and prepares himself. What might it have been like to be in that room when Jesus entered? Can you see the expression on his face? Was he tired? Joyful? Pensive? Can you see the love in his eyes? He held so very much inside his heart as he entered into the upper room that momentous night.

JOURNAL

Describe in your journal what your thoughts and experiences have been during your prayer time. Write Jesus a letter in your journal concerning the things you feel. Listen to see if he has anything he wants to reveal to you. Let your love flow to the Lord. He longs for these times of communion with you.

37 – "This is the New Covenant in My Blood"

Because I live, you also will live.
On that day you will realize that
I am in my Father, and you are in me,
and I am in you.
John 14:19b-20

- During the Passover meal and dissension among the disciples over greatness and Jesus' response (Jerusalem, in the upper room): *Luke 22: 24-30*
- Washing the disciples' feet (Jerusalem, in the upper room): *John 13:1-20*
- Identification of the betrayer (Jerusalem, in the upper room): *Matthew 26:21-25; Mark 14:18-21; Luke 22:21-23; John 13:21-30*
- Prediction of Peter's denial (Jerusalem, in the upper room): *John 13:31-36; Matthew 26:31-35; Mark 14:27-31; Luke 22:31-38; John 13:37-38*
- The Lord's Supper Instituted (Jerusalem, in the upper room): *Matthew 26:26-29; Mark 14:22-25; Luke 22:17-20; 1 Corinthians 11:23-26*
- Questions about his destination, the Father, and the Holy Spirit answered (Jerusalem, in the upper room): *John 14:1-31*
- The vine and the branches (Jerusalem, in the upper room): *John 15:1-17*
- Opposition from the world (Jerusalem, in the upper room): *John 15:18-16:4*

- Coming and ministry of the Spirit (Jerusalem, in the upper room): *John 16:5-15*
- Prediction of joy over his resurrection (Jerusalem, in the upper room): *John 16:16-22*
- Promise of answered prayer and peace (Jerusalem, in the upper room): *John 16:23-33*

A CONTEMPLATIVE VIEW

Apostle John . . .

I am leaving, Jesus told us, in many ways, all through the meal. Oh, how he loved us that last night! "My children," he said, "I will be with you only a little longer. You will look for me, and just as I told the Jews, so I tell you now: Where I am going, you cannot come."

His words nearly broke our hearts. He looked at me, sitting beside him, and all I could do was look at him and shake my head. I was lonely already at the mere thought of his absence. How could we ever do without him? And he knew how I felt. I could see this by his expression when he looked at me, so full of compassion, so wise. He seemed to know my heart at any given moment. But he continued on, in an even voice, as though well rehearsed. I suppose he'd waited a long time to say the next words that fell upon our sorrowful ears.

"A new command I give you: Love one another," he said, "Just as I have loved you, so you must love one another. By this all men will know that you are my disciples, if you love one another."

He said this with great emphasis, and it made me realize how serious this was. This very night was probably our last time with him!

I drew closer to him and took hold of his arm. I wanted to ask him, "Why? Why must you go?" But Peter asked a different question before I had the chance.

"Lord, where are you going?"

Jesus didn't answer right away, but looked down at the table. When he looked up again he said we would all fall away that very night on account of him, according to Holy Writ. He quoted the prophet Zechariah [13:7], saying, "I will strike the shepherd, and the sheep of the flock will be scattered."

Disbelieving these stinging words, Peter asked why he couldn't follow, saying that he would lay down his life for him.

I ached for Peter when Jesus answered, "Will you really lay down your life for me? I tell you the truth, before the rooster crows, you will disown me three times."

Jesus shocked us when he said we'd all fall away.

We knew now, without doubt, that Jesus was the Messiah. And we all knew that his kingly destiny was written about in Scripture. He was meant to restore all things and rule on David's throne. But he kept insisting that he would lay down his life.

During the meal, he took in his hands unleavened bread and his cup of wine, saying, "Eat this bread . . . drink this wine ... this bread is my body given for you, for the forgiveness of many. This wine is my blood, shed for you. This is the new covenant in my blood. Do this in memory of me."

And we took from him both the bread and wine. He bound us all together with him forever that night, and it would continue to be our covenant with him.

That night was like no other night in my life. For me, the hardest part was that I couldn't bear his leaving us. Like a father knowing he's dying, Jesus spoke parting words to us: "Do not let your hearts be troubled. Trust in God; trust also in me. In my Father's house are many rooms; if it were not so, I would have told you. I am going there to prepare a place for you. And if I go and prepare a place for you, I will come back and take you to be with me that you also may be where I am. You know the way to the place where I am going."

Thomas reasoned that we didn't know where he was going, so how could we know the way?

Jesus answered, "I am the way and the truth and the life. No one comes to the Father except through me. If you really knew me, you would know my Father as well. From now on, you do know him and have seen him."

Philip said, "Lord, show us the Father and that will be enough."

Jesus replied, "Don't you know me, Philip, even after I have been among you such a long time? Anyone who has seen me has seen the Father. How can you say, 'Show us the Father'? Don't you believe that I am in the Father, and that the Father is in me?"

Never had he spoken so clearly, without figurative speech. We were astonished. Seeing this, he said, "You believe at last!"

Yes, we believed. He confirmed what I'd wondered but hadn't dared to dream. He was, in reality, God-with-us! Our beloved rabbi and friend was God-in-our-midst, laughing with us, surprising and amazing us, speaking God's ways to us . . . But now, now he was about to leave us.

Before our meal had ended, I laid my head upon his chest and heard the beating heart of God.

Surely, this is why he came to us—so that we can all, anytime we want, hear and know his heart.

WONDER JUST A LITTLE

So much happened during Jesus' last supper with his disciples—for the evening was far more than a night of conversation at a table. In reality, in just a few hours' time, Jesus had planted everlasting truth into the rich soil of the human heart—thereby forever establishing his kingdom of heaven.

The kingdom of God is a kingdom within one's heart. From his lips flowed words that would sustain his followers until his return. He gave encouragement, promises, revelation about himself, wise and practical instructions, hope, and specific warnings. He humbly and lovingly served them—showing them how to love and how to be great. He warned about things to come. Up until this night, all the persecution had fallen upon him; but afterwards, it would fall on them—for his sake.

Jesus disclosed the full reality to them—that in seeing him they'd seen the Father. How Jesus' own heart rejoiced when he saw, at last, that they finally understood. He explained that his own would abide in him—and didn't have to strive or worry. Giving tremendous hope to them, Jesus inaugurated the coming of God's kingdom, which would continue to come through him and in them. He had come to do more than to establish a kingdom; he had come to give himself to the world. The Son of God, the disciples were beginning to see, was the Reward they would all be willing to die for. And the Lord promised that he and his Father would come to them and abide in them. He would not leave them as orphans; soon, they would know him even more.

WHAT DO YOU SEE?

Read the Scriptures listed in this chapter and meditate upon the things that happened that Passover night. Imagine yourself as an invisible visitor in that room. As the scene unfolds before you, notice the Lord, the room, the table, the men. Perhaps the disciples were fearful to be in Jerusalem with Jesus, for they must have realized how dangerous it was to be there with him. And yet, perhaps whenever they were with him, they'd learned not to be afraid. He'd wondrously and repeatedly proven to them that he could keep them safe.

What is Jesus like when he first begins their Passover meal? What do you see when he takes off his outer clothing and begins to wash their feet? What do you suppose Jesus was thinking during the time he did this for them? Is there conversation going on at the table as Jesus goes from one pair of feet to another? Or, do the men sit in wonder, silent with their own thoughts? How did Jesus look, bowed over their feet, intent on his task, either sitting or kneeling on the floor, holding their feet in his lap? How is he when he speaks about the kingdom of heaven and their parts in it? Watch him. Can you imagine his face and gestures as he discloses his most intimate feelings about how he will "abide" in them and answer their prayers after he is gone? What is his voice like when he talks about the one who will betray him? Can you see Jesus as he sadly tells Peter that he will deny knowing him three times before the night ends?

What is Jesus' body language as he talks about leaving them? Is the meal solemn or, at times, joyful? How do the disciples react to the things Jesus tells them?

How do the frightened disciples react when Jesus warns them to take a purse and a bag, and to carry a sword? This was the opposite of how things had been when he sent them out before. What is

Jesus' body language in response to the two disciples who dash from the table to retrieve their hidden swords for his inspection?

Many things were said and done during the meal. Look for the details. Reflect on the deeper meaning of what happened. What might the singing of the Psalm, ending their time together, have been like? Who led the singing? That alone is a thing to contemplate . . . God singing with men before he goes off to die.

How would it have felt to be with Jesus during his last hours on earth as God living among us as a man?

JOURNAL

How do you feel about Jesus after reading this chapter? What insights have you gained? How does that evening, so many long years ago, affect you today? Ask the Lord to reveal to you what he wants you to know at this moment. Be open to any ideas, images, words, or thoughts that come. Record these, or describe them, in your journal. Sit quietly in the Lord's presence and simply give him your love.

38 – Jesus Prays

After Jesus said this, he looked toward heaven and prayed:
Father, the time has come . . .

Father, I want those you have given me
to be with me where I am,
and to see my glory . . .

I have made you known to them,
and will continue to make you known in order that
the love you have for me may be in them
and that I myself may be in them.
John 17:1, 24a, 26

- Jesus' prayer for his disciples and all who believe (Jerusalem, in the upper room): *John 17:1-26*
- Jesus' agonizing prayers in Gethsemane (Garden of Gethsemane at the foot of the Mount of Olives): *Matthew 26:30, 36-46; Mark 14:26, 32-42; Luke 22:39-46; John 18:1*

A CONTEMPLATIVE VIEW

Apostle James, son of Zebedee . . .

The soft glow of the oil lamp gently lit the face of our Master. We were about to leave the upper room. His expression was warm and serene when he said, "I have told you these things so that in me you may have peace. In this world you will have trouble. But take heart! I have overcome the world."

After he said this, he looked up toward heaven and prayed. Whenever Jesus prayed out loud in our midst, I was transported. At those times, it felt as though he took us to heaven with him. I can still hear his beautiful voice as he prayed that last time with us. Long and heavenly, his words of intercession and communion with his Father revealed a heart full of hope, vision, and care. First, he prayed to his Father for his own glorification, then for us, his disciples, and lastly, for all those in the future who would believe in him.

I've come to see his prayer at that time as a bridge he was crossing. He was leaving us to cross over to his Father and return to his heavenly glory. But during that moment of prayer, we stood on that bridge beside him. We looked into heaven with him.

I know that he always intercedes for his own—and will continue until we all become answers to his prayer. For he prayed that we who were his would see him in his glory and be there with him. Yes, he prayed that we would rejoice with him in his glory—I know he prays this still, for those yet to join him.

And he prayed that we would all become one, even as he is one with his Father.

Our hearts had soared during his prayer.

But everything changed suddenly in the darkness of the olive grove. His prayers changed just as drastically. We could hardly bear to listen.

After listening to his anguished cries, John, Peter and I fell asleep during the long stretch of lonely silence that followed.

Jesus had asked the three of us to come apart from the others to keep watch with him while he prayed.

We know now that his agonizing prayer in the garden was another bridge: between our damnation and God's salvation. This was a bridge we could not bear to share with him. He had thrown himself down upon that bridge—and he was alone. In our despair, we could not bear to keep watch with him, so we fell asleep.

"My soul is overwhelmed with sorrow to the point of death," he had confided to us as he took us deeper into the garden so that he could pray more privately. He knew we could hear him. Surely, he knew. And I don't know why or how we could have fallen asleep.

But in so doing we added disappointment to his terrible grief.

The garden was so dark. Gloom and despair hung heavily in the air all around us. We were there hiding from the authorities, or so I thought. But Jesus wasn't hiding—he was waiting. He knew his betrayer would lead the rulers and soldiers to arrest him in the garden, as he knew the rest of us would desert him—and scatter to safety. That is why he brought us to the garden, away from the upper room. If we had stayed there, surely, we would have been arrested with him.

"Are you asleep?" Jesus sadly asked us, not once, but three times, each time stepping away from his prayer-bridge to check on us. He wanted us to be near him. He didn't want to be alone.

What good were we to him? I don't know. As a man, he needed us. As God, he knew the terror that faced him. We didn't know—so we left him there alone on that terrifying bridge.

Finally, Jesus' prayer ended, and he crossed the bridge. "Not my will, but your will be done."

WONDER JUST A LITTLE

How wonderful that Jesus' prayer in the upper room was remembered and recorded so that we could "hear" it. It gives us faith and hope. Surely, it is our glimpse into not only our Lord's heart, but into heaven. When Jesus prayed this prayer, he was looking beyond his death and resurrection to the time when he would be in heaven, in his glory.

Jesus' prayer was drastically different when he was in the Garden of Gethsemane. There we see him, in his humanness, calling out to his Father, overwhelmed with dread.

Had the darkness of evil descended upon him? Was the devil torturing him? Was he overwhelmed because he realized all that was about to happen to him?

God the Father sent an angel to strengthen him. But Jesus was beyond the angel's help, for he prayed more earnestly and began to sweat blood. What does this show us? It means that Jesus, who had lived his entire life in obedience to his Father, was being asked to do something he didn't want to do. Jesus, human being, full of life, wanted to live! It is what we all want.

But Jesus had come to die a terrible death by crucifixion. He was the Lamb of God, slain from the foundation of the world. His mission was to show God's love, to give everything he had, for our salvation. Jesus loved his Father, but humanly he certainly did not want to face terrible pain and shame and death.

Truly, this is where Jesus surrendered himself to *the Cross*. It happened here in the darkened garden just as much as on the rocky hill called Golgotha. To die to self is to "take up one's cross." It is the choice to live for God and not for oneself. It was in this, the final surrender, that Jesus learned obedience.

God learning obedience? Yes, even to the point of death.

All this he did to save us. All this to prove his love for us. He would rather die for each one of us than live without us. And here we see him make that terrifying, costly choice.

In the Garden of Eden, Satan tempted Adam and Eve to disobey God. They chose to do what they wanted, and not what God wanted. They brought death and sin upon themselves and all their offspring when they said "no" to God and "yes" to themselves.

In this second Garden, Jesus redeemed their sin—and all sins committed since then by those who put their trust in him. He said "no" to himself and "yes" to his Father. "Not what I want, but what you want to be done," Jesus said.

And in that prayer, Jesus surrendered himself. He crossed the bridge that would take him from life to death—for us.

WHAT DO YOU SEE?

Jesus' two different prayer times are covered in this chapter: 1) Jesus' beautifully graceful, high priestly prayer with his disciples in the upper room after the Last Supper; 2) Jesus' prayer and agony in the Garden of Gethsemane. Pay close attention to what stirs your heart the most. It is an art to learn to recognize and respond to these personal Holy Spirit stirrings. If you are *drawn* to both prayers, you may wish to meditate upon both.

1. Meditation for Jesus' Prayer in the Upper Room:
You may wish to read the entire account of the Last Supper

before reading and meditating upon his closing and final prayer with his disciples. The account sets the stage for how Jesus' heart must have felt. Pay close attention to this part of the prayer: "My prayer is not for them alone. I pray also for those who will believe in me through their message, that all of them may be one, Father, just as you are in me and I am in you. May they also be in us so that the world may believe that you have sent me. I have given them the glory that you gave me, that they may be one as we are one: I in them and you in me. May they be brought to complete unity to let the world know that you sent me and have loved them even as you have loved me. Father, I want _____ (put your first name here), who you have given me to be with me where I am, and to see my glory, the glory you gave me."

Now, imagine seeing Jesus in his glory. Yes, cross that bridge in prayer as he did, to see yourself in the future. Let this vision be all God wants for you, right at this moment.

2. Meditation for Jesus' Prayer in the Garden of Gethsemane:
Suppose you were able to go to the Garden of Gethsemane and support Jesus during his travail. What would you say to him? Here's your chance. Imagine the scene. Don't be afraid to be yourself with him. Imagine you have an angel escort, as you space-and-time travel. You and the angel walk past the three sleeping disciples. Next, you come upon Jesus. The angel introduces you to him as someone from the future, and that is all he says to the Lord about you. Then the angel leaves you alone with Jesus. By the light of the moon, you look upon each other's faces. Time for Jesus stands still; time for you is to be with him at this moment. Imagine what would happen. If given this chance, what would you say to him?

JOURNAL

Record in your journal about this time of meditation and what thoughts or ideas ministered to you. Prayerfully listen to the Lord with a ready pen. What is on his heart that he wishes to reveal to you? What do you wish to say to him? End by sitting for a few minutes, quiet and attentive to his loving presence.

39 – The Kiss of Death

Jesus, knowing all that was going to happen to him,
went out and asked them,
"Who is it you want?"
John 18:4

- Jesus betrayed, arrested, and forsaken (Gethsemane): *Matthew 26:47-56; Mark 14:43-52; Luke 22:47-53; John 18:2-12*
- Trial—the first Jewish phase, before Annas (Jerusalem, courtyard of Annas): *John 18:13-14, 19-23*
- Trial—the second Jewish phase, before Caiaphas and the Sanhedrin (Jerusalem, house of Caiaphas): *Matthew 26:57, 59-68; Mark 14:53, 55-65; Luke 22:54a, 63-65; John 18:24*
- Peter's denials (Jerusalem, courtyard of Caiaphas): *Matthew 26:58, 69-75; Mark 14:54, 66-72; Luke 22:54b-62; John 18:15-18, 25-27*

A CONTEMPLATIVE VIEW

"Why

Why did it have to be a friend?
Who chose to betray the Lord?
And why did he use a kiss to show them?
That's not what a kiss is for.

Only a friend can betray a friend.
A stranger has nothing to gain.
And only a friend comes close enough
To ever cause so much pain . . ."
                                    Lyrics by Michael Card

Simon Peter . . .

Through the night shadows, Judas led a mob of men with weapons and torches to the olive garden. Jesus stood beside me, having wakened me for the third time, saying, "Are you still sleeping and resting?"

I looked up at him, sorry that I had disappointed him again. His eyes looked straight ahead, towards the garden entrance. "Enough!" Jesus said, "The hour has come. Look, the Son of Man is being betrayed into the hands of sinners. Rise! Let us go!"

The three of us sprang to our feet in time to hear and see movement. It wasn't one of the other disciples in the cave; this man had a torch. We had taken the only torch with us.

The way this man quickly approached between the rows of trees told us that he must have known the garden's main pathway.

Jesus said to us, "Here comes my betrayer!" But all I saw was Judas coming toward us.

I wondered, "Who are these people with him . . .?" I looked back to the Master, whose eyes were fixed on Judas—the look on Jesus' face . . .

It was Judas! Judas was the betrayer!

Still unmoved beside me, Jesus waited for him to come closer. When the two were nearly face-to-face, Jesus said, with a sorrowful voice, "Friend, do what you came for."

Without hesitation, Judas replied, "Rabbi!" He took Jesus' shoulders in his hands and leaned forward, touching his lips to the Master's cheek.

"Judas, are you betraying the Son of Man with a kiss?" the Master asked, his voice cracking from the sting of such a deed.

This was Judas' signal to the soldiers—so that they would know which man to arrest. It was an act of quiet, deadly violence against the Creator of life. But this I have seen in retrospect, when I remember and look back upon that night so full of contrasts.

Without a trace of remorse, Judas kissed Eternal Life goodbye.

To Jesus, it was surely the "kiss of death."

Immediately, soldiers came up from behind Judas and tried to seize our Master. Enraged, I drew my sword and wildly struck out at them in his defense. I cut off the ear of a man, who turned out to be a servant of the high priest. Jesus quickly rebuked me, saying that he could ask his Father for legions of angels if he chose to. He touched and healed the man's ear. I backed away, filled with fear.

Within minutes the soldiers bound Jesus and took him out of the garden, hemmed in by guards all around him. He looked like a criminal being led away.

Everything happened so fast. I didn't know what to do. The others fled. I hid myself at a safe distance and followed them to the house of Caiaphas to see what would happen to Jesus.

I was so angry at what Judas had done, but soon I found that I was not, in any way, a better man.

That night, in the courtyard of the high priest, after much loud cursing for effect, and denying my Lord for the third time, I realized that Jesus had turned and was looking right at me. The memory of his pain-filled gaze is forever etched in my mind. I had denied him just as he predicted I would—and which I had profusely argued I would never do.

I believe that being betrayed by Judas and I hurt Jesus more than did the thirty-nine lashings, the beatings, the crown of thorns, the nails in his hands and feet, and even more than the pain he suffered while he hung on the cross.

I know Jesus. I know his heart. I know what is important and what he would die to have. He wants us to believe in him and remain faithful. If we do, we will inherit eternal life. If we do, he will have us, and we will have him. I saw the disappointment in our faithlessness in his gaze as he turned to look at me.

What Jesus had said about me was true—the devil wanted to sift me as wheat. Jesus said he had prayed for me, and when I turned back, that I would be strong for my brothers. But how, I asked myself in the hours of my deepest grief, could I be strong for anyone? In a matter of hours, I was broken in pieces, and had become mere fragments of the man I'd been. I wept and lamented, for I could see no way out! *What on earth would I do if I could never see Jesus, my Lord, again? What on earth would I do if I came face to face with him again? How would I ever be able to look him in they eye after what I had done to him?* I was a man torn asunder by my sin, and yet I loved my Lord more than my life.

Jesus knew my heart, and he came for me. In moments, with one long, silent gaze from my risen Lord, I was his again. I was his lost sheep found.

I can strengthen my brothers in this: there is nothing we can do that will ever keep us from his love. He is our one and only hope. If we believe, he is able to make all things work out for our highest good. He can redeem anything and anyone. That is why his name is Jesus—the Savior. And that is why he let us cause him so much pain.

WONDER JUST A LITTLE

Judas had preached and healed in Jesus' name as one of the chosen Twelve. He saw how readily Jesus forgave and loved people. He walked beside God as a man. They were close friends. As we know, friends share hopes, struggles, and dreams. They listen to and they help each other. Friendship is based on trust. Judas, in the disciples' community, was in charge of their ministry's money. Jesus trusted him with much.

Ponder a moment the parable Jesus told—the one about the Master who entrusts different sums of money to his servants while he goes away; and the way in which the servants "invest" their Master's funds. Think about Judas having been given, literally, all of his Master's money. Judas didn't invest any of it, but actually stole from his Master. Remember, also, Judas' anger over the "wasted" spikenard? Greed—not generosity toward the poor—was his motivator, and part of his downfall. It played an important part in his final act of treachery.

How bitter a realization it was for Jesus as he watched one of his closest disciples "serve mammon" instead of him. Judas knew Jesus as his close friend and Master for about three years while they ministered and traveled together. We know how close we become to someone we travel and live with on the road. There's an intense, in-your-face closeness that can't help but develop. There are joys, hardships, and challenges, all creating many memorable times. Friendships are made, or broken, because iron sharpens iron. Judas and Jesus knew each other's idiosyncrasies, habits, attitudes, responses, beliefs, and thinking. They could anticipate what the other would think, say or do. Scripture records, in Psalm 41, "Even my own familiar friend in whom I trusted, who ate my bread, has lifted up his heel against me."

Do you feel the passion and sorrow in these words? Truly, the more one loves the more one grieves over love grown cold.

Scripture tells us that God is a zealous, jealous God! He is "that tremendous Lover!" All this was in Jesus' heart, for he was God. How he ached for Judas to stay true and faithful.

Surely, Jesus felt the painful loss of his friend as he watched his negative attitude develop. Many times Jesus mentions his concern about his friend. In Capernaum, after most of his followers leave him, but not any of the Twelve, Jesus comments that one of them who has stayed, is "one who has a devil." He only said it because he was deeply grieved by Judas even then.

Yet, Jesus didn't turn Judas away. Why? Do you think he hoped Judas would come around? Here is a great mystery to ponder: About Judas, Jesus said, "The one who will betray me . . . it would have been better if he had not been born." This comes from the lips of Judas' own Creator! Here we see a mystery involving predestination and free will. This is a great wonder, hard for us to understand. But it is true that our choices determine our own outcomes. And it is true that God wants everyone to come into eternal life with him. We have been given great power. In giving us freedom to choose, God has chosen to relinquish his power over us. For love cannot be love unless there is freedom! Freedom is a costly gift.

Judas was meant to be an apostle. The Lord called him to be an apostle, and that was "the plan" for his life. However, Scripture records a different destiny. Perhaps if Judas had not fallen away, the Scriptures would have been written differently.

How Jesus agonized over the loss of this one man's soul. What went wrong for Judas? How could it happen? How and why did he embrace death instead of life? Even his name has died—for who would ever name a child after him?

Then we have Peter—emotional, predictable, spontaneous, lovable Peter. His sin against his Friend, in contrast to Judas, ended by bringing him closer. It strengthened their love relationship. Jesus redeemed Peter's sin. Peter, finding out the truth about himself, became truly humble and dependent solely on the grace and forgiveness of his Lord. Two similar sins, but two drastically different outcomes. One is hurled headlong into the eternal fires of damnation, forever separate from his Lord. The other is given the "keys to God's kingdom," with the apostolic authority of shepherd of the flock.

May we all become like Peter, in that when we fail (for we will fail and fail and fail), we will turn to look into the eyes of our Savior and see nothing but love.

WHAT DO YOU SEE?

There are four accounts of rejection in this chapter. Two episodes of denial and betrayal happened in the high priests' courts; first with Annas and then with Caiaphas. Read John 18:13-14, 19-23. Imagine Jesus as he is brought to stand before the priests for questioning. Let the responses spoken by Jesus sit in your heart. Ponder them. What do you hear? What do you see?

Jesus came first to his own and they rejected him. During these two formal hearings and the trial that follows, we see betrayal, denial, and rejection of a nation's own, much-desired Messiah.

Can you imagine the pain the Lord felt over his own people's rejection? They denied him so utterly that they wanted him dead. And they hated him so violently, that they wanted him to suffer excruciating pain. Did they have any idea how much he suffered by their rejection? Jesus loved them so much that he suffered more for their sakes, knowing that their rejection of him would mean they would be forever lost and condemned. He had a future in glory. They did not. He loved them so selflessly that he thought more about them than he did about his own pain.

Imagine what it was like for Jesus while he waited through the

long hours of the night as a prisoner. His hands and feet were probably tied and he was kept under guard. Imagine this scene of
betrayal—as humankind betrays and rejects its Creator. Ask the
Lord to give you insights into what this ordeal was like for him.

JOURNAL

Record in your journal what the Lord has shown you during your
reading and meditation. Think of ways in which you have rejected or
betrayed him. Tell him how you feel about those times. So often our
indifference and busyness stands in our way of experiencing closeness with the Lover of our souls. Sit attentive and quiet with the
Lord, open to whatever is in his heart towards you right now.

40 – Condemned

"Are you the Son of God?"
"You are right in saying I am."
Luke 22:70

- Trial—the third Jewish phase, before the Sanhedrin (Jerusalem): *Matthew 27:1; Mark 15:1a; Luke 22:66-71*
- Remorse and suicide of Judas Iscariot (In the temple and the potter's field): *Matthew 27:3-10; Acts 1:18-19*
- Trial—the first Roman phase, before Pilate (Jerusalem, at the Praetorium—the palace of the Roman governor): *Matthew 27:2, 11-14; Mark 15:1b-5; Luke 23:1-5; John 18:28-38*
- Trial—the second Roman phase, before Herod Antipas (Jerusalem, before Herod Antipas): *Luke 23: 6-12*

A CONTEMPLATIVE VIEW

A Jewish chief priest and member of the Sanhedrin . . .

My colleagues and I had determined to bring the Rabbi from Galilee in for trial. His formal excommunication was imminent. However, in this case, Caiaphas, our high priest, had execution in mind. This seemed more reckless than I had felt necessary until Caiaphas reminded us of a prophecy spoken months before our decision to arrest this dangerous man. For more than two years we had discussed the Nazarene problem. Then it escalated to the point that his execution seemed our ideal, and only, recourse. We loathed the shedding of any Jewish blood, but we could not tolerate the dangers that he was exposing our nation to. He set himself against all authority, answerable to no one except himself, preaching on his own authority in God's name. His soft view of God's law was a threat to our faith and traditions. In only three years, he had won the populace over—the uneducated thousands who knew not the dangers of our precarious political situation as an occupied people under subjection to Rome. The temple and our barely-tolerated freedoms under the Empire's rule were put in jeopardy by the teaching and actions of this unorthodox, disrespectful renegade. The man, Jesus, was himself a threat to everything sacred. His blasphemy could not be tolerated, nor could it go unpunished. A false prophet, a lunatic, or a devil I knew not what, but he was certainly not our Messiah!

For months, whenever we tried to test him or bring him in, the man had slipped away from us. Many of us were convinced his powers to heal were from Beelzebub, to deceive and to destroy our nation. It was up to us, the overseers of the faith, to purge Israel of all liars and false prophets in the name of the Holy One of Israel. We would not rest until we brought an end to him.

Surely, God was with us because of how easily he was delivered into our hands on Passover. I considered these things as I watched him during his trial. He stood in front of us, a pitiful specimen of humanity. Guilty beneath the gaze of the High Priest, he stood defenseless. Then we heard blasphemy from his own lips. At first, things didn't go well for us because the witnesses couldn't agree. But I watched him—he was unmoved by the various accounts that were given about him. I was disappointed that he did not cry out about his accusers or beg for mercy from us. His self-confidence irritated me.

The tediousness of bringing in eyewitnesses who couldn't agree was a waste of time. When things seemed to be going nowhere, I noticed his eyes went from man to man in the room. I wondered what he was thinking. Did he smugly believe he would walk out a free man? We would never let him go. Yet he seemed so sure of himself; he had no fear. This irked me, for I began to worry that we couldn't justify his death sentence with the evidence we had. We knew he was guilty. We had to get him to talk! Silence was his own best defense.

Caiaphas forced him to finally speak. "I charge you under oath, by the living God, to tell us if you are the Messiah, the Son of God."

It worked! Jesus answered, "Yes, it is as you say." Then, with his audacious way, Jesus added, "But I say to all of you: In the future you will see the Son of Man sitting at the right hand of the Mighty One and coming on the clouds of heaven."

His words brought me both relief and rage. You can imagine the commotion in that room that followed those words! He had clearly blasphemed in all of our ears. Several people were so distressed that they tore their robes. But to be sure we had sufficient evidence for the death penalty, Caiaphas pressed him further, asking, "Are you, then, the Son of God?"

The fool looked at Caiaphas, and I could see he knew, without any doubt, that we had him now. We all knew he wouldn't deny it. The man was full of himself.

Silent at first, the Nazarene must have been counting the cost. Several voices shouted the same question to him, demanding his answer. We waited only moments. He answered: "You are right in saying I am."

I am! I am! My mind reeled at his unmistakable admission. Now he would pay for his self-proclaimed equality with God. We condemned him at once.

Nicodemus, a Pharisee . . .

As a secret follower of Jesus, I had hoped he was the Messiah. I expected him to display his power in the assembly of the Sanhedrin. I'd seen him perform signs and wonders. But he did nothing to convince us of his right to David's throne. I wondered why he willingly put up with the trial at all. But then after he gave his final answer to us, the whole place charged at him. My respected friends would have stoned him on the spot if we had been in a place where there were stones to pick up. Instead, they beat him with their fists and staffs.

The High Priest told us we must hand him over to the Romans for the death penalty. It was against their law that we condemn our own people. The Romans must do it for us.

Also, we couldn't execute Jesus secretly because he was too well known. Part of cleansing us from his false teachings and claims was to make a public display of his death—so that our people would know he was cursed of God for misleading them.

But I think he was handed over to Pilate mostly because of envy. He had won the hearts of the people and had turned many sinners toward God. Something the scribes and their like couldn't do. Jesus had a way of showing the religious "elite" who they really were, and they didn't like what they saw. No, the fruit of Jesus' words and actions caused people to adore him or despise him. The sinners came in droves. The religious couldn't compete with him. They couldn't even stand up to him. He tangled them up in their own traps.

What really irritated them was that he didn't need their approval: he knew that he was a man of God. Jesus spoke with authority because he had authority—straight from heaven. Most were so far from God, they didn't recognize God's mouthpiece when they saw him in front of their eyes.

No, most of my closest friends wanted Jesus to suffer, to suffer the pain and agony of crucifixion. They were mad with envy and hate. There was nothing I could do. I was sick to my stomach as I watched the "respectable religious leaders" beat the gentle preacher from Nazareth without mercy. While the temple guards held him, angry, cowardly men took turns beating him. Afterwards, the guards dragged him outdoors and they themselves beat him even more severely. I followed them to see what they might do to him and was overwhelmed by the sight. I literally ran home, begging God to send angels of mercy to his Anointed One. But, even while I prayed for him, I fought away my doubts.

If Jesus was the Messiah, then why was this happening? If he was not, by what power had he performed his miracles?

In time, my doubts were put to rest. It wasn't easy following Jesus. Never was, never would be. He even warned us about this.

WONDER JUST A LITTLE

Can you imagine?

Can you imagine? We made God taste terror and cry.

Can you imagine? We tied the Creator's hands behind his back.

Can you imagine? We struck God's face and bloodied his wondrous, holy eyes.

Can you imagine? We stripped and flogged God Most High.

Can you imagine? We accused *The Truth.*

Can you imagine? We blindfolded the *Light of the World.*

Can you imagine? We placed upon the *King of Kings* a painful crown.

Can you imagine? We put a heavy cross upon God's back.

Can you imagine? We condemned God for being himself.

Can you imagine? We put the *Giver of Life* to death.

Can you imagine what we did to God?

Can you imagine why God let us?

We made God taste terror and cry. Can you imagine why God let us?
So that he could save us from every fear and comfort us.

We tied the Creator's hands behind his back. Can you imagine why God let us?
So he could ransom us and set us free.

We struck God's face and bloodied his wondrous, holy eyes.
Can you imagine why God let us?
So we would long to see his face, to look into his eyes of grace.

We stripped and flogged the Most High. Can you imagine why
God let us?
To take away from us our shame, sins, sickness and blame.

We accused *The Truth*. Can you imagine why God let us?
To save us from the lies that would destroy us.

We blindfolded the Light of the World. Can you imagine why
God let us?
To light our path to *Life* and lead us homeward.

We placed upon the King of Kings a painful crown. Can you
imagine why God let us?
Because his head became the ground of Eden's cursed thorns.

We put a heavy cross upon God's back. Can you imagine why
God let us?
So that the holy weight he bore that day would take our burdens
away.

We condemned God for being himself. Can you imagine why
God let us?
So that in the end, we'd forever enjoy and know him.

We put the Giver of Life to death. Can you imagine why God let
us?
So that we could come alive and live because of him.

Can you imagine what we did to God? Can you imagine what
God did for us?
Can you imagine?

WHAT DO YOU SEE?

Art helps us, if we aren't disinterested or too numb, to see the moving, dramatic realities of what we call "Christ's Passion." From the Last Supper to the Resurrection, artists and musicians have tried to transport us there so that we might better see the wonder and beauty of God, our Savior, and his love. We would do well to ponder these images with our thirsty souls. Ask to see God's love, so fully and profoundly shown, during his Passion. Then come and feast upon the love of God, at his table of abounding grace. Nowhere is his love so graphically shown to us than in these final hours when Jesus suffered and died.

The following questions are meant to bring you into your time of meditation:

Consider that the Lord chose to fulfill his destiny during the Roman occupation of Israel, when crucifixion was common. Did he have to go to such an extreme? Ask him to show you his passionate, beautiful "giving of himself" in how, when, and where he did so.

In these accounts of his rejection, his trial, and his claims, ponder with the Lord not just what happened, but how and why. Prayerfully imagine yourself in the assembly at the time and place when Jesus was condemned. Look closely at him. Watch his movements. Listen. What does he say and not say?

What might he have been thinking during his trial? Was he in communion with his Father? How do you think he felt? Can you see his facial expression and his body language? How does it feel to see him struck and physically abused? Watch how he endures the violence without defense or retaliation. How does this make you feel towards him?

Nowhere in the Bible are the words, "Jesus loves me, this I know," better described than during the events surrounding the Passion. Enter into your meditation with expectation, and desire to see the wonder and greatness of God's passionate love for you. Take your time. He longs for you to delight in him and his amazing love for you.

JOURNAL

From your time of reading and meditation, what aspects of this leg of Jesus' journey to the cross most stirred your heart? What would you say to Jesus if he walked into the room where you are right now?

41 – "Behold the Man!"

Wanting to release Jesus,
Pilate appealed to them again.
But they kept shouting,
"Crucify him! Crucify him!"
Luke 23:20-21

- Trial—the third Roman phase, before Pilate (Jerusalem, at the Praetorium): *Matthew 27:15-26; Mark 15:6-15; Luke 23:13-25; John 18:39-16a*
- Mockery by the Roman soldiers (Jerusalem, at the Praetorium): *Matthew 27:27-30; Mark 15:16-19*
- Journey to Golgotha (from the Praetorium to Golgotha): *Matthew 27:31-34; Mark 15: 20-23; Luke 23:26-33a; John 19:16b-17*
- First three hours of crucifixion (Golgotha): *Matthew 27:35-44; Mark 15:24-32; Luke 23:33b-43; John 19:18, 23-24, 19-22*

A CONTEMPLATIVE VIEW

"Behold the Man!"

O Lord, my Love, my All!
When I look upon that shameful pedestal
Where stood your manly form rejected and forlorn
I see your brokenness from our abuse and scorn

"Behold the Man!" all judgment cried
We did not know 'twas God we crucified
What wondrous things you earned for us that day
When we took your holy life and breath away

You endured so much for the sake of winning me
I am overcome by your brave humility
And in those glory hours of surrender and defeat
You spent your life entirely, so I'd be free

O Lord, my Love, my All!
My words to you are inadequate and small
I cannot tell you more than this
That you have won the world such joyful bliss

I love you more than words can ever say
And I thank you for what you did that day
And when I love and long for you in prayer
I see your beauty and your goodness there

I cannot tell you more than this
That you have won my heart such joyful bliss
"Behold the Man!" It is a holy call
To look upon you, Lord, my Love, my All

**

Pilate, the Roman governor . . .

As far as I was concerned, the young man who stood in front of me for judgment was nothing but a religious fanatic—a dreamer of dreams. He was no criminal. No, he was innocent in and of himself. But because his own people hated him, he was a threat to me.

Of course, nobody knew this but my wife. She knew how I must carefully tread through the political tides and waters between Rome and my post. I dared not upset the fragile peace with these fickle, ill-tempered, demanding Jewish priests.

To make things worse that morning, my wife sent word to me about a dream she'd had the night before, warning me to have nothing to do with the innocent man, Jesus, who had been brought to me. I am not a religious man, but I fear bad omens!

By the gods of Rome, I was sick of these Jews and all their ridiculous rituals and rules. They were the most unmanageable, unreasonable, irritating people to govern in the whole of the Empire. I loathed them all—and their temple and the bloodthirsty god they served. They sacrificed doves, bulls, lambs and goats to him. The place was not a house of prayer, but a slaughterhouse. The smoke of the sacrifices put a hungering in everybody's belly. It was repulsive. They lavished their money and services on this god. It wouldn't be long before Rome would take their gold and temple treasures and raze their beloved Jerusalem to the ground. I felt this in my bones. We were, all of us, standing on uncertain, quaking ground. So, looking into the demanding faces of the chief priests and the calm one, their captive, I wondered what he'd really done. It was maddening to think he might be a good man caught in their trap of envy. It surprised me a little that I cared something for him—for usually I cared nothing for any of them.

Why did his own people want him crucified? I'd often heard reports of how they execute their own lawbreakers. They stone people to death. I know Herod took the law into his own hands with the Baptist. The Sanhedrin usually hid its problems from me. They wanted to take care of their own business. Why was this one such a threat that they would bring him to me? Taking their captive aside from them, I searched this out. I asked him, "Are you the king of the Jews?"

He answered with a question, irritating me at once with his impudence. "Is that your own idea, or did others talk to you about me?" he asked.

"Am I a Jew?" I retorted. "It's *your* people and *your* chief priests who handed you over to me."

He hardly blinked at my outrage. I circled him, glaring at him, sizing him up.

"What have you done?" I asked. I had to get to the bottom of it and I didn't like his unwillingness to defend himself. Given the chance, anyone else would have pleaded with me for his life, claimed his innocence, and accused his accusers. I had taken him away from the wolves outside and had given him a chance to be set free. But what the man, Jesus, did was unnatural.

He still said nothing to defend himself. This is when I saw foolishness. Here I had the power over him, to crucify him, or let him go. It didn't faze him. When I said as much, he answered that I had no authority over him except that which was given to me from above.

By the gods, I hated these religious, superstitious cases. And in Jerusalem, they were plentiful. It seemed to me these Jews could tie everything that happened in life to the gods; well, in their case, to their *one* god. I never understood why, in their sacred temple, their god stayed hidden in some mystical dark room where no one was allowed. But they went about sacrificing and dearly giving to him, always trying to appease him. From the Praetorium, we could look down into their temple courts and see everything that went on. These people worshiped this god of theirs and served him dutifully.

Regardless of what I felt about the Jews and why this Jesus had been handed over to me, I think he realized I wanted to help him. I tried to get him to acknowledge whether he was a king or not. And he finally answered, "My kingdom is not of this world. If it were, my servants would fight to prevent my arrest by the Jews. But now my kingdom is from another place."

I exclaimed, "You are a king, then!"

Did he know this could mean trouble with Rome, I wondered. I realized he didn't really care what trouble he was in. He answered that he was a king and for that reason he had been born into the world, to testify to the truth. After hearing this, for a moment or two, I feared the gods and recalled my wife's warning about him. I wondered, *What is the truth here?* Picking up on his last words, I asked, "What is the truth?"

Predictably, he gave me no answer. I walked away from him. It was folly to try to reason with a man like this.

I had to be very careful. I owed my position as governor to a friend who had recommended me to Caesar. Since then, my friend had been found guilty of severe mistreatment of the Jews in Rome and had been executed for it. The powers in Rome knew that I, too, despised these people. I was being watched. My ability to control and fairly govern these people would be my gain or my ruin. It meant I had to play games with these chief priests and with Herod, their puppet king who answered, as did I, to Rome.

I didn't know how to play this particular game out. I tried to reason with the man's accusers. I also sent him off to Herod, who sent him back to me. Why did they think their reasons for the death penalty were valid? Why were they so envious of him? Would I make enemies of the multitudes if I crucified him, or if I let him go?

I turned him over to the gathered crowd to make them decide his fate. Then the verdict would not be my burden. I hoped that they would, by their numbers, overrule the priests accusing the man. I was stunned to hear the multitude turn against the accused. It was not just the priests now, but everyone was against him. Then I tried to spare Jesus from crucifixion by making the people pity him. I had him flogged, and then stood him before them all. Certainly, after seeing how severely he had been punished, they would show mercy. They must have known he had done nothing to deserve the cross.

I stood Jesus before them. He was a pitiful sight, dressed in Herod's purple robe, with a crown made of thorns on his head. This was a mock king, complete with a thorny crown, his face battered and his body bleeding from the lacerations suffered during his beating. Surely the man was punished enough for his foolishness. To the crowd I said, "Behold, the man!"

But they cried out all the more, "Crucify him! Crucify him! Crucify him!" I remember looking at him. His eyes were filled with tears and he looked down after our eyes met. I saw no anger, no fear. He was amazing. It was a pity, but I had no choice. I washed my hands of the matter in front of them all; this way I could not be held responsible by anyone. If Jesus from Nazareth was the King of the Jews, or of some other-worldly place as he indicated to me, then he took his title to the cross and to his grave.

WONDER JUST A LITTLE

The verdict was unanimous—except for the few followers who loved Jesus and could do nothing to help him. Our loving, wondrous Lord was sent to the cross, just as he had said he would be—just as was foretold through the writings of the prophets of old. The Lord himself had come to earth, to teach and to heal, but most importantly, he came to save. Jesus did more than *show* us his love, he *became* that love. God himself became atonement—performing the highest act of love. The Son of God came to "lay down his life" for his friends. We need to consider that the abuse and torture didn't just "happen" to him. He chose to sacrifice himself. Jesus knew hatred would bring him to this terrifying end.

Jesus had not stepped down from his position on the throne of heaven. He was the sovereignty of God in action, even on earth. He had simply come in humble disguise. He was one with his Father. They were in perfect union.

Only a perfect life could ransom the imperfect.

Only Life, in the form of a man, could overcome death for mankind.

Only the Creator could create a way for us. He came to reclaim our hearts and bring us home.

Jesus' crucifixion was a magnification of the worst of the shame, pain, rejection, and death human beings suffer. All this had come to us through the sin of disobedience. Disobedience and self-ishness had brought darkness and evil into our lives. We could no longer see God or know him and his love—not the way we were meant to. We had lost sight of who our Creator really was, and who we were *meant* to be.

Fear, sin and death have been with us since the days of the first sin in Eden. Jesus was the promised Seed to come—the Son of Man and the Son of God. He came to restore us back to himself, giving us eternal life. Through his sacrifice, he took away the sting of sin and death from us. As Savior, he paid the highest price—the giving of himself—to save his creation.

A quick chopping off of his head wouldn't have been enough. A few stones hurled at his body wouldn't have been enough. No other method of execution would have been payment enough.

As enemies of God, we gave him everything death and sorrow could offer, and he gave us everything Life and Joy could offer. In so doing, we would have the choice, the possibility, of becoming his own. We would be his enemies no longer, if we looked upon "the

Son of Man" and believed in him. We would be strangers no more.

Only the wise who are on the side of truth hear his voice. Only the foolish look at the cross and mock. Only the dead stay afar from his cross, going about life without a care. The Truth surrounds us in this world. We can hear his voice, if we listen, if we will but look upon his saving form with faith.

Who was that thirty-three year-old man who stood before Pilate ready and willing to die? Who was that gentle teacher, who had for years been a simple carpenter, who did nothing but good all his life? Who was that willing Sacrifice that took all our shame and fear away, heaping all upon himself that holy Passover Day? Who was called the Lamb of God by his forerunner, his witness, the prophet called John? Who became the Passover Sacrifice and was slain on that very feast day? Who called himself the Bread of Life and on the night he was betrayed, gave it to humankind to remember him by? Who, like a sheep to the slaughter, went to the altar of sacrifice without a fight? Who, having no beginnings, was born to a virgin and overcame the power of death? Do you know his name?

> *Who has ascended into heaven, or descended?*
> *Who has gathered the wind in his fists?*
> *Who has bound the waters in a garment?*
> *Who has established all the ends of the earth?*
> *What is His name,*
> *and what is His Son's name,*
> *if you know?*
> (Proverbs 30:4)

He is the unrivaled, glorious treasure of our eyes!
Jesus, fairest Lord Jesus!
Behold the Man!

WHAT DO YOU SEE?

As you read the Scripture passages, enter into your time of meditation with expectation and faith. Jesus longs for you to know what he has gone through for you. This is why we know so much about it. Of all that is written concerning Jesus' life, the most thorough writings are about his last week—especially his Passion. We have been given many details, for God wanted us to have them. We cannot consider or contemplate it enough. No matter how long we have known Jesus or looked into these things, we can never understand fully the depth of love and grace he poured out for us during those awe-full hours of his suffering and death.

There is so much to see and ponder. Watch Jesus as he stands before Pilate and Herod; and as he hears the people cursing and crying for his blood. Walk beside him as he stumbles, in his weakness, beneath the weight of the cross. Watch as Simon of Cyrene is made to carry it for him. Watch as the soldiers drive nails into his hands and feet, and then go about the practical duty of hanging him on the cross. Does Jesus cry out? How does he accept this final, dark and painful part of his mission? Does Jesus cooperate with the soldiers? Does he "lay down his life" or fight for it in the end? How does he fight this holy battle? How must he feel when the soldiers gamble for his clothes? How does Jesus react to the cursing and mocking from the bystanders? Can you imagine the evil spirits of darkness surrounding him? How does Jesus' voice sound when he forgives the men in his hearing? What do they do when he does this? Watch his suffering love as he endures the cross. Take your time. Let the violence of men and the benevolence of our Lord settle into the deepest parts of your heart. There is no greater way to know God's love for you than at the foot of his cross.

JOURNAL

After recording what your time of reading and meditation was like, write a love letter or a poem to the Lord. There is so much of his passionate love to experience while contemplating and remembering what he did for us on the cross.

42 – The Sun Stopped Shining

It was now about the sixth hour,
and darkness came over the whole land
until the ninth hour,
for the sun stopped shining.
Luke 23:44-45

- Jesus' words to his mother and John while on the cross (Golgotha): *John 19:25-27*
- Last three hours of crucifixion (Golgotha): *Matthew 27:45-50; Mark 15:33-37; Luke 23:44-45a, 46; John 19:28-30*
- Witnesses of Jesus' death (Temple and Golgotha): *Matthew 27:51-56; Mark 15:38-41; Luke 23:45b-49*

A CONTEMPLATIVE VIEW

"This is a mystery, that Christ can be the obedient,
glorious love of God and the full measure
of our disobedience, both at once."*

John, the "beloved apostle" . . .

I was the only disciple of the Twelve to see the Master suffer and die. But no matter how many times he had told us about his upcoming ordeal, I was not prepared for any of it. I had grown used to the signs and wonders he worked, and what I was made to witness at his cross seemed impossible. My entire world, my life, everything, came crashing down.

I truly had believed that Jesus could do anything. He seemed invincible to me. With all my heart I believed he was the promised Messiah destined to reign forever. Yet, how many times did he tell us that he would be betrayed, handed over to his enemies, suffer, die, and rise?

We couldn't imagine what he meant. Often he spoke to us in parables and riddles.

But when he was taken prisoner, when he was tried and found guilty of blasphemy, when he was beaten and dragged through the streets of Jerusalem, when he was handed over to the Romans and flogged and mocked, when he was given a cross to bear and led to the hill of execution . . . I forgot his warnings. I fell into despair and pity for him—a grief too hard to bear.

I held his mother close to me while struggling to hold myself together for her sake. Seeing us, Jesus nodded his head in a gesture that asked us to come to him, up to his cross. Clinging to one another, we did so. We could see how hard it was for him to breathe, let alone speak.

His battered, suffering face was full of compassion—for our pain, not his own! His words were few.

"Dear woman, here is your son," he said to his mother. She bowed in reply and clung tightly to my arm. Looking at me, he said, "Here is your mother."

The two of us loved him so deeply. And, from then on, we became mother and son. I could never take his place for her. But we experienced his love through each other the rest of our lives.

There were others near his cross. The Magdalene was there. She was the woman Jesus always enjoyed having around. With that loving, bidding look of his, the Master called her to come to him as his mother and I had.

Mary Magdalene . . .

My beloved teacher and friend, who had set me free from evil spirits and an indecent life of madness and sin, hung now over the fires of hell! Flames of torture licked at his feet and sent violent spasms through his body. Blood steadily dripped from his wounds and traveled in red streams down the splintery wooden stake. Small pools of rich, red liquid collected on the ground below his cross from his wounds.

Iron spikes impaled his feet—the same precious feet I'd anointed with perfume and kissed once—they were crossed together and fastened to the stake. I could not believe how terribly he suffered, when I came so close to him. His breathing was pain-filled grunts and involuntary, quiet groans—which he tried to control for my sake when I drew near him. The weight of his body bent him at his shoulders and his knees. His head hung, as though bowed in submission, for he lacked the strength to hold it upright for long. No, a head was too heavy a thing for him to bear. Even so, the stubborn thorny crown, tangled in his hair, did not release its shameful hold. O, my King!

As his body hung wounded and naked on display, those who hated him gloated. I heard their venomous cursing mouths let fly without mercy. I couldn't understand why anyone would hurl such abuse on him . . . No, I couldn't understand any of this. Why such hatred against a man so good? Why such violence against a man of God? His hands had the power to heal, as did the words from his mouth. I never met a kinder, more generous man. None so true.

All he had ever done was good. Even while he died, his goodness shone.

For three, long hours the Sun of Righteousness, the Light of my life, was swallowed up by hatred and the power of darkness. And eerie blackness fell upon us all. It was no storm, for there were no clouds. The sun stopped shining.

When I could no longer see his face, all that held my gaze was the light from the soldiers' fire licking at the darkness near his fastened feet.

**

"My God, my God, why have you forsaken me?
Why are you so far from saving me,
so far from the words of my groaning?" (Psalm 22:1)

" . . . I am a worm and not a man, scorned by men and despised
by the people.
All who see me mock me; they hurl insults shaking their heads:
'He trusts in the Lord; let the Lord rescue him.
Let him deliver him, since he delights in him.'" (Psalm 22:6)

" . . . Many bulls surround me; strong bulls of Bashan encircle
me.
Roaring lions tearing their prey
Open their mouths wide against me.
I am poured out like water, and all my bones are out of joint.
My heart has turned to wax;
it has melted within me.
My strength is dried up like a potsherd,
and my tongue sticks to the roof of my mouth;
you lay me in the dust of death.
Dogs have surrounded me;
a band of evil men has encircled me,
they have pierced my hands and my feet.
I can count all my bones;
people stare and gloat over me.
They divide my garments among them
and cast lots for my clothing." (Psalm 22:12-18)

WONDER JUST A LITTLE

Lord of mercy! Lord of justice!
What mystery is this that you
died in agony and grief,
suspended between the two?

What happened to Jesus at Golgotha was horrific, yet wonderful, ghastly yet glorious. But was it truly the Father's will for Jesus

to suffer so and die?

"Thou shalt not kill."

The commandments of God were given to us so that we might know right from wrong. Can you imagine . . . We killed the Giver of the commandments—the Creator of life? Our sins nailed the image of God, God Incarnate, to a tree.

Why, oh why, did he go so willingly?

Jesus said that he came to lay down his life as a ransom for many. God himself became a perfect and holy living sacrifice. He paid the highest price that could ever be paid: God's own life.

But Reason asks: How can someone else's death be payment for what I have done?

He wasn't just "someone" else – He was *Life* itself.

Besides, what Jesus has done for us goes way beyond reason. He himself calls it, through the infallible inspiration of Scripture, "the foolishness of the cross." And it is **the only way** to forgiveness and eternal life.

Our way to eternal life was purchased at a very high price. God laid himself down, a perfect offering, for sin. He took upon his holy, glorious self the punishment and shame, filled with torment and pain, and became the one punished in our place. Surely, this sacrifice is the most extravagant, costly trade: God's life for yours.

God became a man so he could pay the price and bring us back to him. The penalty for our sins has been paid by him. This is the "wisdom" of the cross.

"Surely he took up our infirmities and carried our sorrows, yet we considered him stricken by God, smitten by him, and afflicted.

"But he was pierced for our transgressions, he was crushed for our iniquities;

"The punishment that brought us peace was upon him, and by his wounds we are healed.

" . . . Yet it was the Lord's will to crush him and cause him to suffer, and though the Lord makes his life a guilt offering, he will see his offspring and prolong his days, and the will of the Lord will prosper in his hand. After the suffering of his soul, he will see the light of life, and be satisfied; by his knowledge my righteous servant will justify many, and he will bear their iniquities.

"Therefore I will give him a portion among the great, and he will divide the spoils with the strong, because he poured out his life unto death, and was numbered with the transgressors. For he bore the sin of many, and made intercession for the transgressors." (Isaiah 53:4-5, 10-12)

How can it be that God broke into our world through our violence towards him, so that he could lavish upon us his tremendous grace, love, and joy?

The Light was covered by utter darkness—for three hours. The Father rejects Sin through the suffering of his Son as Sin; and now the Father grants us acceptance through the Son. We rejoice as we embrace this wondrous mystery.

Walter Wangerin, Jr. writes:

> "Here is a paradox, both impossible and true.
> "Jesus is rejected by God, is cut completely off from God, is hung on a tree and thereby cursed, divorced at all points from his Father. *And yet:* it is in this same Jesus, at this same moment, precisely *because* of his sacrifice and death, that God is most present to the world! It is in Jesus *on the cursed tree* that God's supreme intentions towards the world are made manifest: that he hasn't come to curse, but rather to love and to bless.
> "God is not here with Jesus. Yet God is indeed here, in Christ, reconciling the world unto himself!
> "God and his sin-corrupted Son are as removed from one another as hell is from heaven.
> "Yet the whole passion is of holy design! Cursing is integral to that design. And the Father, verily absent, is also verily here, accepting the sacrifice.
> "This once we can have it both ways and can delight in the manic breaking of the rules of the universe. This once the creatures, we created ones, can rise up *in* creation to peer *beyond* creation

through a magic window at the Uncreated One, the Creator. Here is a window through which to gaze into Heaven, to know and believe in the nature of God. Here, in paradox. Here, in conjunction of impossibilities. Here, on Golgotha.

"And here is a door through which God has crossed infinitely to enter our finite existence, flooding the dungeons with light. Here is a door through which we by faith may enter Heaven, a doorway made of nails and wood, a crossing, a cross.

"But deepen further this paradox. Ask: when were the windows most darkened for Jesus, that he could see nothing of God the Father? Answer: On Golgotha. And by what was the great door bolted shut and locked against his entering in? By the wood and the nails of the cross.

"Christ's unseeing is our sight.

"For it is on Golgotha that a centurion spins around and stares at the man in the middle, just as that man dies, exactly as Jesus gives up the ghost and slumps forward from the cross.

"But all at once that centurion sees as though light burst upon his eyes, as though the veil between bright heaven and dark earth had been torn in two from the top to the bottom. The centurion sees better than he did, and more than he ever did before: he sees God! He sees the very nature of the love of God! The dying one is the other one's window, and what has been veiled is now revealed, and a pagan whispers with the solemn weight of conviction, confession, faith: 'Truly, this man was the Son of God!'*

"For God so loved the world that he gave his only Son, that whoever believes in him should not perish but have eternal life."
John 3:16

WHAT DO YOU SEE?

You are at the cross of Jesus. Imagine the scene and listen to the sounds. Feel the wind swirling around you on that lonely, gruesome mount. Watch what the soldiers do. Listen to the cursing of the passersby, and from one of the two others who are crucified, suffering and dying. Watch as Jesus' loved ones come to him. Listen to the few things Jesus speaks from the cross. Feel the terror as darkness falls around everyone in the middle of the day.

When Jesus says, "I thirst," be the one to bring him the sponge with the wine-vinegar. Watch as he sucks and swallows the vile drink. This surely is a symbol of the bitterness which is all that the world had to give him, while at the same time he gave everything he had for us.

Take the thought "I thirst" with you into your time of journaling. Watch Jesus die. What is this like? How does this make you feel? How would you like to quench his thirst right now?

JOURNAL

God thirsts for you. He longs to have close communion with you. It is the reason he has come and died for you. Spend time with him now and share yourself openly with him. Be open to what he wants to share with you. Tell him of your feelings. Ask him how he feels too. Be open to whatever the Lord wants to reveal to you. If you have never given your life to him, do it now. If you would like to live a life of closer intimacy with him, tell him of your intentions. This is the reason he suffered and died for you.

---

*From *Reliving the Passion: Meditations on the Suffering Death and Resurrection of Jesus as Recorded in Mark* by Walter Wangerin Jr., Zondervan Publishing House, ©1992.

*From *Reliving the Passion* by Walter Wangerin Jr., Zondervan Publishing House, ©1992.

43 – Triumph Through Death

The curtain of the temple was torn in two
from top to bottom.
Mark 15:38

- Witnesses of Jesus' death (Temple and Golgotha): *Matthew 27:51-56; Mark 15:38-41; Luke 23: 45b, 47-49*
- Burial—Certification of Jesus' death and procurement of his body (Golgotha and the Praetorium): *Matthew 27:57-58; Mark 15:42-45; Luke 23:50-52; John 19:31-38*
- Jesus' body placed in a tomb (The garden tomb at Golgotha): *Matthew 27:59-60; Mark 15:46; Luke 23:53-54; John 19:39-42*
- The tomb watched by the women and guarded by the soldiers (Bethany, Golgotha, and the Praetorium): *Matthew 27:61-66; Mark 15:47; Luke 23:55-56*

A CONTEMPLATIVE VIEW

A Roman Centurion on duty at Golgotha . . .

Most of the criminals we crucify are examples of what happens to those who cross the will of Rome. We hang them on display, naked, to die a slow, tortured death—while their own people watch. For effect, we install the stakes for these hangings by city gates, usually on platforms or on high ground. Most of the ones we kill are thieves, murderers, insurrectionists and the like.

How the bravest man I ever saw came into my hands to be

crucified was none of my concern. I was a soldier with orders, as were the men under me. We hung him for treason in between two murdering criminals. Above his head we hung the sign that identified him and his crime: "King of the Jews." Later, I heard an onlooker say he was someone they had hoped was the Messiah. I'd heard about this—that these people expected a deliverer to rise to power and they'd be done with Rome. We laughed at them. But then I heard someone mock him, saying: "Son of God, come down from your cross, if you can!"

I wondered if the man claimed to be a god . . . like our Caesar . . . but I shrugged it off.

Evidently, the man had riled up the temple priests so much they had handed him over to us to kill for them. The man was a threat, they said, to peace. But the one we hung in the middle was no rebel. He was quiet; and seemed like a good man—not like the typical rabble-rousers we execute.

His hands opened to us. Eyes without hate. Not a single curse word. He *gave* himself to us to nail down.

Maybe he wanted to get it over with. I don't know, but for the first time during a crucifixion, I wondered how I would act in the man's place. How would I do being stripped and impaled onto wooden beams and hiked up into the air? How would it feel to hang in such torment while people stared? I knew I wouldn't be anything like him. He went without a fight. I thought less of him for it—until later. In the middle of the afternoon, when the day should have been the brightest, pitch dark descended on us. We built fires and sent a man to bring torches out to us. It was such an eerie darkness. We drank to ease our nerves.

The one in the middle continued to amaze me. He said little from his cross, but the few words he spoke were said without any hint of anger. An unbelievable thing, I thought. And, in his dying moments, he mustered up unnatural strength, impossible to have at the end. Here was a man who had been, for hours, too weak to lift himself. Then, all of a sudden, he stood tall against his nailed feet, and cried out to his god, calling him Father.

I wondered, who was his father? Did he pray to the dead? Then, I remembered the man had claimed he was the Son of God. His shout still lingered in my hearing: "It is finished! Father, into your hands I commit my spirit."

It seemed to me that he died choosing to, for at that moment he did not look or sound like a dying man. And that was not all. What happened next gripped me with fear—the earth, the sky, and the wind all seemed to respond to his cry.

The moment the man cried out and died, the very hill we stood on split into fissures and large pieces of the mount, just below us, huge chunks of limestone, broke apart and rolled to the roadside. The whole city shook. Most terrifying of all to me was the wind swirling around us. It was an eerie, threatening wind that cast sand in our eyes and sent up showers of sparks from the hot coals of our fires. Thunder boomed overhead, but there was no lightning, nor any sign of clouds or rain. Then, within minutes, everything became deathly still. The sun came out, and then fell fast in the western sky. It cast a long shadow of him on his cross. I gazed up at him, filled with dread. So much had just happened.

I remembered what he had said hours before: "Father, forgive them for they know not what they do." I knelt on the ground, removed my helmet, and proclaimed to everyone on that mound: "Surely, this man was the one he claimed to be—he *was* the Son of God!"

An angel of the Lord, standing by in heaven . . .

We, the Savior's hosts of angels, heard his cry to his Father in heaven. Soon, the Son, of his own choosing, would die.

A shroud of darkness fell—the Light of heaven and earth no longer shone. God's Son hung in the center of an abyss—a dark, painful void of utter separation from his Father. There was nothing and no one to help him—not even us—his tens of thousands of adoring angels. Although in our hearts we loved and worshiped him, we, too, kept silent.

He had become Sin as well as Grace. It was a mystery now revealed, for this was new to us. Both judgment and mercy had come to mankind through our Creator.

Then, at last, we watched him stand tall against his nailed feet and cry—for all of Heaven, Time, and the universe to hear: "It is accomplished! Father, into your hands I commit my spirit."

At once, he let go of his body, and his spirit came out from it. And his head, his dear head, lost the crown of thorns in that final bow. At once he was with us in our world of the spirit. He was glorious! He was Light, triumphant, and full of blinding holiness—full of zeal! With a shout, he descended from our sight, into the regions of hell.

None of us could follow him—he was going as both a man and as God—where none of us could go.

Satan and his hordes at the cross were so astounded by the sight of him that they fled in an uproar of cries and of terror, so that even on earth the impact of these things was felt.

Never were any of us so ecstatic. We worshiped our Lord Jesus. We were in holy awe of him. We knew he would return to his body on the third day—and we waited for him. Until then, we knew that the Lord of Lords had triumphed over Sin and Death, having accomplished all that he had set out to do. In unison and in thundering praise, we sang throughout the heavens: "Glory to his name! Holy, holy, holy is the Lord, God, Almighty!"

A Jewish priest on duty in the temple . . .

On the day of Passover, while I ministered in the temple, an ominous darkness fell. As a Levite priest on duty, I reacted the only way I knew—I lit lanterns. Everyone was afraid. After about three hours, an earthquake shook the ground beneath our feet. It was so violent, we feared the temple would come down.

I remembered what the Galilean preacher had said about destroying the temple and raising it in three days. Was it just coincidence that the man was at that moment dying on a cross outside the city? I feared what this might mean. He was a great magician, a powerful worker of evil—or he was who he claimed to be.

With a deafening sound, the veil in the temple was torn apart, from top to bottom. The "Mercy Seat" of the Holy of Holies was exposed. This was the holy dwelling place of the *Presence*—the place of God's glory—which our eyes were forbidden to see. Never had anything like this happened. None of us knew what to do. We were terrified.

The chief priests who had gone out to watch the crucifixion of the condemned man, Jesus from Nazareth, had returned pounding their breasts, and muttering prayers for God's mercy. And here was the way to the "Mercy Seat" opened before us. Falling to my knees, I cried, "My God! My God! Have mercy on us and do not, by the holiness of your presence, destroy us!"

Then startling news came to us in the temple. People who had died were seen walking around Jerusalem!

"God of Heaven and Earth, what is happening?" I cried. "Is this the day of the Resurrection? Is this *that* Day?"

For most of my peers, the fear and alarm didn't last very long. When the darkness lifted and the sun came out again, the elders of our people said that nothing but an earthquake had occurred. The man, Jesus, had died like any other man. "There was nothing to fear," they said. But I thought to myself, *What about the rising of the dead that undisputed eyewitnesses had seen?* And, more, *What about the rising of faith, with hope, in me?*

WONDER JUST A LITTLE

When Jesus descended into hell after his death, he did so in victory and power. He took back from Satan what Adam and Eve, through disobedience, had relinquished. The war Jesus fought meant his own death instead of ours. He, as a son of Adam, reclaimed what would have been forever lost; now, instead, he opens wide the way to life and heaven. Forever. These are the keys to freedom from sin, and they open wide the prison doors.

Did Satan know what would happen upon the death of Jesus? Did he know what Jesus was accomplishing through his painful death on the cross? Did Satan think he could destroy the Son of God?

What about the angels of Heaven? They saw mysteries unfold before their eyes. How they must have honored their Creator on the day he died, giving himself so fully to reclaim what was lost because of Rebellion, which had started in heaven. They had witnessed the plan of redemption unfold, for through God's own hand and labor, his great love, justice, and mercy was made known. They saw the true character of God, revealed through the Son.

What can we learn from God's Plan of Salvation? What did the angels see? It is this: Using force, God could have destroyed Satan, as well as Satan's plans against the children of earth. But forceful or destructive power is Satan's way, not God's. God's way is the prevailing power of the universe, and it is based on love, truth, and goodness.

Look at the way Jesus fought evil with good, overcame darkness with light, and surrendered to death to win eternal life. The most passionate act of love the world has ever seen was when our courageous Savior defended us with the weapons of forgiveness, gentleness, and his own surrendered life. Jesus, the Lord of the universe, armed with the power of his love, overcame sin, death, and hate—forever.

Have you ever wondered where Jesus went after his death? He called it "Paradise" to the thief who suffered on a cross next to him. Scripture says he "preached" to the souls there and led them out to heaven. This is not a fantasy tale or some mystic story. This happened. Can you imagine the scene when the Lord of Glory came to set the captives free? How wonderful it must have been for Jesus, too, to taste the reward of his suffering and death so soon.

What was God telling his people when he tore the veil in the temple?

"Come unto me . . ." Can you hear the voice of Jesus?

"Yes, come! I have made the way for you to come to me." The atoning death of Jesus made it possible for all to come now, very near.

WHAT DO YOU SEE?

Read the Scriptures listed for this chapter. Ask the Holy Spirit to be your guide while you enter into this historical scene in prayer. Imagine the time when Jesus died. His head falls—his life goes out from his pain-raked body, and then what happens next? In the spirit-world, what might this have been like? Imagine Jesus, full of glory and light. Let the eyes of your heart follow Jesus in his descent to the underworld.

If you wish to pray further, return to the cross, to the moment when Jesus' body and head fall with the weight of lifelessness. Disciple John is there. He is looking at his Master. He has seen him suffer. He watches as the soldier thrusts a spear in his side. What is going through his heart and mind? What is it like for those who are his enemies? Imagine the darkness, the earthquake. Mary Magdalene is there, weeping. What are the soldiers doing? Imagine the fires, the wind, the shaking ground. What about the believing thief? How must he feel?

Now, look at this time through the eyes of Jesus. It is nearly finished for him. Does his voice sound from a heart full of fear, or joy? This was the moment for which he was born! Allow him to share the moment, what it meant to him, with you.

JOURNAL

First, record in your journal your experiences from your time of reading and prayer, describing what things most moved you. What does it mean that the "temple veil" has been torn from top to bottom? This dramatic event shows us the heart of God. How he longs for us to understand the depth and breadth of his love and grace. In your journal, list the many different ways God has given you to understand him and what he has done to win you—to not only save you, but that you might really *know* him.

44 – He's Alive!

"It is true!"
Luke 24:34

- The tomb visited by the women (Bethany and Golgotha): *Matthew 28:1; Mark 16:1*
- The stone rolled away (Golgotha): *Matthew 28:2-4*
- The tomb found to be empty by the women (Golgotha): *Matthew 28:5-8; Mark 16:2-8; Luke 24:1-8; John 20:1*
- The tomb found to be empty by Peter and John (Golgotha): *Luke 24:9-11, 12; John 20:2-10*
- Post-resurrection appearance to Mary Magdalene (Golgotha and Jerusalem): *Mark 16:9-11; John 20:11-18*
- Post-resurrection appearance to the other women (Jerusalem): *Matthew 28:9-10*
- Report of the soldiers to the Jewish authorities (Jerusalem): *Matthew 28:11-15*
- Post-resurrection appearance to the two disciples traveling to Emmaus (On the road to Emmaus): *Mark 16:12-13; Luke 24:13-32*

A CONTEMPLATIVE VIEW

In a Garden

It began in a garden, long, long ago
When the Creator gave *Life* and walked with his own

Now, here in a garden his holy Seed lies
Sown in the earth, for love, he has died

This, his Seed, buried and hidden from eyes
Is about to break forth with Heaven's surprise
In a garden, the Creator had always foreseen
In a garden, to walk again, with his redeemed

"Where are you?" God called for his own long ago
"Where is he?" she cried for the Seed that was sown
In a garden, the Creator had always foreseen
In a garden, to walk again, with his redeemed

Mary Magdalene, one of the "close" disciples . . .

"Woman, why are you crying? Who is it you are looking for?"
These were the first words from the risen Lord.

He was ready to spring his surprise on me. At first, I didn't realize it was *him*—not until he said my name, "Mary." My name, so
gentle and loving on his lips.

Oh, could it be *him*? Could it be? Were my eyes playing tricks
on me? I wondered these things. Yes, yes, it was *him*! My Lord, my
rabbi, my friend! Yes, it surely was him.

I had watched him suffer and die. I had followed the men who
buried him. But now, with him alive and walking around . . . I was
the happiest woman alive.

"He's alive! He's alive!" I proclaimed to his men. But their
eyelids were weights of lead. They refused to hear what I said. I
told all that had happened to me when Jesus, in the garden, came
looking for me. From the sunshine, from the dawning new day, he
had sent me to them.

"Go, tell my disciples you have seen me."

Peter, one of the Twelve . . .

You cannot imagine the regret and despair I suffered at having denied my Lord. But he came to me when I was alone. In that moment I knew he still loved me. In that moment, I knew I would live. He's alive, and now, so am I.

John, one of the Twelve . . .

"Peace be with you!" These were the risen Lord's first words to me. I was in the upper room with the others. At first, seeing Jesus terrified us. We thought he was a ghost. He did not use the door—all of a sudden he stood in our midst.

My sorrow and despair had taken its toll. I was the only one of the Twelve to see him suffer and die—to carry him. I cannot describe the burden this was to carry him to a tomb. Jesus dead? It just couldn't be—it seemed impossible to me.

He had suffered so. And I suffered still. Now, here he was, standing less than fifteen feet from me. Alive.

His eyes found mine. It was then I believed. And all my sorrow and grief, with a flood of tears, was released. Within minutes, I embraced him. He was real.

Thomas, one of the Twelve . . .

"Put your finger here; see my hands. Reach out your hand and put it into my side. Stop doubting and believe." These were the risen Lord's first words to me.

It's hard to believe such impossible things. How could he have risen from the dead? How, indeed, did he know that I had not believed when the others told me about him?

"My Lord and my God!" I cried out to him and fell to my knees in worship.

"Because you have seen me, you have believed; blessed are those who have not seen and yet have believed."

These telling words to Thomas are also the first words of the risen Lord to you and me.

WONDER JUST A LITTLE

Death couldn't hold onto Life any more than the grave could hold onto Jesus.

It was predawn, in a garden cemetery, when Life swallowed Death once and for all.

"I am the Resurrection and the Life," Jesus had said. And he forever proved it.

An angel came from heaven, rolled back the giant stone and sat down upon it, waiting for Jesus to come out. Oh, to have seen Jesus step out of that tomb! What did he look like?

By the time Mary arrived, things in the garden looked normal. Except . . . the soldiers were gone. And the stone was rolled away. And the body of Jesus was gone.

In that quiet, little garden, God was walking around!

And he looked like a gardener.

Mary! Don't you want to shout at her? It's *him*! It's Jesus!

"Why are you crying?" he asked, just playing with her, ready to burst with his surprise. But because of her sorrow, he ended his tender charade. He said her name: "Mary."

His voice—what was it like? Was it loving . . . inviting . . . play-ful . . . tender? Yes, surely, it was all of these. At once, she knew him. So what does she do? She throws herself at his feet—in *possessive* worship. She clings to him like she will never, ever let him go! And, indeed, she never will.

No, Jesus, don't ever leave again! She says through her prayer of clinging.

No, he has plans for her . . . plans for the two of them . . . plans for each of us.

Soon she would be able to "cling" to him in a whole new way— in Spirit and Truth. She would forever and ever cling to him. But, just then, in the garden, she must let go of him.

His voice, loving and playful, said, "I have not yet risen to my Father."

He laughed softly. He is so blessed by her show of affection. He can't move because she's on top of his feet, clinging to his ankles . . . holding him in place as she pours her heart out in worship and love.

"Don't cling to me. I have not yet ascended to my Father." Does he think she will keep him from going? She must let go! But not for long... He will send the Holy Spirit . . . He will not leave her an orphan . . . He will come to her again! And she will cling to him in an even better way.

And so he says, "Go instead to my brothers and tell them, 'I am returning to my Father and your Father, to my God and your God." They, from then on, would know the Father on the same intimate level as the Son. Jesus couldn't have been more delighted in the telling of that news.

WHAT DO YOU SEE?

While Jesus is in the garden with Mary, it seems he doesn't know just what to do with himself. First, he wants her to go and tell his disciples he will see them in Galilee. Then he shows up in the upper room wanting to be with them, asking them to touch him, enjoying their surprise.

Humanly speaking, can you imagine how Jesus felt after his resurrection?

Jesus is bursting with the reality that he has made the way open for his friends to call "his Father their Father, his God their God!" He has revealed the love of the Father to them—he has redeemed humankind back to God. His mission was successful. He was ready to return to heaven but he was not ready to leave them just yet. He loved them so much he wanted to show himself to them and share his triumphant joy with them. This is the heart of Jesus. He wants, more than anything, for us to see and know him.

After reading this chapter's Gospel accounts of the resurrection, imagine what it was like for the Emmaus disciples on the road when Jesus joined them. Jesus let them think he was a stranger. Why do you think he did that? Can you sense the delight he was feeling? He wanted to show these two disciples, not of the Twelve, how he had just fulfilled the Messianic Scriptures concerning all that he had to accomplish. What does this tell you about the Lord? What moved him to show such favor to these two "unlikelies"? What might it have been like to walk with the risen Jesus and hear these revelations straight from his own mouth? What was Jesus like when he sat with them at the table and broke bread? Can you see this? What does this mean to you today?

JOURNAL

Record in your journal the thoughts and experiences from your time of reading and meditation. What would you do if Jesus were to walk into the room where you are right now? Can you imagine this? Right now he is with you as surely as if he has appeared to you. Spend time with him; let your faith arise. Can you sense his presence? Surely, he wants to reveal himself to you just like he did to Mary in that garden two thousand years ago. Your "garden"—that spiritual garden in your heart—is a trysting place to meet with the Maker, the Keeper, and the Lover of your soul.

45 – Saying Goodbye

And surely I am with you always,
to the very end of the age.
Matthew 28:20b

- Report of the two disciples to the rest (Jerusalem): *Luke 24:33-35; 1 Corinthians 15:5a*
- Appearance to the ten assembled disciples (Jerusalem): Mark 16:14; *Luke 24:36-43; John 20:19-25*
- Appearance to the eleven assembled disciples (Jerusalem): *John 20:26-31; 1 Corinthians 15:5b*
- Appearance to the seven disciples while fishing (Sea of Galilee): *John 21:1-25*
- Appearance to the eleven in Galilee (A mount in Galilee): *Matthew 28:16-20;1 Corinthians 15:6*
- Appearance to James, Jesus' brother [location unknown]: *1 Corinthians 15:7*
- Appearance to the disciples in Jerusalem: *Luke 24:44-49; Acts 1:3-8*
- The Ascension—Jesus' parting blessing and departure (From Jerusalem to the Mount of Olives in the vicinity of Bethany: *Mark 16:9-20; Luke 24:50-53; Acts 1:9-12*

A CONTEMPLATIVE VIEW

James, a brother of Jesus . . .

When Jesus appeared to me after his resurrection, the last thing he wanted to do was say "goodbye." I saw this in his eyes, heard this in his words, experienced this within his embrace.

In fact, I know he didn't want to leave at all. Actually, the truth is, his coming to earth was to say: "Here I am." God came here to be with us, to bring us closer to him and to bring us into the kingdom of heaven.

As Jesus' brother, I sorrowfully confess, I didn't believe he was anything more than my brother. It's hard for me to admit how stubborn and closed my heart was towards him. And so, when he appeared to me after his suffering and death, seeing him alive from the dead nearly killed me. All reason, all logic, fled! I was taken out of myself, lifted to stand in a place I knew not. I wept from both overwhelming sorrow and tremendous joy.

I would have been happy to die and go with him, once I really knew him.

The moment he appeared, the truth of who he is, as well as the depth of love I saw in his eyes, flooded over me like a tidal wave. Weeping, I worshiped him. The astounding realization of his Person unmanned me. Changed me. Revolutionized me. I am no longer who I was. Nor is he any longer who he was to me.

He knew that I hadn't really known or understood him before. He forgave me. Then he asked me to come to him, as his true brother, in the Holy Spirit. And so, I proclaim to you, in Spirit and in Truth, Jesus is my Lord.

Many days after he appeared to me, I was with about five hundred others, on a mount in Galilee, when my Lord came to me again. When he stood in our midst, with heaven's love and joy shining from him, he gave us a commission that would last to the end of our lives, as well as to the end of time. He said, "All authority in heaven and on earth has been given to me. Therefore, go and make disciples of all nations, baptizing them in the name of the Father and of the Son and of the Holy Spirit, and teaching them to obey everything I have commanded you. And surely I am with you always, to the very end of the age."

Not many days later, I was with my "brothers and sisters" in Jerusalem, on the Feast of Pentecost. On this day, in that upper room, the wind blew indoors and tongues of fire descended upon us. It was the special day he'd promised would come: the Feast of First Fruits. We were the Holy Spirit's first-fruits. Glory to God! We were given a sign that God's kingdom had come. God's kingdom was upon us! In other languages we sung. Truly, the God of our fathers, the Spirit of the Holy One, had come—first through his Son, my brother, and now though the wind and the fire.

Peter, the apostle Jesus called his "rock" and "shepherd" . . .

The day Jesus led us up the Mount of Olives for the last time was also the last time I saw him. From then on, the "water" I'd walk on would be just as uncertain as the waves of the sea I'd stepped across that time I ventured out to him in faith.

With certainty I know he will always be with me.

On the day he ascended into heaven, when he disappeared from sight into the clouds, my heart groaned because I knew I'd sorely miss him. And yet, I also rejoiced because the Son of God had come and I knew him intimately. I always would. Forever. You see, everything Jesus had said proved true. And so now I can believe everything he told us—especially his promises.

If he said, "You will deny me," I did. If he said, "Throw your nets on the other side for a catch," there would be fish in our nets. Along those lines . . . he once said, "Go to the lake and throw out your line. Take the first fish you catch; open its mouth and you will find a four-drachma coin." It was the money we needed for the temple tax. Do you think I felt foolish with my line in the lake? Guess what? I paid our taxes with that four-drachma coin. Oh, he made me laugh. He could do anything he put his mind to—that creative mind of his!

Truly, Jesus was always good for his word—no matter what he said.

In parting, he said this to us: "You will receive power when the Holy Spirit comes upon you; and you will be my witnesses in

Jerusalem, and in all Judea and Samaria, and to the ends of the earth."

Those were the last words, physically speaking, he said to me. And now through the spreading of his Word, through the testimony of his many servants, many believe.

Even as you read this, he is fulfilling those very words.

Truly, Jesus is with us—with you—to the end of the age. We can count on it.

John, the one everyone named "the beloved" apostle of Jesus . . .

Jesus appeared to me in my old age and he showed me future things.

It is with great joy I write the words that he spoke to me that day: "Behold, I am coming soon! My reward is with me, and I will give to everyone according to what he has done. I am the Alpha and the Omega, the First and the Last, the Beginning and the End . . . I, Jesus, have sent my angel to give to you this testimony . . . I am the Root and the Offspring of David, and the bright Morning Star."

And the Spirit and the Bride say, "Come!"

And let him who hears say, "Come!"

Whoever is thirsty, let him come; and whoever wishes, let him take the free gift of the water of life.

The grace of the Lord Jesus be with you.

WONDER JUST A LITTLE

Well, what do you think? We have reached the end of this book. But it is not the end of the story—far, far from it. You see, the story of Jesus and the testimony of his life with us goes on. The incarnation of God goes on. In us. In you. Isn't it amazing? What an extravagant wonder this is. God in us! Take a few minutes and let that truth settle deeply inside your heart. In fact, his incarnational life in us is the reason Jesus came to earth, is coming, and will come again. He wants to *be with us* so closely, so intimately—in fact, no further away than the air we breathe.

The wonder of it all is this: Jesus never said "Goodbye."

WHAT DO YOU SEE?

Imagine witnessing one of these recorded appearances Jesus made to his loved ones before he ascended into heaven. Pick your favorite one. What is it like to see the resurrected Jesus? How does he look? What does he say? What is his tone of voice when he speaks those final words? What are the most important truths he wants to leave with us? Knowing that Jesus is the living Word of God, which of his final words do you appreciate the most?

In your time of meditation, visualize what it would have been like to see Jesus physically ascend into the clouds and out of sight. Why do you suppose he left us in this particular way? He could have simply disappeared. Why do you think Jesus chose to leave in such a dramatic way? While you are looking up, angels have the final, final word. What do they say? How did they say it? What would it have been like to have seen and heard the angels give such a wonderful promise? What do you see?

JOURNAL

Don't say goodbye to your journal. Using the ideas presented in this book for meditation and writing, perhaps you may wish to go back and find other important events of the Scriptures that you would like to "relive." The experience of reading and praying with Scripture can be a profound way to experience Jesus in the now. So, right now, what does your heart wish to do with this journal? Would you like to write a poem or a letter of thanks and praise to Jesus? Do you simply want to listen with a ready pen? Whatever it is, let your heart lead you—surely, your love for Jesus will lead you to him. Always.

Printed in the United States
1133900005B/235-252